On the Ballot in Louisiana

Running for President to Fight National Decay

Bill McGaughey ran for President of the United States in the 2004 Democratic primary in Louisiana. His five-week campaign during February and March, 2004, took him to more than sixty cities or towns in the state. Attracting 3,161 votes from Louisiana Democrats, he finished fifth among seven candidates. Protection from outsourcing of U.S. jobs to low-wage countries was his main issue. McGaughey has published seven books on subjects ranging from work hours and international trade to world history and political campaigns. His thesis is that world civilization is currently focused on entertainment and this shapes the requirements of modern campaigning. A 1964 graduate of Yale University, he lives with his wife, Lian, in Minneapolis, Minnesota, where he owns rental housing.

On the Ballot in Louisiana

Running for President to Fight National Decay

by Bill McGaughey

Thistlerose Publications
Minneapolis, Minnesota, USA

Thistlerose Publications

Printed in United States of America

Published by Thistlerose Publications, 1702 Glenwood Avenue, Minneapolis, MN 55405, USA

Library of Congress Control Number   2004110137

Publisher's Cataloging-in-Publication
(Provided by Quality Books, Inc.)

McGaughey, William.
     On the ballot in Louisiana : running for president to
  fight national decay / by Bill McGaughey.
     p. cm.
     Includes index.
     LCCN 2004110137
     ISBN 0-9605630-6-7

     1. Presidents--United States--Election--2004.
  2. McGaughey, William. 3. Presidential candidates--United
  States--Biography. 4. Primaries--Louisiana--History.
  I. Title.

E905.M34 2004   324.973'0931'092
                                       QBI04-200337

Acknowledgments

Thanks to persons who have reviewed the manuscript and made comments or corrections, including Andrew Griffin, Jeff Crouere, Jonathan McIntosh, Pam Russell, Johney Turner, Ted McManus, Leonard Gray, Bob Holeman, Cheryl Jacob, Chad Hebert, Emilie Bahr, Seth Fox, Edwin Roy, Eleanor Evans, Jessie Boyett, Mark Rainwater, Mike Jones, and Steve Bandy. Thanks to the people of Louisiana for hosting an open primary and to all those I met while campaigning in that beautiful state in the winter and spring of 2004.

Table of Contents

Part IV

Illustrations

(Dates when photographs were taken are in parenthesis.)

p. 313   Author wearing Mardi Gras beads while addressing conference of International Society for the Comparative Study of Civilizations (ISCSC) in Fairbanks, AK, on "Doing Politics in the Entertainment Age" (6-12-04)

p. 323   Author addressing ISCSC conference in Fairbanks, AK later in talk   (6-12-04)

p. 331   Author addressing ISCSC conference in Fairbanks, AK still later (6-12-04)

p. 343   Fair Trade rally at Minnesota State Capitol in St. Paul, MN   (4-21-01)

p. 366   Map of Louisiana drawn by author (largest cities)

p. 367   Map of Louisiana drawn by author   (interstate highways)

FRONT COVER

Lower left: Author with white hat photographed outside Logan's Roadhouse restaurant in Alexandria, LA   (3-9-04)

Background: Sample ballot of Democratic presidential primary election in Louisiana provided by Louisiana Secretary of State

BACK COVER: Author eating bowl of gumbo soup at restaurant near New Orleans (2-24-04)

Part

CHAPTER ONE

The Unsettling Big Picture

In the course of the past five or six thousand years, humanity has passed through four historical epochs on the way to the present time. The first was an age of political empire when monarchs developed the arts of state craft and made war upon one another. Then came an age of world religion when prophets and philosophers created ethical systems to guide society. A third age of world history came about as post-religious society pursued wealth and secular knowledge. A fourth began in the 20th century as attention shifted to popular entertainment. The development of computer technology suggests that a fifth age may now be on the horizon.

Within this historical context, institutions of power have arisen. Powerful men have exerted control over human society in, first, creative and, then, destructive ways. Each sees himself as embodying the most advanced form of civilization as if what he represents will last forever. But the lesson of history is that nothing which lives continues to develop in a straight line. All is subject to processes of growth and decay.

Right now, the United States of America is rightly considered the most powerful nation on earth. The ideological priesthood that surrounds it proclaims that the American nation is exempt from serious problems by virtue of a destiny which it calls "American exceptionalism". We have the world's largest economy. We are its only military superpower. People from every nation on earth are living in our midst and we treat women humanely. History itself may have come to an end, some say.

All this is, of course, nonsense. We Americans are no more immune to historical processes of decay than any other people. In fact, it is happening before our eyes. Economic and social decay is rapidly proceeding. If the American people allow themselves to be squeezed by doctors and lawyers, if we have a system of "deep-pockets justice" which targets parties with money while a criminal underclass ravishes our cities, if our people are only prospects to be sold commercial products, or we despise the types of persons like ourselves and begrudge them a comfortable living, then we have a problem with self-esteem. Yet, Americans want so much to believe.

Look around you. Our economy has ceased being a creative force for the betterment of people's lives and has instead become a slave master, strapping people into long hours at work, stagnant wages, failing health-care arrangements, and increasing personal debt. Today's premier growth industries center around gambling, corrections, and medications to treat anxiety and depression. We owe other nations huge sums of money from our chronic trade deficits. We cannot protect our territorial borders from illegal immigration. And now the United States is bogged down in Iraq because of a war which we thought was liberating but which most other people think was waged to get our hands on Iraq's oil.

We speak of the "American dream" as if it were a result of our own wise policymaking. Where is that "dream" for today's young people, urged to spend large amounts of money up front for a college education to qualify for one of today's high-paying jobs, if U.S. employers will simply purchase low-cost labor from abroad? They are fast becoming a generation of suckers. The average college student has a $17,000 student loan needing to be paid after graduation. That expenditure is to be met from the relatively high salaries that college graduates expect to receive. Yet, the same educational institutions that take young people's money are bulwarks of the "free trade" ideology that says American labor must compete on the basis of cost. In a high-cost society, Americans cannot live on Third World wages. But their government refuses to protect them even as the drum beat continues: Go to college. Have we no shame?

We say we live in a democracy but we tolerate the making of fundamental policy decisions by that branch of government which is least responsive to the people. We let appointed judges usurp the supreme decisionmaking authority in government. Nowhere does the U.S. Constitution give judges that power. Marbury v. Madison was an act of judicial usurpation. Brown v. Board of Education let questionable sociology overturn not only the Constitution but decades of case law. Roe v. Wade found a Constitutional right to privacy based on imagination rather than fact. The prevailing view is that "the Constitution is what the judges say it is." No, the Constitution is what the document itself says. Behind the robes, the emperor has no clothes.

This shall not stand. I join the deliverers of a "doom and gloom" message who say that the American empire must reform itself and shape up if it is to avoid the ignominious fate of many others like it in the past. Our "enemy" is not an external one but wrong ideas which we ourselves have accepted. America is its own worst enemy. It lacks moral leadership. It lacks an appreciation of its own people. For a nation which once sent a man to the moon, its subsequent goals and achievements have been disappointing indeed.

But now we are dragged into a kind of compulsory optimism about the future of this society. Granted that Ronald Reagan's optimistic temperament was for him a source of personal strength, it does not follow that all who would criticize government policies are pessimistic purveyors of "doom and gloom." In times of war, this attitude extends to questioning their patriotism. No, some policies deserve to be criticized because they need to be changed. Neither the current government nor its policies are synonymous with the interests of the American people. "Optimism" that equates with irrational wishfulness does not serve those interests well. It is the substitution of junk politics for honest thought.

The dominant political forces in our country today are ones which exploit the mass of its people economically or which, being a group apart, see the majority population as an oppressor of themselves. Politicized relationships reach inside the family. These postures weaken the society, undermining its morale. Ours is a false patriotism if it consists only of hoopla and does not have the courage to face the threat from within. This type of community cannot stand. It will fall to the tellers of lies. It will crumble from within.

Even so, there is in America a residual democracy which says that our nation is ruled by its people. There is a legacy of political openness which says that anyone who meets a rather broad set of qualifications can be elected President and govern this vast, rich country of 300 million people. I decided to put that theory to the test. In the spring of 2004, I ran for President of the United States. By the time you read this book you will know that my bid for the Presidency was unsuccessful; but perhaps you will be interested in the attempt.

CHAPTER TWO

A Nation Held in the Grip of Lies

While the truth sets a people free, lies demoralize and enslave. We are a nation held in the grip of lies. These are multiple lies that are sternly and deliberately enforced. Let me be specific. There are at least three categories.

First, I would refer to the adjectives "racist" and "anti-Semitic" (and, to a lesser degree, such terms as "sexist" or "homophobic") which inhibit discussion related to particular racial or religious groups. In demonizing persons who express politically incorrect views, these one-sided labels turn any reasoned argument into an ad hominem attack. The point is not to allow an honest airing of differences that would contribute to social understanding but, in fact, to prevent this, implying that there is only one morally acceptable opinion and those who think otherwise are human filth.

Whites who say anything negative about blacks are candidates for the "racist" label. The same is true of non-Jewish persons who say anything negative about Jews; they are considered perpetrators of "anti-Semitic hate". Any statement found offensive by self-styled representatives of the black or Jewish communities is interpreted to mean that the person who expressed it has an unfocused, all-consuming group hatred which controls his thinking. He is someone who wants to lynch blacks or is another Hitler.

These are lies. With respect to race, the lie consists of judging white people as a group for their perceived attitude toward blacks when the Civil Rights movement was based on the principle that it was wrong for whites to make any blanket judgment of blacks. White acceptance of that principle - that it was wrong to be prejudiced against blacks - has led to and even more strident and pervasive form of prejudice directed against themselves now. Some day, I may be hauled into court as a perpetrator of "hate crimes" for even thinking this way.

It is untrue that whites alone have those hateful or disparaging feelings toward members of other racial groups that are associated with "racism"; yet, when the same tendencies are observed in African Americans, they are either ignored or defined out of existence. The lie also consists of disregarding evident facts in policy discussions. We pretend that the high crime rate within the black community should not affect police attitudes toward individuals suspected of crime. We assert that affirmative action represents "equal justice under the law." The concept of a "protected class" is an abomination; all classes of people should be equally protected.

With respect to anti-Semitism, an "anti-Semite" can be anyone who accuses Jews of nearly anything, especially in alleging their hidden influence in society. While this term has the ring of clinical precision to it, anti-Semitism is used with reference to Jews exclusively, ignoring the fact that Arabs and Palestinians are also Semitic peoples. The concept of anti-Semitism falsely suggests that the world revolves around the Jewish people - that the enemies of Jews are the enemies of humanity - and we must all engage in narrow sectarian fights to aid this particular people.

I do not think it a stretch to say that American Jews are disproportionately represented in influential positions in Hollywood, the news media, and other opinion-setting institutions; or that the same institutions emit consistently negative messages regarding fundamentalist Christians or "anti-Semitic" types of people while being sympathetic to the state of Israel. Yet, to suggest a pattern in any of this would be said to reflect anti-Semitic "conspiracy theories." Such intimidating influences help to perpetuate the lie that the U.S. Government is aiding Israel because it is a democracy rather than because a ruthless, well-financed interest group is pushing for this. Our relationship with Israel is the genesis of America's problems with terrorism and may well have contributed to the U.S. decision to invade Iraq.

One has the impression that this is a dirty subject. (No wonder people avoid discussing it.) I must hate Jews or I must hate blacks to express this sort of opinion. Or, if I present a more restrained criticism, it must mask more sinister feelings. Let me say, in defense, that the allegation of racism or anti-Semitism is a political act - and I reserve the right to criticize any political statement. As an American citizen, this is my right and I will exercise it.

Because this whole area is charged with such rancor, I feel obliged to state that my purpose is not to build a case against Jews or black people but to seek a basis of fair and open discussion. The current arrangement serves only to drive people's thoughts underground. Human relations are a two-way street. No group of people monopolizes virtue or vice. Negativity lurks in everyone's heart. Yet, even as I object to the "racist" or "anti-Semitic" label, I must distinguish those who would irresponsibly use such language from individuals in the groups they purport to defend. There are innocent persons on both sides who may not wish to be dragged into this kind of discussion.

A second type of lie is that expressed by the U.S. business community in regard to its relationship with government. I would characterize this as the "heads I win, tails you lose" philosophy. Business officially supports the idea of free markets and open competition. Government should "get out of the way" of what can be accomplished in this environment. Low taxes and minimal regulation of business are the best policies.

Business does not want people to notice that its numerous lobbyists in Washington and at the state capitols, along with its huge campaign contributions, are focused on securing special favors from government. As part owner of the Texas Rangers baseball team, George W. Bush did not become rich from winning pennants or shrewdly managing the team roster; he did this by convincing the Texas legislature to use taxpayer money to build a new stadium. Profits are not made by maximizing competition but by persuading government to impose regulations that will restrict the competition or by providing direct subsidies or lucrative contracting opportunities. Money is also made by private interests when costs or risks are externalized to the taxpayer and business cherry-pick the more profitable parts of the operation.

We need to cut the tax rate on capital gains, they say, to stimulate capital formation and create jobs. In fact, most big employers purchase capital equipment for the purpose of eliminating jobs as human labor is no longer needed. The stock market is a place to gamble as much as it is to raise new capital for business. It's untrue that most people work long hours do so of their own volition or that massive layoffs lead to a healthy long-term restructuring of the economy. The reality is that, after layoffs, the "lean and mean" organizations work their remaining employees to the bone and costs are cut further through outsourcing of employment to low-wage countries. The CEOs then reward themselves for a job well done on behalf of the shareholders.

It's a lie that "free trade" policies will help the U.S. economy grow or that we can afford to part with our manufacturing industries by specializing in post-industrial, "brainpower" functions. And, of course, a college degree is needed to develop the cognitive skills to cope with challenges in that environment! And, chronic trade deficits are of no concern so long as foreigners use their dollars to buy our assets and debt. Workers who lose their jobs to free trade must believe that there is nothing we can do about globalization. That's a lie - we could impose tariffs. That option is dismissed not by reasoned arguments but by dire warnings delivered by media pundits or academic hired guns about "economic isolationism", "protectionism", or "building a wall around America". Nonsense, a tariff is only a tax; the free-traders must attack straw men to make their case.

Some say the problem of trade deficits could be solved by including labor standards in trade agreements; yet it is no violation of any internationally recognized labor standard for workers in China or Bangladesh to be paid so little. We lie to ourselves in thinking that our failure in the trade area is due to "unfair competition" by evil foreigners. No, this is a failure "made in the USA". Public officials charged with protecting our national interest are asleep at the switch; or, they have effectively taken bribes.

A third lie has to do with the assassination of John F. Kennedy. U.S. Government officials have concluded that President Kennedy was assassinated by a lone gun man, Lee Harvey Oswald, who fired three shots with a rifle from an upper-story window of the Texas School Book Depository building. A blue-ribbon committee headed by former Chief Justice Earl Warren came to that conclusion. Most "responsible" observers concur.

Yet, an overwhelming body of evidence uncovered mostly by free-lance investigators suggests otherwise. Even a subsequent Congressional investigation concluded that four shots were fired, some at angles inconsistent with Oswald's presumed location. A lone gunman shooting from above and behind Kennedy could not have produced that result. We have medical testimony and even photographs of a front entrance wound in the dead President's neck. We have eyewitness accounts of a hole in the front windshield of the Lincoln in which the President was riding, now mysteriously removed. We have evidence that the FBI and Secret Service controlled every aspect of the investigation.

Each particular piece of evidence deserves to be questioned, of course. The idea that top U.S. Government officials could have had advance knowledge of the President's assassination or even have been involved in its execution is truly mind-boggling, as is the idea that the nation's chief investigative and intelligence agencies were involved in a cover up. Yet, in totality, critics of the

Warren Commission report have built a strong case with many mutually corroborating details. Many books have been published on this subject. The History Channel devoted a whole week of programming to testimonies that conflicted with the Warren Commission report.

A majority of Americans today doubt the Commission's conclusions. Still the U.S. Government, forty years after the assassination, refuses to release key evidence about it. Some respected organization needs to spearhead a continuing investigation. Since federal agencies are widely implicated in a cover-up, it cannot be the federal government. News organizations have more credibility. Yet, our nation's top newspapers, television networks, and other media outlets - the History Channel excepted - decline to pursue the story with the persistence it deserves. Someone needs to tell them this is a bigger story than Watergate. There's a Pulitzer prize waiting out there for some enterprising reporter who can crack this case.

God help this country if its top political leader could be assassinated in a motorcade and the crime could be covered up for forty years. Are we children who could not handle the news that some government agency or respected political leader was involved in killing the President? Whether or not one agreed with President Kennedy politically, all red-blooded Americans should be troubled by his murder. It's a stain on our national honor. We are not this free and open society where the truth will out but a people easily cowed by authority figures who ridicule "conspiracy theories" and keep the official lies under wraps.

Truth matters. A nation which knowingly gives itself over to lies has a spiritual problem. It has a problem with self-esteem in allowing itself to be so violated. I suggest that it ought to be a priority for patriotic Americans to correct this problem, for lies bore at the society from within. People become demoralized, angry and confused, and are easily misled. Any political activity in which I take part should have a truth-telling component.

CHAPTER THREE

Finding Courage to Speak the Truth

Speak the truth? I am such a dork to think this matters to anyone - one of those simpleminded persons who thinks it his duty to speak the truth. Sophisticated adults know that the world does not always come in blacks and whites but occasionally in exquisite shades of gray. How much good does the truth teller do when he informs a 6-year-old child that the tooth fairy doesn't exist? Should a person on his death bed be told that he has but an hour to live? Regardless of preachings about truth, the important thing is to keep the show going.

Be realistic. There are times and circumstances where lies, while theoretically abhorrent, do actually make sense. For instance, they are a good tool to use for keeping other people in line. Since our country is based on the idea of being on top, we Americans may have a particular appetite for swallowing lies. All that may change, however, when we realize that we are not on top and the lies in which we so knowingly acquiesce are meant to keep us pacified. When the lie teller wants us to keep a little secret, we, like Tonto, can always say: "Whadda ya mean 'we'?"

It did not take me long to realize that, even though I had graduated from a prestigious college, I was not part of the ruling class. My kind seldom is. By "kind", I don't mean gender, race, or socioeconomic class but the type of person who would write books like this. We are these dorky self-styled truth-tellers perched on a soap box, hoping someone will be interested in our wisdom. But I offer experience, too. So this book is a story about my experience in running for President as well as a place to express thoughts about the kind of society I would try to create if by some chance I were elected to that office.

On the day before I set out on a journey to what I thought would be my first primary state, I had a haircut at a barber school in Minneapolis which I often patronize. The student barber was a talkative man, white, about fifty years old, who hailed from Mankato in southern Minnesota. He told me that he had worked for twenty-five years for the flagship firm of a conglomerate owned by one of Minnesota's richest men, the billionaire owner of a professional sports team. I asked him why he had left employment with that firm. It was not that he had been laid off or fired, the man said, but a calculated decision, mid life, to begin a new career.

A problem was that work hours were becoming too long. He had done a business study and found that several barbers in Mankato were approaching retirement age and none were ready to take their place. By his reckoning, he could make the same amount of money per week as a barber as he did with his former employer working twenty hours a week less.

This man had no hard feelings about his former employer. He had been a competent and trusted middle manager. He went on to say that the billionaire's businesses were so successful because he, the owner, expected each company to be profitable. The company manager was held accountable for increasing profits and, if he failed to perform, he was left go. He himself had been an "idea man" who found ways to cut costs and increase profits when profit margins shrank. I was struck by the fact that the billionaire employer had paid this man such a meager salary after twenty-five years and was working him so hard that he was willing to trade all this for the beginning life of a barber.

Thinking ahead to my forthcoming political campaign, I began to associate his situation to what seemed not uncommon for so-called "management" employees. There is something in American culture which makes us identify with and support our leaders no matter how shabbily they treat us. All they need to do is tell us that we are part of management, that we are part of a privileged group.

One might guess that my own career path has been different. I was an outspoken, free-spirited type of person who objected to the unflattering messages about white males conspicuously displayed in the work place. I was involved in a union drive. My employer, a public-transit agency, cut me loose in the spring of 1996 after sixteen years of employment, three weeks before I would have become eligible for continued health-insurance coverage. This ended a twenty-five year career in accounting with a number of public and private entities.

Before leaving the last job, I purchased real estate in an inner-city neighborhood of Minneapolis. It was across the street from an apartment building where I moved to be close to my employer. I first bought a fourplex owned by HUD and then a nine-unit apartment building adjacent to it. At the time, housing prices were depressed. Street crime was rampant. There was drug dealing in the apartment building.

Inevitably, I ran afoul of the local neighborhood association, police and city officials. Despite my best efforts, my apartment building was blamed for bringing criminals into the neighborhood. The city health inspector condemned my building and a building inspector cited me for costly code violations. I met this challenge through borrowing. After the neighborhood group held a rally to denounce me, I learned of a group of landlords in south Minneapolis who were suing the city for inspections abuse.

I became a stalwart with the group. Although the federal lawsuit did not pan out, the suing landlords turned into an effective political-pressure group. We spoke out at public gatherings, picketed City Hall, protested city-ordered building demolitions, and, most importantly, held a monthly meeting which was videotaped and shown on cable television. There was also a free-circulation newspaper. We became a thorn in the side of city government. Thanks to our incessant propaganda, the public came to realize that buildings do not cause crime; criminals do. Also, top city officials were running real-estate scams.

Of course, such activity led to electoral politics. When no one opposed the mayor's reelection, I announced that I would run. Then I dropped out of the race when a better-known candidate friendly to our cause stepped up to the plate. Four years later, in 2001, the head of our landlord group became a mayoral candidate. Unexpectedly, he suffered a heart attack, became bitter about the lack of campaign support, and dropped out both as a candidate and leader of the group. I filed for mayor to fill his shoes.

My campaign was short but active. I passed out numerous fliers denouncing the city's housing policies while carrying a picket sign around town. Election day was traumatic on two counts. First, my campaign efforts gained a pitiful 143 votes, which was good for twelfth place among the twenty-two candidates. Second, and more important, the Pentagon and World Trade Center were attacked on that day. For it was September 11, 2001. The terrorist attacks produced lasting trauma for our nation and the world. My personal disappointment with the primary results was more than relieved when, in November's general election, Minneapolis voters replaced the mayor and a majority of City Council members.

My take on politics was shaped by experiences had as a member of the landlord group. As a political-pressure group, we had failed in all the conventional ways. We failed in our lawsuit. We failed to pass a bill introduced at the state legislature. We failed to elect any of our members to public office. Yet, the group was a big success. What we had achieved had to do with perceptions of truth. We had turned the discussion around from stigmatizing landlords for neighborhood crime to making the public see that the police needed to accept ownership of this problem and it was improper to use inspections as a crime-fighting tool.

Once lamb for the slaughter, we inner-city landlords became a feared player in city politics; a reporter once called us the only effective opposition to the city's one-party government. And we did this, again, not through legal victories but by speaking the truth as we knew it. We learned that an individual speaking out in public on matters of which he has personal experience can be a powerful instrument for change.

The landlord group was filled not with policy wonks but with persons willing to say what was on their mind. As a result, it had a certain energy and power. We did not try to be the "good guy" or control our public image. If someone called us a group of "slumlords", we accepted the label. When an ill-meaning person would say "I realize that you personally are one of the 'good' landlords; we are talking are talking about the many 'bad' ones", I would respond, "my neighborhood group considers me a slumlord".

I was saying, in effect: "Don't try to divide us." That way we could live without fear. Without poking into one another's business, we trusted each other. There were no fights over parliamentary procedure. There was no haggling over issues. Each member of the group did what he or she could to aid our common enterprise.

The essence of our operation was, as I said, to speak out on aspects of city policy. The televised meetings provided a way to amplify our testimony. However uncouth we may have seemed, these meetings had a ring of authenticity. These were real people speaking out on matters of real public concern, not bureaucrats speaking jargon. As a result, persons aspiring to public office gravitated toward our group; and, when some of them got elected, we had clout.

All this time, neither the *Star Tribune*, Minneapolis' daily newspaper, nor the weekly alternatives gave us any recognition or credit for what we had accomplished, even in our key role in unseating the City Council President. We slumlords were, by definition, incapable of doing anything good. Political liberals hated and despised us. Conservatives, while courting our political and financial support, may have considered us beneath their dignity. We were these greedy maggots who provided housing for the poor, not as an act of charity but to make money. I'm sure that the lawyers, journalists, educators, religious and business leaders decided that we, in associating with society's underclass, did not have clean hands. But we saw ourselves as a group working to clean up city government and, in our own way, improve society.

Those who saw the landlord organization as an economic interest group, working to increase its own profits, missed the mark. We were mostly small property owners. There were plenty of other landlords with larger property holdings who refused to join us. In fact, they often joined with our critics who, in tagging us as slumlords, hoped to ruin us individually so they could pick up our properties for a song. Yet, our political exertions benefited them as well. Were we dupes and fools, giving our free labor to persons who despised us, or did we have some other motivation?

I decided that our exertions were worthwhile from the standpoint of creating a life filled with camaraderie and high adventure that would be hard to come by in any other way. Whatever others might think of us, we were given the opportunity to express ourselves and to be ourselves politically while also having a noticeable impact on the community. It was Camelot during those brief years when our group held together unselfishly and fearlessly fought all the dragons of the realm. I am not among those who say it might have been better to have given up that experience for the sake of acquiring more riches to take to the grave.

I learned to put a value on speaking the truth for its own sake. I developed a faith that even one person expressing something once will change society in a small way. And, if others follow that person's example, the change can be great. "Monkey see, monkey do," is a powerful influence upon human beings. Courage is infectious. Someone courageously standing up in public to express what he believes inspires the urge to emulation, howsoever other forces work to hold people back. Chief among them, perhaps, is the need to make a living. Bureaucracies and professions that provide an abundant income are subject to pressures that tell people how to think.

In that regard, we independent landlords had an advantage. No one could fire us if we said the wrong thing. We could be as outrageously wrong or politically incorrect as we wanted to be. Our customers, the tenants, would not abandon us if they needed rental housing; and, if the city tried to pull any nonsense similar to what it did to me, the landlord group could retaliate immediately. They knew we had teeth.

So, really, we were in the rather unique position of being able to speak freely what was on our mind. We could exercise the freedom of personal thought and expression which citizens of this nation in theory enjoy but not in fact. It was an enviable situation to have in life. This is what inspired my further venturing into politics. I would aspire to speak the truth because I could. Many others in our community did not enjoy that luxury.

CHAPTER FOUR

A Run for the U.S. Senate

After the exhilarating triumph of the 2001 Minneapolis city election, the landlord group faced a potential crisis. With a new executive director, we had to direct our energies in new ways to serve the landlord community. We could not continue to focus on fighting Minneapolis city government if its top officials were now our friends. The new mayor had attended our meetings three times in the year preceding his election and we had presented proposals to him. Most of our enemies on the City Council were gone. By and large, their replacements were persons whom we had supported. Another problem was that, with rising real-estate prices in the city, some members who had needed our help because they were trapped in bad investments had cashed in and moved on to other pursuits. Our membership was in decline. The combination of these two situations convinced me that we needed a change in direction. For me, it was a move toward the larger political world.

It was easy for the Twin Cities media to hang on to their negative stereotypes of landlords and ignore our positive deeds. It would not be so easy if we scored big in electoral politics. Although what we had accomplished as a landlord group could not be held at a peak, it could, perhaps, translate into other areas. I had the idea of using the landlord group as a model of political activity. The essentials of this model were to be, first, a group focused on action rather than legislation, and, second, one possessing its own media capability. The model could be used by any group having political aspirations, either separately or in combination with others.

I dubbed it "the Orange Party" and prepared orange-colored leaflets for circulation at both the 2002 Democratic-Farmer-Labor (DFL) and Republican state conventions. I myself spent most of a day handing out literature at the Republican convention in St. Paul. The response was minimal. I came to the conclusion that this concept was too esoteric. The name "Orange Party" was either too confusing or unattractive to persons committed to other political parties.

Earlier in the year, I had caucused with the Independence Party, to which Minnesota's sitting governor, Jesse Ventura, belonged. In late June, I received an invitation to participate in the party's state convention to be held in St. Cloud. A reminder telephone call persuaded me to attend. I drove up to St. Cloud by myself, talked with people, and listened to the speeches. What was the Independence Party besides Jesse Ventura? The thrust of its message seemed to be that party members were neither too conservative nor too liberal but were in the political middle. In an age of excessively partisan politics, this was not an unattractive message. Indeed, several high-profile members of the two major parties, including former U.S. Congressman Tim Penny, had defected to the Independence Party and were running as its candidates in the 2002 election.

I grew uneasy, however, as the "neither conservative nor liberal" formulation broke down into "fiscally conservative, socially liberal". That was the posture of status quo politics. Both major parties were pro-business and were at least nominally in favor of fiscal responsibility; and both were in favor of attracting Civil Rights-type political constituencies. That is, they were both committed to fighting white racism and advancing women's equality issues. Both were under the thumb of big business or similarly endowed special interests. In addition to the conceptual problems, I wondered if a third party could survive if it failed to differentiate itself sufficiently from the two major parties.

The Independence Party state convention took place on July 13th. July 16th was the filing deadline for the 2002 election. I decided to run for U.S. Senate, challenging the party-endorsed candidate in the primary. Being a person who had attracted only 143 votes in the Minneapolis mayoral primary, this was an ambitious step for me but I plunged into the campaign with enthusiasm. None of my landlord friends supported me. My new wife and stepdaughter, too, were skeptical about this venture. Even I admitted that I was deficient in many of the personal qualities befitting a successful political candidate.

The basis of my challenge was dissatisfaction with the party's political orientation. The Independence Party needed to offer a clear alternative to the two major parties. In what way? There were, I thought, two separate sectors of political conflict - the economic and the social/cultural - in which liberal and conservative positions were defined. As I sized them up, the Republicans were primarily a party of business and the Democrats were primarily a party of Civil Rights. In other words, the Republicans were economically conservative and the Democrats were culturally and socially liberal. Yet, each party had a recessive aspect mirroring the dominant aspect of the other party. The Republicans were not opposed to Civil Rights and the Democrats were not opposed to doing favors for big business.

My idea was that an Independence Party candidate should take the opposing position on both counts. So I devised a campaign platform calculated to oppose both parties simultaneously and in equal measure. My campaign consisted of two statements: (1) "I believe that the Federal Government should reduce the standard workweek to 32 hours by 2010," and (2) "I believe in the full citizenship, dignity, and equality of white males (and of everyone else, too)."

For a campaign prop, I carried a picket sign upon which the two statements were printed on opposite sides.

Unlike the mayoral campaign, I did not walk about carrying this sign; but I did use it in photos distributed to newspapers. The main one was a photograph of myself displaying the "white male" side of the sign in front of a statue of Paul Bunyan and Babe the Blue Ox in Bemidji. The campaign itself was targeted mainly to newspapers in the outstate (non-metro) area.

During a one-month period, I drove 5,500 miles to cities and towns in Minnesota. I gave each editor or reporter literature about my two issues and a standard pitch to explain myself as a candidate. I was also a guest, along with two others, on a midday interview show on Minnesota Public Radio on the Friday before the election. I also placed, or attempted to place, small retail ads in the two large Twin Cities newspapers. To my great disappointment, the *Star Tribune* declined to accept my campaign ad so long as it contained the words "dignity for white males". It also refused to cover my campaign.

Despite the news blackout in Minneapolis, I did all right. I finished second in the primary with 8,482 votes, or 31% of the total, compared with 49.5% for the party-endorsed candidate and 19.5% for a third candidate. This experience gave me confidence that I knew how to campaign. The same publicity techniques applied to races for electoral office as for promoting landlord issues. I did not need much money or a base of campaign supporters but could handle the job myself. On the other hand, I realized that, while such an approach might gain a certain number of votes, it is not enough to win election to a major office.

Yet, my two issues had struck a nerve. Old-style politics centered on differences in economic class. Today's conservatives denounce "class warfare" while practicing their own version of it. My proposal for a shorter workweek provided some balance.

Beyond its economic benefit, this idea appealed to persons concerned with the time squeeze on personal and family life. The new-style politics is all about gender and race. In upholding the dignity of white males, I was jumping into the social and cultural wars that have followed the Civil Rights movement, siding with that faction most under attack. It was a novel position likely to stir passions one way or another.

I would suggest that questions of gender and race, while muted, have defined the U.S. electorate in the past several elections. Al Gore received 92 percent of the African American vote in the 2000 contest, and a larger share of the female than of the male vote. White males voted for Republicans. The strategy of the Democratic Party has, therefore, been to hold its African American base at all costs while adding to it votes from other groups which see themselves as being disadvantaged. The Republicans play a more subtle game of appealing to white and male voters by not being like the Democrats with respect to blacks and feminist women while actively courting the Asian and Hispanic voting blocs. The last thing either party wants is to have someone like me stirring the racial muck, forcing this question out into the open. They would rather have their respective constituencies obediently pull the party lever in response to unspoken appeals. That made my mission all the more compelling.

Some have asked me: Why don't you seek a smaller office first, like a seat on the City Council, where you might stand a chance of winning, rather than starting your political career with a run for higher office? It's a good question. The answer gets back to our discussion about the two kinds of politics. The first kind has to do with passing laws, winning court cases, being elected to public office, or persuading elected officials to do something. The second kind has to do with changing public opinion by speaking out at public meetings, protesting, and demonstrating. I have cast my lot with the latter.

The fact is that I enjoy the life of political action more than I would being an elected official. I hate meetings governed by the rules of parliamentary procedure and all the arcane details that go along with this. Who would want to spend a life that way? But speaking out, even in a hostile environment, is both a useful and personally stimulating type of experience. That is my own higher calling. It's a way to serve the truth. Therefore, even if the apparent goal is out of reach, the exercise of running for U.S. Senate or for President does provide a platform for expressing one's views on matters of importance to our nation.

If I ran for City Council, my campaign might be of interest to persons in certain neighborhoods. A campaign for mayor might interest a larger group of people. It might also interest the larger newspapers and radio or television stations. The downside is that impossible pursuits of elective office lack credibility. Even when such a distinguished individual as former Minnesota governor Harold Stassen ran repeatedly for President, he became an object of ridicule. That was perhaps because he had fallen so far from his previous situation in becoming an insignificant contender in the presidential race. As a political nobody running for high office, I would invite a different kind of ridicule which would arise from the seeming lunacy of taking my own quest seriously. My greatest challenge would be to convey a sense of credibility. Necessarily that would lie in becoming the bearer of a message which voters would otherwise not receive.

Most political campaigns stress building an organization. I could not do that for the simple fact that few, if any, supported my candidacy. I was in a more primitive phase of political change. The most effective means of bringing my ideas to the attention of others was through action. I would run for public office even with a set of issues so reviled that no one dared show support. While the immediate election could not be won, this was building a base for future victories. I needed faith that my ideas had some degree of validity and were not personal fantasy. But it was important to do something about those beliefs, not just talk. Action was the key.

In 1991, I was a human-rights observer of a union election at the Cuautitlan Ford plant near Mexico City. The official union, supported by the government, was being challenged by a union slate supported by most of the workers. Such situations are susceptible to fraud. Since I do not speak Spanish, I relied for information upon an American journalist living in Mexico named Matt Witt, who later became editor of the Teamsters' national publication. Something which he told me as we were lunching in the hot sun outside the plant gates became for me a kind of epiphany.

Witt said that most people think the way to change society is to petition a powerful organization to do something. That approach is invariably unsuccessful. At most, one gets a polite brush off. Power listens to nothing but power. The alternative is to take the matter into one's own hands. Just do something. Protest, demonstrate, go to Mexico to see if the elections are fair. Even if you are an individual seeming to have no power, your action will force the big players to take into account what you are doing. Your gravitational force, however small, will force them to change. Action, not words, is the road to change. I never forgot that conversation.

I think that one of the most important problems facing the United States is the intimidating environment that keeps our people in bondage to lies. There is no law which says that people must believe or heed those lies. They are enforced through intimidation. The person himself or herself chooses to obey the lies. Admittedly, "the system" punishes disobedient individuals. You could lose your job for saying the wrong thing. You could be ostracized by your friends. But, in the United States of America, you are not put in jail or killed for refusing to submit to these lies. The U.S. Constitution protects free speech. It also prohibits official establishments of religion which I would interpret in a broad sense as prohibiting any type of compulsory moral belief.

Yet, Americans submit fearing the consequences of expressing the wrong moral, social, or political opinion. Recalling Matt Witt's comments, I would say that the most effective response is not to complain about it to the government but, feeling confidence in one's self, say to the world: This is wrong! Shout it to the roof tops. Tell anyone who will listen. You will, of course, be exposed to ridicule, but I doubt that the police will be called. While I appreciate the courage of black conservatives in challenging the current racial paradigms, I think it important that white people, too, weigh in on this question, whatever their views.

In my opinion, the highest political calling is to speak the truth in public. I run for high political office not to be elected but to achieve the more important result that has to do with changing perceptions of truth. Though I speak to the media to amplify the message, my basic act is to demonstrate my refusal to submit to intimidation. I will not repeat or heed the lies, even if others will. Anyone willing to pay a price can do this. It's another expression of patriotism - loving one's own country enough that one is willing to suffer ridicule and personal abuse to put one's community on a firmer footing of truth.

The odds are, frankly, that few will listen. Immediately, it may seem a futile gesture. However, such gestures, if repeated, have a cumulative effect. At some point - perhaps quite suddenly - the world will be won over to a new and more truthful point of view. This, in turn, could further blossom into laws, official policies, and the rest. Wouldn't that be a more satisfying political achievement than being elected to high office?

CHAPTER FIVE

Doing Politics in an Age of Entertainment

Political campaigns are about communicating with voters. The candidates practice "retail politics". They go into small-town cafes, churches and union halls or walk down streets shaking hands with people. Face-to-face communication is best but it is also least efficient from the standpoint of time. Each person who shakes hands and talks with a candidate may remember that fact while making decisions in the voting booth. However, to run for high office by such techniques alone is like trying to paddle across the ocean. In theory, that's possible but a better way would be to mount a sail and let the wind drive the boat forward. Using a sail to propel a boat across a body of water is like letting media publicity deliver one's message to voters in a political campaign. One has to seek publicity, distasteful as that may be. One must mug before the camera and court the favor of media people.

It used to be that commercial newspapers would cover political campaigns as a part of their news reporting. Stories would be written about the candidates' stance on issues as an indication of what their policies might be if elected to public office. The voters would compare the candidates in this way. They could pick whichever future they liked best. However, such a model of political coverage is archaic. We are living in an age of entertainment. Entertainment sells newspapers and newspapers print what sells. Political issues bore today's readers; they prefer personalities and the "horse-race" aspect of campaigns.

There is a further concern about giving away free publicity. Why cover a campaign as news when the candidate might be willing to communicate through paid ads? The skimpier or more distorted the news coverage, the more a campaign might need to do advertising and, therefore, the richer the newspaper might become. This motive conflicts with the fact that political campaigns provide news content which is why readers subscribe to newspapers in the first place. The public expects the media to fulfill their traditional function of informing voters about candidates and issues during election campaigns. For the most part, newspapers do. Radio and television broadcasters are another matter.

The advent of the electronic media has had a major impact upon our society. It has, in fact, created a new civilization - the fourth of the great world civilizations that have arisen since civilization itself began. Paradoxically, this "civilization" is focused on popular entertainment. The third civilization, which we are now leaving, is based on the print culture. The idea of the newspaper editor or reporter investigating corruption, crusading for justice, or digging for yet undiscovered truths belongs to the earlier tradition. So does the idea of democracy, which is a market-like process for picking governments. So do political issues. The print culture created structures to convey serious thought. They have begun to decay.

Today's journalist is out to deliver entertainment. He or she mines the "human-interest story" found in, say, destruction from a major flood or tornado. Newspaper reporters like to interview the person who has lost everything because that catches readers' attention. Television is the medium which does this best. Here human tragedy appears in living color. We can watch the tears flow from the victim's eyes or, better still, how the victim bravely holds back tears to keep up appearances. Political candidates wanting television coverage need to know how this medium works. They need skills of the experienced entertainer.

I once had that conversation with Minnesota governor Jesse Ventura, who as much as anyone embodied a politician of the entertainment age.

Some thought it scandalous that this man, a former pro wrestler, could be elected governor of a state. Did Minnesotans have no self-respect? Such an attitude reflects values of the previous civilization.

Ventura was matter-of-fact about this question. I suggested in the book that politicians with entertainment backgrounds were in synch with their age. Therefore, such people today tend to be successful political leaders. Yes, the Governor commented, to be a politician was much like being an entertainer. It helps if government leaders have entertainment skills. In fact, he said in a later interview, because one function of government may be to entertain people, public subsidies for sports stadiums might be an appropriate use of taxpayer funds.

However that may be, entertainer celebrities have one advantage over ordinary politicians: They can easily attract free television coverage because the public is already interested in them. There is a happy conjunction of the broadcasters' need to maintain ratings and the candidate's need to be covered in a political campaign. The public is more interested in these entertainer celebrities as personalities than as persons advancing serious issues. In Reagan's case, that may be less true. But a politician such as Ventura or his friend, Arnold Schwarzenegger, wins votes simply by being who he is. Though a fresh face in politics, the voting public considers him an old friend.

Commercial television has a great influence on voters. One study found that eighty percent of Americans get most of their news from television. Minor candidates, of course, find it hard to get television coverage. To reach the voters, these candidates may have to pay for television commercials. But to advertise on television, a campaign needs money - lots of it. To get money, the candidate must either be independently wealthy or attract campaign contributions from wealthy persons or interest groups which are buying political influence.

As an issues-focused candidate without much money, I was at a disadvantage in this political milieu. Free-spirited candidates out to expose the lies that vex this society have little chance of interesting the big contributors. If one told the truth about certain subjects, their contributions would dry up. Therefore, the financially viable candidates, who are considered the main contenders for office, will lay off attacking the sacred cows. They will assiduously practice special-interest politics. It falls, then, to the little guy to say what really needs to be said about conditions in this society. Only they are free to speak the truth.

A recent study in Seattle found that infants exposed to heavy television viewing tended to develop shorter attention spans than those who watched little or no television. It was alleged that the unrealistically fast-paced flow of images and sounds on television "rewired" the human brain. The brain became less capable of functions requiring patient study of objects. Small children in that situation later exhibited problems of "having difficulty concentrating, acting restless and impulsive and becoming easily confused." One should realize that today's voters, who belong to the television generation, may not be conditioned to follow complex, rational arguments. They need to be persuaded in some other way.

Karl Rove ran the 2000 Bush campaign with that in mind. He focused the campaign on "character, not issues". Many voters subliminally make their voting decision on the basis of which candidate has the better personality. The candidate debates are a showcase of personalities interacting with each other. George W. Bush came across as a down-to-earth guy with a good sense of humor where Al Gore was a bit too mechanical and stiff. Political issues have little to do with it. An advisor to President Reagan, Roger Ailes, once said that "likeability" was the "magic bullet" in politics. If people like you as a person, they tend to ignore the disagreeable things you represent. The "likeable" candidate would be someone like John Edwards as compared with a nerdy, issues-centered candidate like Dennis Kucinich. Unfortunately, I also fall into the latter category.

Communication by television is also about branding. Branding is about repetitiously presenting a consistent image. The more viewers see a television commercial, the more the product image sticks in their mind. Political candidates, too, are branded. Their facial image appears often on the television screen. Their TV commercials project

a simple message. Clear labels are attached to the candidates: President Bush is "a strong, steady leader" while John Kerry is a "tax-and-spend liberal from Massachusetts." On the other hand, Kerry is an authentic Vietnam veteran who courageously rescued his buddies from harm while George W. Bush's military record was suspect. The discussion seldom gets any deeper than this. The voters need to know one or two salient facts about the candidate and a entire campaign can be built around this.

My idea of changing values is out of place in an environment where people are conditioned to think in stereotypes. The voters already know who the "good guys" and "bad guys" are. They know which opinions are respectable and which are not. If I am hoping to present a complicated argument that goes against the prevailing view of gender or race, I immediately become a suspected front man for the Royal Society of Wife-Beaters or the Ku Klux Klan. Countless news reports and movies have told people in advance what to think of me. I can hardly hope to reverse their opinions in the short time which I might have, if lucky, to express myself on television. That takes repetition and costs money.

I would be working against decades of hard attitude-building by the Hollywood image-creating machine. Hollywood peddles dramatic stories. Most stories have a moral theme. There are heroes and villains in the drama. The rub lies in associating these morally charged characters with certain demographic types. Nowadays, for political reasons, one seldom sees a black man portrayed as an ignorant, shiftless character, but, more often, as someone - say, a member of a commando SWAT team - with great personal strength. The villainous characters are typically non-Jewish white males. Thuggish police officials from the American South circa '50s or '60s are standard fare. These formula-driven scripts of the entertainment world shape political thinking today. The branding process associated with popular entertainment has tended to denigrate groups consistently shown in a bad light. The convergence of news and entertainment is especially strong in the social area.

Economic questions are often complicated. Getting to the truth requires a detailed discussion in which contradictory evidence may be considered. Political campaigns do not have time for that. The best way to persuade is by using authority figures. You need a man or, increasingly, a woman who possesses evident credentials and is well groomed. That person needs to seem judicious, expressing a moderate position in lofty, vague terms but not sparing the metaphorical characterizations. On the other hand, you lose it if your witness becomes angry or goes into too much detail. As always, people want the image of a winner. Huey Long used to dress up in expensive suits with flamboyant neckties to impress his audiences. Today's presidential fashion is the casual look, which signals that the candidate, while rich, is a man of the people.

It's enough, when discussing economics, to hurl one or two well-chosen labels at the opposition. Those who cite the bad consequences of free trade are "protectionist"; and, says the chorus line, "protectionist policies won't work." Why they won't work needn't be answered - we've run out of time. An economist from an Ivy League college who says those trade policies won't work is presumed to know his subject. If the free-trade critics persist, then, of course, they want to "build a wall around the country." However well-intentioned, they are "ostriches with their heads in the sand", ignoring the reality of a global economy. Inevitably, television debates on this kind of issue lead to ad hominem attacks.

A sign posted next to a driveway not far from my home says: "Don't even think of parking here." In politics, there should be a sign that reads: "Don't even think of advocating tariffs." Everyone knows that tariffs are protectionist and protectionism is no good. Our citizens are so well trained by the media that they instinctively know what is and what is not an acceptable opinion. As a result, you will seldom hear respectable candidates for public office expressing certain views even if the facts point in that direction. They will inch toward the forbidden position but never cross the line. I guess that function is left to dummies like me. With no reasonable chance of being elected, I can afford to play the heretic. Since the media mostly ignore me, I would actually welcome being attacked by another candidate or by a media commentator for the publicity it might gain.

I think the important thing is to make a principled statement on an issue of public policy. It is to be seen standing up for what one believes in and, therefore, setting an example, even at the risk of being labeled a "kook". To speak one's true mind, even once, sets a precedent for the future. In my opinion, the high political ground is to speak out where contrary opinions are needed to challenge the consensus of lies.

Meet Bill McGaughey, another candidate for President seeking the Democratic Nomination
Ask the right questions!
says candidate Bill McGaughey

CHAPTER SIX

Seeking a Political Identity

My campaign for U.S. Senate left me with issues in two different areas. They were chosen to differentiate me, as an Independence Party candidate, from candidates of the Democratic and Republican parties. The issue chosen to give voters an alternative to the Republicans was an economic one: I was in favor of legislation to reduce the workweek. The issue chosen to differentiate myself from the Democrats was a stance on identity politics: I was for the "full citizenship, dignity, and equality" of white males. In other words, I was positioning myself as an economic liberal and a social/cultural conservative. I was taking the weaker side in both areas. For, it seemed to me, that both the Democrats and Republicans, as well as Independence Party members, were largely pro-business (and anti-labor) and in favor of white-male guilt. That was also the position of corporate America.

Before beginning a campaign, it was important for me to consider my political identity. What would be the partisan image that I would convey? How might people perceive me as a candidate? I was not an elected official with a voting record. I was associated with no identifiable faction of either major party; neither was I in the mainstream of Independence Party politics, whatever that might be. With the exception of belonging to the landlord group, I was associated with no special-interest group. I was just out there doing my own thing. I was, in the summer of 2003, a 62-year-old white man, six feet tall, moderately overweight, married, with a stepdaughter in college, who had worked in the accounting field for many years but who now supported himself from owning rental properties in Minneapolis. Behind me lay a reasonably successful campaign in the Independence Party primary for U.S. Senate and its legacy of the twin issues.

Both issues were controversial. Neither enjoyed a significant base of popular support. I embraced them for different reasons. The economic proposal grew out of a long-standing personal interest in questions that related to shorter working hours and trade. I had researched this area and published books on the subject. My first book explored the economics of shorter-work-week legislation. I had also coauthored a book on this subject with Eugene McCarthy. My book on trade was one of the first anti-NAFTA books on the market.

My interest in "white-male" identity politics grew out of personal experiences had while living in the Twin Cities with its socially and culturally liberal politics. Feminism is strong here. The area's racial politics reflect the legacy of Hubert Humphrey, who, as Mayor of Minneapolis, delivered a stirring speech at the 1948 Democratic National Convention in favor of Civil Rights. I spent the 1980s and 1990s working for a public-transit agency which, like previous employers, strongly endorsed affirmative action and the idea that white people had oppressed black people and men had oppressed women over the centuries. I came to see a connection between the derogatory self-image foisted upon me and the lack of economic opportunity which I and many others have experienced in such environments.

Which direction to go? It might be that the Independence Party, following a disappointing result in the 2002 election, would look to me and my approach for guidance in resurrecting itself. Toward that end, I wrote a book about myself and the campaign titled *The Independence Party and the Future of Third-Party Politics (Adventures & Opinions of an IP Senate Candidate)*. This paperback book, published by Thistlerose Publications, had an eye-catching cover with a picture of me in suspenders standing before the giant wooden statues of Paul Bunyan and Babe the

Blue Ox in Bemidji, Minnesota. I was carrying the sign which promoted dignity for white males.

In the book, I tried to combine stories about the Senate campaign, discussions of issues, and my personal background in a coherent work. The approach was inspired by Ray Whebbe, editor of a free-circulation newspaper in Minneapolis called *The Watchdog*. He advised me to downplay issues and instead present my experiences during the campaign as an adventure story. He would give the book publicity in his newspaper. I also expected to sell copies by renting the Independence Party membership list. My hopes to inspire a broader discussion within the party were dashed when the Fifth District chair told me that, contrary to an earlier understanding, I could not rent the party's membership list since that would violate confidentiality rules. Its email newsletter did mention my book's publication but no one responded to that announcement.

I attended the Independence Party's two-day state convention at a community college starting August 2nd. While the people there were friendly enough, this gathering brought the same processing of detail which had driven me up the wall the previous year. It was bogged down in an endless discussion of party platforms, rules, procedures, and the like. Party members debated ninety-seven separate platform issues, broken down between "cornerstone" and "supporting" planks, on subjects ranging from racial profiling to campaign-finance reform to smaller class size in public schools to electric-gas hybrid vehicles to privately owned casino gambling to support for a unicameral legislature. My chief rival in the previous year's Senate primary, Jim Moore, whom I now supported, was elected the party's state chairman.

The fact of the matter is that I had decided to run for President in June. It had become clear that my expectations of stimulating a discussion of ideology and orientation within the Independence Party were misplaced. There was no forum for that. There was, instead, the same philosophical difference between me and other party members as before. I wanted the party to go with one or two core issues which would give it an identity apart from that of the two major parties. Party leaders wanted to hammer out a multifaceted platform defining the party's ideals which would then become its identity. It seemed to me that the Independence Party was letting procedure get in the way of a coherent message. All this minutiae came across as a blur.

Having to get my own message out, I needed to hit the campaign trail. The problem was that the Independence Party would not be involved in a statewide or national campaign until 2006. A national organization called "Committee for a Unified Independent Party" (CUIP) had held a conference in New York City at the beginning of the year which I attended. Would CUIP provide a forum for fundamental policy discussions from a perspective of political independents? I came to realize that this group was more interested in advancing its organizational agenda than in having two-way discussions. The political universe seemed devoid of opportunities to discuss the kinds of issues that matter to people. The only party with a live contest in the next several years was the Democrats.

In the U.S. Senate campaign, I had opposed the Democrats in advocating "dignity for white males". If I became a Democrat, would I have to change my views on this subject? No, it should be possible to participate in a Democratic Party primary while remaining faithful to one's political convictions. One way would be to seek the Democratic nomination for President but remain an Independence Party member. I checked with the Federal Election Commission and learned that the agency had no objection to that posture. Others had done it before.

Another possibility was to become a Democrat but run against what I perceived to be the core Democratic position: the politics of gender and race. I would be a candidate out to change the party's philosophy. I could argue that the Democrats' special appeal to African American and feminist voters was alienating the broad majority of white and nonfeminist voters who perceived it as being divisive and unfair. All the Republicans had to do was to stake a "moderate" position on social issues - one slightly to the right of the extreme position taken by the Democrats - and voters would flock to that party in droves.

My first instinct was to remain with the Independence Party. I had recently published a book with that party's name in the title. Voters do like to see some consistency in party affiliation. On the other hand, I felt that party identities were overrated. Political parties are not like a religion where one must remain faithful to a particular set of beliefs but a tool to persuade government to act in a certain way. Beliefs and positions evolve. For me to become a Democrat, there would be no need to embrace the party's current ideals. A party is whatever its members want it to be. And elections help them make that choice.

My two issues - a shorter workweek and dignity for white males - offended different groups with different degrees of emotional intensity. The second issue jumped out. So strong is the revulsion to racial or gender prejudice in our country today that to say one is in favor of white-male dignity is thought to mask hatred for other groups. Simply put, it's not respectable to say anything like this. Thought to represent the unhooded face of group violence, such views are like political pornography. Like regular pornography, however, they attract attention.

In contrast, it is not such a shocking thing to be in favor of shorter working hours. While the business community may not like it, American politics has a well-established tradition of considering issues antithetical to business. At most, one is regarded as a naive idealist in supporting such schemes. I would not be hated, just not receive campaign support. On the other hand, the idea that I, as a candidate seeking the Democratic nomination for President, would run on a platform of advocating dignity for white males would raise immediate hackles. What to do?

All this had to be considered in light of my own demographic nature. I am male. I am white. I had the advantage of a "good" education. In our society, people like me are a dime a dozen. Was I complaining that white males experience disadvantage in the same sense that blacks or women claim to have suffered? The very thought makes many people angry.

Let me say this. Women, blacks, and others unlike myself have concerns which are as valid as mine; but they are not more valid. I am no cipher unless I choose to be. I don't mean to suggest that anyone should pay special attention to my concerns. If someone like me is "successful", then people would pay attention. But an older man like me, who in the course of many years has failed to distinguish himself through notable success in a career, is passed off as delusional if he thinks that he might become or do something great. There is no support system for this kind of aspiration.

The fact that our society's power structure disproportionately consists of well-educated white men such as myself confuses the issue. One would assume that my kind of person is favored in this society. Once that might have been true, but not any more. Fifty years of the politics of social disadvantage, which celebrates and promotes the struggles of disadvantaged people to realize their dreams, have created an attitude of contempt for those in the old guard.

White women today seem to specialize in putting white men down. And black men tell me that their black women put them down. We all put people down like ourselves. Maybe we hate ourselves? Yes, I think that's so. What one would call self-hatred is rampant in our society. When self-hatred is king, there is little advantage in belonging to a group that is powerful. The power structure merely focuses its self-hating energies on you.

I remember how, years ago, people expected great things from me. (Or was it only my mother who cared?) Today, I find fewer who show any interest in what I am doing. I found few who took me seriously when I said I was running for President. Even my close friends thought this was a nutty project. I tried to argue that, even if I could not expect to be elected, it embodied a serious purpose. Eyes would glaze over. Granted, I had 62 years to prove myself and demonstrate that I could be someone. If I could not do it in all this time, what made me think I could now? Let me say just that, because I am running out of time in my life, I thought I might like to run for President. What else is there to do in one's old age?

The Gospels say that "a prophet is not without honor except in his home town and among his kinsmen and family." After years of trying to convert the people of Mecca to his religion, the prophet Mohammed had to go to Medina to find worldly success. If the principle of self-hatred affected Jesus and Mohammed, it could affect anyone. I am certainly not in their league, but I do have some personal pride. I have done some interesting things in my life. Let not anyone living in my home town try to take this away from me.

I wrote an insightful book on world history, for instance. I found that, while no U.S. newspaper would review it, an African reviewer described the book as "an excellent job, an epoch-making phenomenon in the art of history writing" and a reviewer in India said my book represented "a brilliant analysis of the march of world history." A reviewer in Pakistan called it "a valuable book which covers the entire expanse of recorded history with great clarity, care and erudition." No college in America would accept it but a school in Hong Kong did. A Chinese-language translation has outsold the English original.

Unable to find a wife from among my own people, I found one in China, not a destitute refugee but an attractive and successful career woman. As an upper middle-class woman from Beijing, she might have had any number of desirable men there but instead she took me. Self-hatred might be present among all peoples. Also, I was lucky.

What this told me was that, if I ran for President, I could not assume that my own state, Minnesota, would be a hotbed of support for my candidacy. Any type of evident overreaching is discouraged in our starched Lutheran culture. Unless I already was someone politically, I would be shunned. The same might be true of neighboring states such as Iowa (scene of the nation's first caucus) and Wisconsin. People there would see me as someone like themselves and resent the fact that I was running for President. But, if I went to New Hampshire, South Carolina, Louisiana, or another distant place to campaign, my candidacy would not grate so much on people's nerves. They would simply take me as any other candidate and try to size me up objectively.

Therefore, the campaign's marching order must be: Hit the road. Fan out to other states to deliver your message. Travel to exotic new places and see what happens. Don't just stay home.

Part

CHAPTER SEVEN

The Kick Off on June 20, 2003

In America, almost anyone can run for President. The Constitution requires only that one be a U.S. citizen who is at least thirty-five years and was born within the territory encompassed by United States.

The immediate cause of my running was the fact that the chairmen or chairwomen of Democratic state party organizations would be meeting in St. Paul, Minnesota, on June 20th and 21st, 2004. This event would be a showcase for the Presidential contenders. If I were a candidate, I could not afford to miss this opportunity; it forced me to make a quick decision. First I needed to make a ten-day trip to the east coast to visit my father and brother, both in nursing facilities. On June 5, 2003, I sent a letter to Mike Erlandson, chair of Minnesota's Democratic-Farmer-Labor Party, announcing that I would be a candidate for President seeking the Democratic nomination. I sent him a copy of my Independence Party book. Copies of this letter and the book also went to three newspaper reporters in the Twin Cities.

In the letter, I brashly declared that "I am running because I believe that the Democratic Party has lost its way and none of the other candidates for President are addressing the core issues." My letter also stated: "While seeking the Democratic nomination, I remain a member of the Independence Party of Minnesota. If I win the nomination or an important primary, I will immediately switch affiliation to the Democrats. I wish to affiliate with a political party whose orientation roughly matches that of the Democrats in Franklin D. Roosevelt's time. I would urge the Democrats to focus upon the security and well being of average working people and to abandon the politics of gender and race." I asked to be included on the list of candidates scheduled to appear before the Association of State Democratic Chairs.

After returning from my trip on June 18th, I printed fliers announcing my candidacy and had a sign made by a commercial printer. On one side, the sign said: "Meet Bill McGaughey, another candidate for President seeking the Democratic nomination." The other side presented a restatement of the Senate campaign's themes: "McGaughey's politics of TWO ENDS. (1) An end to Class Warfare, especially by the Rich. (2) An end to the Politics of Gender and Race." Having this prop, I faxed a press release to twenty-five newspapers and radio or television stations in the Twin Cities which said that I would be announcing my candidacy for President of the United States outside the Radisson Riverfront Hotel in St. Paul, site of the Democratic party officials' meeting, at 10:45 a.m. The first candidate presentation, Howard Dean's, would begin at 11:00 a.m.

I drove to St. Paul from my home on Friday morning, June 20th, parked in a ramp near the public library, and walked several blocks to the hotel. The other candidates' supporters were out in force. Howard Dean had the largest and most vocal group of supporters. The Kucinich and Kerry campaigns were also well represented. In contrast, no newspaper reporters or television crews seemed to be looking for me. I glanced at my watch - it was 10:45 a.m. I was then completely surrounded by boisterous Dean supporters standing near the hotel entrance. No one paid the slightest attention to me. To tell the truth, I made no campaign announcement. I simply stood there with my sign, taking in the scene. It was an inauspicious beginning to what I had hoped would be a rip-roaring campaign.

As the day progressed, I overcame my initial embarrassment and began to talk with others gathered on the sidewalk. In addition to supporting the candidates, many who carried signs were promoting a cause such as gay rights or peace in Iraq. I gave them my literature and they gave me theirs. A young black man named Craig who said he was with the District of Columbia Democrats was interested in my view of racial politics. I gave him a copy of my book with its provocative cover. Hurrying to the airport to catch a flight home, he graciously accepted the copy.

The candidate appearances, held in the hotel's downstairs ballroom, were closed to the public. However, a Dean coordinator told his supporters that she thought the event organizers would let some of them in to hear the presentations. I followed this crowd down the escalator and into the ballroom. Evidently, the plan was for each candidate to make a 45-minute presentation to committee members followed by questions. After placing my picket sign against the wall, I stood with others in the back of the hall listening to Howard Dean. He seemed to be doing well. The ballroom was packed, with a few empty chairs in the back.

As I said, Dean was the first presenter. Dennis Kucinich and Al Sharpton also attended the event in person. Two of the presidential candidates, Senators John Kerry and Joe Lieberman, who were being kept in Washington to cast a vote on the bill for prescription-drug benefits, made presentations by satellite. Rep. Dick Gephardt also appeared before the group by satellite. The other three - Bob Graham, Carol Mosely Braun, and John Edwards - did not participate.

Interesting as this was, my purpose was to have meaningful interaction with the candidates, the press, or other significant individuals. My best bet for such an encounter was not in the ballroom but outside near the hotel entrance. Howard Dean, a smirk on his face, had already greeted his supporters there. I was hoping that others, especially Al Sharpton, would come outside to greet the crowds. I went back outside the hotel.

During one of the dull moments spent standing on the sidewalk, I saw Walter Mondale walk past me, engaged in conversation with another man. Soon afterwards, a vivacious, blonde-haired woman with a compact video camera approached me. "Isn't that Walter Mondale?," she asked. Indeed it was, I said. This woman evidently wanted to talk with Mondale. She went off in pursuit but he escaped. Then she came back to me, showing an interest in me and my sign.

She said her name was Alexandra Pelosi. She was a documentary maker for HBO who was traveling around the country covering the 2004 presidential race from a human-interest standpoint. Yes, I admitted, I was a candidate for President of the United States. This was the first day of my campaign. What were my campaign plans, she asked? Did I intend to enter any of the primaries? In truth, I did not yet have any plans. However, I answered that I thought I would go to Iowa. "Oh, can I go with you?," she asked. I had the presence of mind to say "yes".

I later learned that this was the daughter of House Minority Leader Nancy Pelosi of California. What's more, she had made a name for herself when she had followed George W. Bush around on the 2000 campaign trail and had produced a critically acclaimed documentary. I did not know that then. Ms. Pelosi soon demonstrated her talent for staging scenes. A cinematic agent provocateur, she recruited nearby persons to engage in discussions with me, the presidential candidate, who presumably wanted to get votes. The hotter the controversy, the better. I had to prove my campaign skills on the spot.

The first recruit was a shirtless, blond-haired young man who ranted about abortion. The Democrats were the pro-abortion party, he said; and, since I was running as a Democrat, I obviously favored that position. I weakly protested that abortion was not my issue. It did not matter. The Democrats were for abortion, and one of their motives might be to kill off as many black babies as possible for population-control purposes. In a loud voice, he demanded a response from me. As Pelosi diligently recorded the scene, I tried to state my own "moderate" position on abortion. None of my answers satisfied. Eventually, this man grew tired of browbeating me and went away.

Pelosi next brought over two middle-aged black women who were officials with a state party organization. I let them know that I was an Independence Party member who was seeking the Democratic nomination. "You can't do that," one of the women said. I was confident that I could, having consulted with the FEC on this matter. So I boldly remarked: "If I can't run for President while remaining an Independence Party member, I might as well drop out now. My campaign is over." From behind the camera, Alexandra Pelosi teased: "This is your first day of campaigning and already you're through."

We also talked about race. One of the women challenged me to give a single example of white males being harmed or victimized by the system. After a moment's reflection, I told her of my own experience. I was an inner-city landlord with predominately black tenants in a racially mixed neighborhood. A number of years ago, my neighbors persuaded the city to condemn my building because of alleged criminal activity there. The drug dealers and gang members were predominantly black. Instead of focusing on the criminals, the politically liberal neighborhood group went after me. I thought race might have something to do with that. It's OK to make crime an issue, I said, if you put a white face on it, but not to focus on the black criminals. My answer did not please this woman. She went away in a huff, refusing to talk with me any more.

Pelosi commented that I had struck out with these first two sets of voters; I would have to be more persuasive than that. I next went up to a mild-looking young white man with glasses and explained the situation to him. I went into a sales pitch covering the basic points of my campaign. Pelosi asked him if he would consider voting for me. He would. Wow, I now had a one-out-of-three batting average.

There was a short recess when I was allowed to relax. Pelosi then reappeared with a graying, kindly-looking man whom she introduced as Art Torres. This was State Senator Art Torres, chairman of the California Democratic Party. Perhaps taking me for a white racist, he began by observing that Hispanic people, too, were white. I responded that I was not against anyone, black or white. We talked about my candidacy. I had come from the Independence Party, I said, but would be willing to switch to the Democrats if I won the nomination. "That's mighty generous of you," Torres remarked.

Despite this exchange, we had a pleasant conversation. I liked Torres. He was open and direct, and he gave me his business card. I, in turn, gave him a copy of my paperback book, *The Independence Party*, which he asked me to autograph. My inscription, in part, read "toward a better Democratic Party". I also gave a copy to Alexandra Pelosi, who at first was reluctant to accept it, as journalists sometimes are. Pelosi did not have a business card on her but she wrote down her phone number and email address at HBO in my notebook. Then she gave me another address at "journeyswithgeorge" which she thought might work better.

After this exhilarating experience, I went back inside the hotel for a cup of coffee. Some of Gephardt's campaign staff manned a hospitality room off the main lobby. I introduced myself as a candidate. They politely responded that they were already committed. I ran into several old friends and acquaintances - the grandson of my old landlady from thirty years ago and an old-guard member of the DFL state central committee from north

Minneapolis where I live now. Dennis Kucinich passed by, pursued by reporters.

I went back downstairs to try to get back into the ballroom. This time, party staff would not let me enter. I hung around the exhibit tables in the hall. Then, carrying my sign, I ran into the Hennepin County Attorney Amy Klobuchar whom I knew from activities related to the landlord group. Except for criminals, of course, she always makes people feel comfortable. We talked for awhile. There were a few others whom I also recognized. At length, I went back outside hoping to run into Al Sharpton or another candidate. Dennis Kucinich was meeting with his supporters. He gave a fiery stump speech and then shook people's hands, including mine. I thought he was squinting to read my sign as he gave his speech. His supporters included many of the Wellstone type of Democrat. Sharpton never appeared.

It had been a satisfying day but I was growing weary. I returned to the parking lot to grab more copies of my book. However, the crowd was thinning out by then. I spotted WCCO-TV State Capitol reporter Pat Kessler near a truck with a satellite dish. In my fatigue, I greeted him as "Skip Loescher", a Twin Cities television reporter of twenty years ago. He said his name was "Kessler". I knew that. In fact, we had spoken more than once during my Senate campaign. Pat Kessler was jotting something down on a note pad. Even so, he took time to talk with me and accept a copy of the Independence Party book, which I autographed. Now the crowd was really thinning out. I walked back to the parking lot and drove home.

CHAPTER EIGHT

An Event in Des Moines

I had been a presidential candidate for less than a day and already I had a promise that my campaign would be covered by HBO. This was like money in the bank. As the days went by, however, I realized that Alexandra Pelosi had not made a specific suggestion about which events she might cover. It was up to me to propose something. Exercising my powers of creative imagination, I sent an email to the "journeyswithgeorge" address. I offered her a choice between three concepts: (1) "debate Al Sharpton", (2) "hunt for skeletons in Bill McGaughey's past", and (3) "recreate the 1945 meeting at the Elbe River between American and Russian soldiers." In her response, Pelosi picked the last concept. In retrospect, it seems the least contentious.

Since I had told Pelosi that I planned to campaign in Iowa, the event had to take place there, of course. Race relations would be its thematic focus. What does "a meeting at the Elbe River" have to do with race? Well, it's about soldiers representing two politically opposing systems putting their animosities aside to embrace as human beings engaged in a common purpose, the defeat of Nazi Germany. My staged "meeting" would symbolize two hostile races approaching each other in a spirit of reconciliation while retaining their integrity. Besides appealing to World War II veterans and Russian immigrants, the "meeting at the Elbe" would be physically appropriate because a river runs through Des Moines, Iowa's capitol and largest city. The fact that a "Cold

War" followed the original event was of little concern to me. We're amateurs at staging political theater.

If the theme was racial reconciliation, however, I needed to enlist African American participation. My idea was that the black participants might approach the Elbe-like meeting point from one direction and whites approach it from the other. How to find black participants? The NAACP was a logical place for recruiting them. Because Des Moines has no local chapter, I wrote a letter of invitation to the national organization. What other organizations might be contacted to supply participants? I had no idea. I had never been to Des Moines before. I therefore ordered a copy of the Des Moines telephone directory from Qwest Dex and wrote down the names, addresses, and telephone numbers of organizations such as churches, labor unions, and fraternal organizations which might have a possible interest in the event. I mailed out a number of letters enclosing fliers. None panned out.

Pelosi had suggested in an email that my event be held during the Iowa State Fair. She expected to be in Des Moines for the eleven-day period, August 7th through 17th, when the fair took place. Several of the other presidential candidates would be attending. I picked Saturday, August 16th, which gave me more time to prepare. Thinking that I might need to scout the territory, I drove down to Des Moines from Minneapolis to look things over. I parked in a lot near the Civil War monument to the south of the Capitol. Walking down Walnut Street toward the river, I spotted what seemed to be an ideal location. This was a small park on the east bank of the Des Moines River called the Simon Estes Amphitheater. A steel-tubed arch stood in front of a small concrete plaza surrounded on three sides by a grass lawn sloping down to the river. How could I reserve this spot, I wondered? It was best to have a backup location. Across the river, in downtown Des Moines, was an-

other small park next to the civic center with modernistic sculp-
ture and a fountain.

The only other logical place for my
event was on the grounds of the Iowa
State Capitol. I was directed to Judy
Lowe of the Administrative Services department in the (Herbert) Hoover Building who handled reservations for events
on the Capitol grounds. She was a help-
ful person who gave me a reservation
form and laid down the ground rules:
Stay on the sidewalks and obey traffic

lights during the march. Do not have any stick-based signs at the
rally. During the 1950s a little old lady with such a sign had poked
someone at a rally so the state had adopted this regulation. However, pole-based signs were OK.

The Simon Estes Amphitheater was my first choice for a
location because it best fit the theme of "meeting at the Elbe".
Back in Minneapolis, I learned that events at this park were scheduled by the Des Moines Parks & Recreation department. I needed
to speak with a woman named Robin. I left telephone messages
for Robin each day throughout the week. When she finally returned my call, she said that space would be available in the early
afternoon of August 16th. I could reserve a four-hour time slot at
the park ending at 4 p.m. when a wedding would take place. The
charge was $500. What!?!

I quickly thanked her and then called Judy Lowe who had
previously told me there was no charge for holding rallies on the
State Capitol grounds. She asked me to fax her my completed
application promptly because she was going on vacation next
week. In time, I received from Lowe a letter of approval to hold
a "Bill McGaughey for President" rally near the Civil War monument from 2 p.m. to 4 p.m. It was copied to several state officials
including the Governor's office.

Since this event would no longer be held on a river bank, its theme needed to change. There would be no "meeting at the Elbe". The element of marching from scattered places to a central point became less important than the rally itself. The event was becoming primarily a free-speech forum on race. It was still important, though, to have a racially diverse group of participants. In my estimation, most officially sponsored discussions of race are contrived. I wanted an event which, like the landlord meetings, would allow each participant to speak freely. If racial radicals showed up, we would seek a Jerry Springer-like synthesis of divergent views where, hopefully, no punches would be thrown. The site of the rally, near the Civil War monument, reinforced the idea of fighting to achieve a resolution of racial conflict.

Word got out to some of my friends and relatives in Minneapolis, who are black, that I was running for President and would be stressing racial themes. My ex-brother-in-law, Alan Morrison, who was working with me to renovate a duplex down the street, offered to convert his pickup truck temporarily into a campaign vehicle. At Menard's, a Midwestern home-improvement store, we spotted a canopy tent with stars and stripes, intended for 4th-of-July celebrations. We could attach this canopy to back of the truck to create a roofed stage for political rallies. Alan called this roving campaign platform my "White-Male-Mobile". It was, however, too much work for a single event. At another home-improvement store, Home Depot, I bought an eight-foot step ladder whose sides were decorated with stars and stripes. Adorned with flags, this became a makeshift podium for the rally.

The biggest challenge was to find persons to participate. I wrote letters to all the other Democratic presidential candidates inviting them to discuss racial issues in Des Moines. I assembled lists of Iowa newspapers and television and radio stations, and mailed or faxed them announcements of the August 16th event. Hopefully, this would stimulate media interest in covering the event or would create advance publicity to bring out people. I belonged to a men's rights organization in Minneapolis. Citing the promised HBO coverage, I proposed that some of its members accompany me to Des Moines to take advantage of the free-speech forum. This might be an opportunity to be heard nationally. However, there was resistance to that idea. A group member, who was white, emailed me: "I suggest you drop the word 'white' from your signs and literature. It puts you in the same category as Nazis and white power groups."

A week before the event, Alexandra Pelosi sent a bomb shell by email. "Dear Bill," she wrote. "I am so sorry to tell you this but it turns out that I am not going to be in Des Moines next Saturday. I hope that doesn't screw everything up for you. Good luck with your event. Alexandra."

For me, plans were too far advanced to cancel the event. Since Iowans were not responding to my appeals for participation, I focused on finding people to ride with me from Minneapolis. Ed Eubanks was the first. He was a friend and a tenant in my apartment building with whom I shared a lively interest in politics. An African American man, he had first suggested that he might play the part of an angry black man in this forum on race to get things going. His presence there would provide assurance that whatever discussion we might arouse would have at least two sides.

An even less likely participant was a former tenant named Randy, a white man, whom I had evicted four months earlier because of his association with drug dealers. One of them had torched the apartment after he moved out. We remained on speaking terms, though, and he agreed to come. Seeking racial and gender diversity, I also leaned on my wife. I thought I had an agreement from her to come until I made the mistake of also inviting my former wife's daughter. Then my wife, who dislikes politics almost as much as she does my former wife, put her foot down. No, she was staying home that weekend. Several others first accepted my invitation and then canceled plans to participate. In the end, we were down to three people: Ed, Randy, and me.

Ed and I got together after 7 a.m. on the big day and drove to Randy's new apartment to pick him up. I had a digital video camera. Randy had a still camera. The car was packed with event paraphernalia such as the red-white-and-blue ladder, tripod, signs, and flags. The 240-mile trip down Interstate Highway 35 took about five hours, not counting the time we spent in stopping at Subway Sandwich in Story Book, Iowa. I had no idea what to expect in Des Moines. We knew that the Iowa State Fair was

winding down that weekend and that the parking facilities near the State Capitol would be used for people to commute to the fair grounds. There was one parking spot left near the Civil War monument. We grabbed it as we pulled into the lot around 1:15 p.m.

I felt obliged to go to the park near the Des Moines Civic Center because our literature had said this was a staging area for the march. It would have been convenient to drive, but I was unwilling to risk giving up our parking spot near the Civil War monument. So, by myself, I walked with my sign and video camera down the hill along Walnut, past the Simon Estes Amphitheater and across the river, and then to the park. It was hot - well in excess of 90 degrees, I thought. No one was waiting there. (Unbeknownst to me, a friend from the men's group, Nels Otto, did drive to Des Moines expecting to meet us at this park. But he arrived at 2 p.m. and we failed to make connections.) I waited for ten minutes for latecomers to arrive. Then, holding the campaign sign high, I walked up Locust Street, back across the river, and up to the State Capitol where I turned right and walked toward the Civil War monument. Ed and Randy were waiting for me in the shade. Although it was a few minutes after our announced starting time, I needed to sit down for a few minutes under a tree to rest and drink water.

Ed and Randy had set up the ladder near the monument and attached two of the flags to it. Another flag and a sign were stuck in the ground. The Civil War monument and Capitol building served as a back drop. Parodying racial stereotypes, Ed clowned a bit as he shuffled his feet and carried the "dignity for white males" sign. I recorded this scene with the video camera. We then attached the camera to the tripod and were ready to begin our event.

As a presidential candidate, I was the kickoff speaker. I mounted the steps on the ladder and, from an elevated position, gave an impassioned speech stressing economic injustice. Race was mentioned almost as an afterthought. It was not a bad performance considering that I was on the verge of passing out from heat stroke. Ed was next. Mounting the flag-draped ladder, he said that, while he did not agree with everything I had said, he did appreciate my thoughts on job creation. Black people would get some of those jobs. Next, Randy abandoned his post as video camera man to give a short speech from the ladder. That was it. No one else showed up to participate. There were no more speeches and no follow-up discussions. We packed up our gear, stashed it in the car, and walked across Walnut Street to the State Capitol, seeking relief from the heat.

The Iowa State Capitol building, always beautiful, was especially beautiful and comforting to us on that day. Its golden dome glistened brightly in the sun. The air-conditioning system worked. Inside, once we were past Security, we were able to purchase cold drinks from a vending machine beneath the Rotunda. Like Alexandra Pelosi, Ed Eubanks took it upon himself to introduce me as a presidential candidate to prospective voters. A young

Asian man visiting the Capitol asked my position on several issues as Ed videotaped the conversation. He gave me a real workout. On my way to the men's room, I passed the "Ronald Reagan conference room", reminding me that President Reagan had begun his career in Des Moines as a sports announcer with WHO radio. After we had cooled down sufficiently, we left the building. Ed, Randy, and I examined the Civil War cannon trained on downtown Des Moines before walking back to the car.

The trip back to Minneapolis was relaxing for us all. Although (to my knowledge) no one else had shown up to participate and no journalists had covered the event, I was relieved. The

important thing was that we had followed through with our plans. Admittedly a farce, this was my first campaign event as a presidential candidate. Ed and Randy seemed caught up in the pretentiousness of it all. I appreciated their support. We had done our thing and captured some of it on videotape for possible future use. Preparations for the Des Moines "race forum" had claimed almost the first two months of my campaign. Now it was time to move on to other activities.

CHAPTER NINE

Campaign Infrastructure

Running for President has a legal side. The Federal Election Commission (FEC) in Washington, D.C. issues regulations for national campaigns which focus on the financial aspect. A phone call to the FEC gets the process started. The Commission mails candidates a thicket packet of materials to explain the process. Presidential candidates have their materials and Congressional candidates have theirs. Each candidate must file a one-page "Statement of Candidacy" within ten days of announcing. The candidate gives his or her name, address, party affiliation, and office sought. The form also asks candidates to designate a "principal campaign committee", including name and address. If there are other committees authorized to receive and expend funds for the campaign, these, too, must be named. Then the candidate signs and dates this statement, and mails it to the FEC. I signed mine on June 30, 2003.

The other required document is the "Statement of Organization". The name and address of the principal campaign committee should match with that on the first form. If the campaign committee has an email address or a web site, these are to be disclosed. Perhaps the most important piece of information on the Statement of Organization is the identity of the campaign treasurer. That individual is responsible for filing periodic reports of financial transactions to the FEC. Money is both the chief enabler and corrupting agent of contemporary politics. In my case, it was largely irrelevant. I was not actively seeking campaign contributions. The FEC does not require committees which have received or spent less than $5,000 to file quarterly reports. Even so, I needed a treasurer. For appearance's sake, it would be good for that person to be someone other than myself. I thought it advisable to convert a small savings account that I had at Wells Fargo Bank into an account for my campaign committee. The treasurer would be put on the list of authorized signers.

I found the campaign treasurer almost by accident. Staying in my parents' former house in Milford, Pennsylvania, I paid a courtesy call on my next-door neighbor. Another woman answered my knock on the door. She was Linda Davis, who did bookkeeping work for the neighbor. Davis mentioned that she was looking for an apartment to rent. My parents' house, now belonging to me, was empty when I was away. This created a dangerous situation. During a cold spell in the previous winter, the pipes had burst. I, therefore, readily volunteered the fact that my house was empty and I might consider renting to her. Davis took a quick tour of the house. She needed a bedroom and another room on the first floor as a studio for her art work. We came to terms. Since Davis was a bookkeeper, I asked if she would serve as my campaign treasurer, assuring her that, if real work needed to be done, I would handle it myself. She agreed. My campaign now had a candidate from Minnesota and a treasurer from Pennsylvania. In other words, it was a national campaign.

I had brought the FEC publications with me from Minnesota. While waiting for my father to have lunch in his nursing home, I studied the booklet concerned with ballot access. Each state had its own method of putting candidates on the ballot. In many states, the Secretary of State decides who the candidates are. A candidate left off the official list has an opportunity to be included by gathering a certain number of supporting signatures. Sometimes the Secretary of State picks candidates whom the national media believes has substantial support. The process varies from state to state.

From my standpoint, I would have little chance of being included on any state ballot if the Secretary of State made the decision. The petition process offered some hope where a modest number of signatures was required. Here, again, the rules vary by state. Alabama requires 500 signatures statewide to be collected between March 1st and March 15th while California requires 500 signatures in each Congressional District. To get on the ballot in Connecticut, candidates not selected by the Secretary of State need to gather a number of signatures equal to 1% of the vote in the previous election.

For me, the best arrangement was to seek ballot access in states which let candidates run if they simply filed an application and paid a filing fee. A few states allow that. The states which seemed most promising from information given in the FEC booklet were: Colorado ($500 filing fee), Kansas ($100 filing fee), Louisiana ($750 filing fee), Minnesota ($500 filing fee), and New Hampshire ($1,000 filing fee). South Carolina's system of ballot access in the primary was said to be "according to (the parties') own rules and at party expense."

Running in Kansas, Colorado, and Minnesota seemed comparatively attractive although, being a Minnesotan, I suspected something was amiss. I called election officials in the most promising states. The Minnesota official told me what I suspected: The law authorizing a presidential primary had been repealed in 1999. Likewise, in Colorado the legislature had repealed the primary law. In Kansas, the presidential and vice-presidential candidates selected by the national convention appear as a team on the August primary ballot. I would not be on such a ticket. That left New Hampshire, Louisiana, and, possibly, South Carolina. South Carolina, I remembered, had been the scene of a grueling contest between George W. Bush and John McCain in 2000.

I knew that New Hampshire had a presidential primary. The aspect which troubled me there was that candidates had to declare party affiliation. The Louisiana Secretary of State's office sent me a packet of materials about the primary. Ballot access in that state was relatively easy except that the filing affidavit and fee had to be received in Baton Rouge within a three-day period. In addition to the filing fee of $750, presidential candidates had to pay an additional fee of $375, bringing the total up to $1,125. I called the South Carolina Democratic Party and spoke with a man named Waukeen Barnes. The filing fee there was $2,500. If I was interested in being a candidate in the primary, he said, I should send him a short email. One files with the party rather than with a state official. The South Carolina Democrats welcomed participation by all candidates, even lesser-known ones like me, Barnes said.

Another possibility, of course, was Iowa. Iowa had a caucus rather than a presidential primary. My first impulse was to include Iowa in the campaign because it bordered my own state. A Democratic Party official in Iowa confirmed that it was not necessary to file. If interested in being a candidate, he said, just send a statement of who you are and the fact that you're running to the state party chair. He advised me to check the party web site to see what the caucus system involved. I knew something about this already since Minnesota, too, had a caucus system.

Eventually, I ruled out Iowa. The caucus system means that there would be no preprinted ballots. Caucuses are simply meetings of party members at the lowest level of organization. Anyone who thinks he or she belongs to the party can attend as a voting participant. Participation in caucuses does, however, take an hour or two on a certain evening as opposed to a few minutes in a voting booth. Caucus attendees can support whomever they want for President.

As a practical matter, party caucuses tend to attract the more committed party members, who would be less likely to favor my type of candidate. Furthermore, even if I attracted some support at the caucuses, lesser-known candidates are seldom able to form a "viable" caucus. They tend to get eliminated in the next round of caucus voting. The final count at each such meeting would probably understate my support if I ran here. Finally, the event in Des Moines on August 16th had attracted no local participation. Evidently, Iowans were not supportive of my candidacy. Maybe the Midwestern self-hating dynamic was at work here.

Because the filing deadlines for the three primary states were in the period between December and February, I did not pay much attention to this aspect of the campaign until later. My inattentiveness cost me the opportunity to run in New Hampshire. For that state, the FEC booklet had said that presidential candidates had to file declarations of candidacy with the secretary of state's office "between the first Monday in December and Friday of the following week." I should have realized that this information might be out of date. Even so, on Friday, November 21, I was shocked to read a news report on the Internet about the two dozen or so candidates who had filed in the New Hampshire presidential primary in time to meet the filing deadline. The end of the filing period was that day. So, I would not be running in New Hampshire. I should try to be careful not to lose my other two opportunities in Louisiana and South Carolina.

Important as it was, the mechanics of filing to become a candidate in a presidential primary did not affect my chances of winning. I had to put infrastructure in place to have a successful campaign. I rented a post-office box in Minneapolis to use as the official address. That would give my campaign a more professional appearance. I could not let on that it was basically a one-man operation. Next, I arranged for campaign stationery. Linda Davis, the treasurer, was also a creative artist. For $15.00, she drew me a sketch of two men and one woman sitting on the back seat of a bus. This created a visual symbol for what I called my "campaign from the back of the bus."

The "back of the bus" theme was meant to put a positive spin on my chief liability as a candidate - that I was not among the nine Democratic candidates for President who were receiving national attention but someone in the second tier of candidates. When I used to ride the bus to work from a suburb twenty-five years ago, I often sat in the back seat of the bus where some of the liveliest discussions took place. This was the image I wished to convey: an engaged citizenry discussing issues of the day.

Another asset I would have as a candidate was my paperback book which would be sold in book stores. If this book was reviewed in daily newspapers, it would create publicity affecting the campaign. Conversely, my campaign for President would expand interest in the book beyond a regional scope. In drawing national attention, this presidential campaign might stimulate book sales in all states. Book sales, in turn, would help the presidential campaign.

Unfortunately, most presidential candidates have books, and mine did not sell especially well. Its title, *The Independence Party and the Future of Third-Party Politics*, clashed with the fact that I was now seeking the Democratic nomination. To my knowledge, the only U.S. newspaper to cover *The Independence Party* was the *Daily Town Talk* in Alexandria, Louisiana. A columnist for that newspaper, Andrew Griffin, picked up my book in an idle moment, started reading the book, found it interesting, and wrote a column.

Another piece of campaign infrastructure was a web site. When I ran for U.S. Senate in 2002, I was able to reserve the domain name, http://www.billforsenate.org. As a presidential candidate, I was pleasantly surprised to find that http://www.billforpresident.org was not yet taken. I quickly reserved this name and went to work creating pages for a web site. I am the proprietor of several different web sites representing various projects or interests of mine. For my world-history book, there is www.worldhistorysite.com; for the publishing company, www.thistlerose.com; for the Orange Party idea, www.orangeparty.org, etc. The web master for them all is a friend,

Mark Stanley, who is a professional web designer and fellow member of a singing group which meets weekly. He has helped me put pages up on the Web, integrate photos with the text, and repair broken links.

Persons visiting billforpresident.org would first arrive at the home page which identified this as the official web site of the Bill McGaughey-for-President campaign. They would then be greeted by the smiling faces of me and my wife Lian, together with a biographical description. The "campaign from the back of the bus" logo would appear farther down in the text. The home page linked to three subsidiary pages - one concerned with issues, one with campaign activities, and one with contact information. On the issues page, the art work showed rays of yellow light converging on a point in the center of the page flanked on all sides by links to other pages which disclosed my position on various issues. Employment and race were the main topics of discussion. Other pages told, for instance, how violence in large American cities (the torching of my apartment) was related to that in the Iraq war or gave Henry Ford's reasons for introducing the five-day, 40-hour workweek in 1926.

I can't say that this web site did much to advance my candidacy. Even though I paid for banner advertising and advice on selecting key words, I have no evidence of significant traffic to the site. Because it was not promptly listed in DMOZ, Yahoo and Google did not search it until after many months. No one contacted the campaign by email from that site; at least, the messages did not get through to me. I received no campaign contributions. Even so, this web site, www.billforpresident.org, may have helped in unseen ways. I assume that such sites are a necessary part of campaign infrastructure in today's political world.

CHAPTER TEN

Campaign Finances and Expenditures

Most successful politicians are seen appearing at megabuck fundraisers or on the phone raising money from contributors. My only campaign contributor was a man who talked with me in front of the Radisson Riverfront Hotel on June 20th and then gave me a dollar. The rest of the campaign I financed myself. It was no use to solicit funds from others since few people supported my campaign. Therefore, this whole area of campaign activity was eliminated; I could focus on the "important stuff".

Mine was, of necessity, a financially threadbare campaign. I would not do much advertising. I was hoping to be interesting and clever enough for the media to deliver my campaign message without my having to pay for it. With no real base of support, I had a tiny budget to pay for advertising and so was forced to try to present myself as a compelling human-interest story. Some editors and reporters probably saw me as the kid who tried to sneak into the show without buying a ticket.

Instead of communicating with voters, I communicated mostly with the media. Such communication is of various kinds. The most expensive and also the most effective means of communication is to visit a journalist in person. However, one can do only so many visits in a day. The daily cost of travel, lodging, and meals must be spread over the number of daily visits to reach a per-unit cost for each contact.

The second most expensive communication method is to send materials by mail. One has the cost of stationery, printing the literature, and, of course, postage. The postage charge is presently 37 cents for the first half ounce or 26 cents up to three ounces for third-class bulk mail (which also requires $150 annual permits). Photocopying can run 5 to 7 cents per sheet for single copies, with quantity discounts at higher volumes. A typical mail piece costs $.60 to $1.00 each at moderate volumes.

A third method of communicating is by fax. This cost is proportionate to the time spent feeding sheets into the fax machine. My long-distance carrier charges me around 8 cents per call for faxing single sheets. Communicating by telephone, another technique, involves the same cost structure as faxing but the time spent talking varies much more widely. Finally, we have communication by email. The cost of delivering such messages is essentially free; it's built into the monthly charge paid to the service provider.

Another "cost" factor is the time that candidates must spend delivering each type of message. This type of cost is roughly proportionate to financial cost. Personal visits are the most time-consuming, followed by sending "snail mail", followed by faxing information, followed by email. Let's say it takes an hour for a typical visit, not counting travel time, compared with five to twenty minutes (depending on how much of the letter can be copied) to type a short letter and another three minutes per letter to type names and addresses on the envelope, stuff sheets into it, apply postage, and seal the envelope.

On the other hand, it takes me, on average, 1.2 minutes to send a sheet of paper through a fax machine and less per sheet when several are sent at the same time. Times spent talking with people on the telephone vary so widely that it would be useless to suggest an average time. Email transmission is nearly instantaneous once you push "send". The time spent composing these messages is a more significant factor. The speed of photocopying machines and of printers attached to one's personal computer marginally affects communication time.

Emails are clearly the cheapest and most efficient way to communicate, both from a cost and time standpoint. However, there's a drawback. Mass-communicated email messages tend to be discounted. If everyone sends this type of message, then well-known journalists may receive dozens of messages in a day and yours will tend to get lost. The very ease of communication serves as its own worst enemy. I was tempted to use bulk email to communicate with millions of people who might or (probably) might not have been interested in my message. However, this so-called "spam" has a bad reputation. In annoying so many people, its use would hurt my campaign. Political journalists, I thought, were fair game to receive unsolicited messages from me. Even so, my communications had to have a certain appeal to get through in a positive way.

My general strategy, developed in the 2002 Senate campaign, was to start with the less personal kinds of communication - letters, faxes, and emails - before moving on to the more personal telephone calls and visits. This I compared with the phase of aerial bombardment before troops enter a battlefield. Such communication can be done efficiently and without painful feedback. But, in the end, wars are won by sending in the ground troops. In the case of political campaigns, the idea is to let people know who you are first and then make individual contact. Therefore, my initial step was to mail out a standard packet of campaign materials. For special events such as the racial forum in Des Moines I sent faxes and emails to Iowa media. However, I knew that to make the sale - persuade a reporter to cover me - I would have to call on my prospect personally.

In retrospect, I did not make enough use of the old-fashioned telephone call. Such communication guarantees that you have the other person's attention. You also gain immediate feedback in knowing his or her reaction to your message and acquiring other information which might be useful. Then, too, you have the other person pinned down in a conversation, willing perhaps to go along with your suggestions out of a desire to be "nice". Seasoned journalists, however, tend to be immune to such pressures.

In truth, I felt telephone calls were personally stressful in the early stages of my campaign. I would become like a telemarketer. I would have to sell the journalist on the absurd idea that he or she should pay serious attention to a political novice running for President. Most would consider this proposition a waste of their time. Communication by telephone would be appropriate if I were communicating legitimate information such as my imminent arrival in their town. Until that time, however, it would be better to broadcast information about my candidacy by letter, fax, or email, and let those who were interested respond.

In communicating with media people it was important to have accurate lists. For $70.00, I purchased a list of 1,100 "national political media" from an outfit which had contacted me through a spammed offer. Bradley Communications, which markets to book publishers, faxed an offer to sell a list of "17,491 key contacts at newspapers, magazines, feature syndicates, and radio/TV talk shows" in its "Publicity Data Base" with unlimited use. The list, encoded on a CD, was marked down to $100 because it was a year old. Other media lists I acquired at the public library. At a library sale, I also purchased a four-volume set of the Gale Directory of Publications and Broadcast Media published in 1999. I also photocopied pages from the current year's Bacon Directory of newspapers, radio, and television, for more up-to-date contacts. Media lists tend to become outdated fast.

The first two data bases could be downloaded to my hard drive. I purchased Filemaker Pro software to access the Bradley lists. My friend, Mark Stanley, converted the other list into a format that could be read. These two data bases allowed me to select certain media people and print their names and addresses on mailing labels. Alternatively, I could select information to make an informal list of telephone and fax numbers and email addresses. Since the other two directories were in print, I used their information straight. With Filemaker Pro software, I typed information from the Gale Directory to assemble my own computerized list of media outlets in key campaign states such as Iowa, New Hampshire, South Carolina, and Louisiana. It was too outdated to be of much use.

The event in Iowa provided the first test of my system. Hoping to attract participants, I faxed press releases about this event to various Iowa media. Many of the fax numbers had incorrect area codes. I corrected these as best I could and resent the messages. In the following week, I emailed messages about the race forum to several hundred media people on the national political list. This went much faster. I began to think of email as a better way to reach reporters than by fax. Additionally, email allowed easier feedback. In the weeks following the Des Moines event, I sent out many different messages to political reporters and others by email, fax, and even mail. I thought that using a combination of communication techniques was best because the messages, coming at the recipient in different ways, would seem to reinforce each other instead of being repetitious.

In the end, it came down to ease and speed of communication. Email was the clear winner. Being technically challenged, I experienced an epiphany of sorts when my wife's friend's husband-to-be came over to our home to help fix her computer. He showed me some new techniques for sending emails. First, you could email a message to several addresses at a time by putting a semicolon between them. Second, to hide the fact that the message was being sent to more than one person, you could type the string of addresses in the blind-copy box marked "Bcc" in Outlook Express. Finally, strings of email addresses - eight or ten addresses, perhaps - could first be typed into a word-processing spreadsheet and then be copied and pasted in the "Bcc" box to send messages to many people. In other words, the "copy and paste" feature on the computer saved me from having to retype the addresses each time a message was sent. This feature could also be used for the subject description and for the message itself.

Once I had created the address strings, header description, and message text in separate files, I could draw upon this stored information to send email messages quickly and easily. First, the files containing the text and descriptive headers were opened. The header and text were highlighted in their respective files. I then proceeded in the following steps:

1. Click on the spreadsheet cell containing the address information and copy it.

2. Click on "new file" in Outlook Express to open a new file.

3. Click on the "Bcc" box and then "paste". (This loads the address information.)

4. Click on the file containing the header description. Now copy this.

5. Paste what is copied into the box marked "subject" in the Outlook Express file.

6. Click on the file containing the text message, which is already highlighted, and copy it.

7. Paste what is copied into the message space below.

8. Click "send" in Outlook Express to send the message.

By following this routine, I found that I could send a header and message to eight or ten email recipients a minute if I concentrated. I created a spreadsheet of about 250 lines whose cells in the left-hand column contained email addresses strung together in this way. These addresses, drawn from several different sources, belonged to newspaper editorial writers, political reporters at newspapers or at radio or television stations, syndicated columnists, and other journalists concerned with national politics. I tried to remove duplicate addresses or those which came back as invalid. That still left around 1,500 messages which presumably went through to the intended recipient. I found that I could do the entire list in half a day. Previously, it might have taken me a day to fax 300 messages or send 600 emails. During the last two months of 2003, I was sending out several messages a week to the complete list. The cost of each email broadcast was minimal.

Greater costs would be incurred when I campaigned in state primaries. In addition to the filing fees, I had to pay for food, lodging, and transportation, and extra minutes on my cell phone. South Carolina's fee of $2,500, though high, was well worth the cost since this race would attract much attention. The Louisiana primary, held on March 9th, would be less important to the nominating process. All the major contenders for the Democratic presidential nomination had been campaigning in primary or caucus states for many months. I, too, might have been active on the campaign trail had it not been for an expensive project which kept me tied to Minneapolis and which hung around my neck like an albatross.

The reason that I was not more concerned with raising campaign funds was that my own financial future depended on finishing the project to renovate a condemned duplex on Glenwood Avenue which I had purchased in May 2002. From the summer of 2002 through 2003, I ordered a new roof, a new paint job, siding for the exterior, a new heating and air-conditioning system, new plumbing, electrical work throughout the house, new sheet rocking for all the walls and ceilings, new bathroom fixtures and kitchen appliances, new carpeting and tile on the floors, new doors, new windows (including egress windows), and a concrete driveway and parking lot in the back yard. As the project went on and on, my personal finances began to look like the federal government's. I ran up credit-card debt, sold assets, and finally took out a $100,000 mortgage on my home, followed by a $50,000 second mortgage.

By the end of 2003, the work was still not complete. Drawn to this duplex by the Taj Mahal quality of its workmanship, a tenant had vacated her previous apartment and was set to move in on January 1st. She had to stay temporarily with friends. Three inspectors had not yet signed off on the work. By the end of the year, the building was still condemned. I had not yet been paid any rent. But time was also running out on my presidential campaign. I did what I could before leaving and left the rest for my former brother-in-law who was the general contractor. Then, on the morning of January 3, 2004, I drove away from Minneapolis, expecting not to return until mid March.

CHAPTER ELEVEN

Campaigning at a Distance

S tuck in Minneapolis, I tried to run a national campaign at a distance, clinging stubbornly to my once-in-a-lifetime opportunity to run for President. I produced a torrent of issues statements that I hoped the media would work into their coverage of the campaign. By regular mail, fax, and, especially, email, I sent these messages to people on the various lists. The best way to narrate this part of the campaign is to take it chronologically. The first two months of the campaign were spent promoting the book, creating the web site, and preparing for the August 16th event in Des Moines. I also did a bulk mailing with an announcement of my candidacy, a four-color book brochure, and two issues statements to political reporters on the Bradley list.

After the Des Moines event, I refocused on employment issues which I felt were my strong suit. In checking the other candidates' web sites, I concluded that none squarely addressed the causes of our "jobless recovery", especially the fact that high-paying U.S. jobs were being sent abroad. I wrote two opinion articles for newspapers. The first, titled "A Challenge to my Op-

ponents", stated that jobs were the main issue in this campaign and that, while most of the other candidates had no idea what was happening in the economy, I did. This went out to several large newspapers on August 21st. Then, on August 25th, I sent out a second opinion article titled "Let's Cut to the Chase on Jobs." Here were my proposed remedies for employment problems: shorter working hours and trade protection through tariffs.

The campaign proper started in early September when I faxed press releases to perhaps a hundred reporters urging that we pull out of Iraq and hand over the problem to the United Nations. One such message was in the form of an open letter to President Bush. Then, a week later, I attacked one of the Democrats' core constituencies in a faxed press release which claimed that the labor unions had "lost their way" in focusing on qualifying for overtime pay instead of trying to reduce work hours. While this did not quite put me in the Bush camp, I was at odds with most Democrats.

Between September 17th and 19th, I laboriously faxed announcements of my candidacy to talk-radio stations around the country. The announcement covered both personal background and campaign issues. The slow pace of faxing messages convinced me that there had to be a better way to communicate. Then, on September 21st, I sent several hundred emails to book reviewers at daily newspapers offering free review copies of my book in case they had not yet received one. I also sent faxes to ninety real-estate organizations pointing out that a Minneapolis landlord was running for President.

On September 22nd, the basic announcement of my candidacy went by email to 600 political reporters on the Bradley list. On the following three days, I sent 1,000 reporters on the same list an email titled "Straight Talk on Jobs". This repeated arguments from my two opinion pieces. I again stressed the fact that highly paid U.S. workers could not compete on cost in a free-trade environment. Protective tariffs and shorter work hours were the answer.

On September 30th, I sent email messages to both daily and community newspapers in key primary states - New Hampshire, South Carolina, and Louisiana - giving interesting facts about myself as a candidate. A day later, I emailed a short, humorous message titled "Clairvoyant President?", referring to the fact that the Google search engine sent persons to the web site for my world-history book who typed in the words "predict the future." If the media people did not like serious position statements, they might go for something like this.

Between October 5th and 7th, it was back to statements on the Iraq war and jobs. Here I used a list of newspaper editorial writers from the Bradley data base, arranged in inverse order of circulation. There was an abrupt change of pace on October 8th when I wrote an opinion article interpreting Arnold Schwarzenegger's election in light of trends in world history. I also sent faxes giving my views on trade and jobs to several hundred editorial writers at medium-circulation newspapers.

A group of short-hours activists, led by Seattle documentary producer John De Graaf, had been working for more than a year on an event called "Take Back Your Time Day." This day, October 24th, was picked because "the date falls nine weeks before the end of the year, making the point that we Americans now work nine weeks more each year than Western Europeans do."

During the period leading up to that event, New York Times columnist Paul Krugman published an article debunking the argument that reduced work time created jobs on the grounds that it reflected a "lump-of-labor fallacy" which economist Paul Samuelson and others had identified. I responded with an opinion article pointing out that this "fallacy", whose argument was based on an early 20th Century public-relations handout opposing the 8-hour day, was itself fallacious and untrue.

I titled this piece "Wizard-of-Oz Economics." The idea was that the news media presented the magnified image of Wizard-like authority figures such as Samuelson, a Nobel Prize winner, to convince the public that certain views had to be true. No, I said, economic proposals had to be considered on their own merits. I was prepared to make an economic argument for the shorter-workweek proposal, whatever Samuelson's opinion might be.

I followed this up with another article, emailed on October 22nd and 23rd, which went into the economics of reduced work time. Titled "Circling Back to the '30s", it made arguments for shortening work time based on the productivity equation (which relates output, productivity, employment, and average work hours). Beyond this, I suggested that U.S. economic policy makers in the 1930s had taken a detour into monetary and fiscal policy and neglected basic labor economics. Contemporary events might force a reversal of that approach.

Next, between October 28th and 31th, I switched back to racial issues with a fax titled "Straight Talk on Race" which was sent to syndicated columnists and opinion-page editors at the larger newspapers. This statement argued that both political parties were exploiting the race issue, albeit in different ways. Racial prejudice, being a matter of personal attitudes, was beyond the scope of effective government action. I also argued that race was being used by the nation's economic elite to beat down poor white people and eventually this would hurt working people of all races.

This was about the time that the above-mentioned computer professional taught me how to send email messages more efficiently. Prior to that time, my campaign messages were sent sporadically by email, letter, or fax. Now faxes and letters were out. So were time-consuming postings of email messages to particular lists. Now I could send emails quickly to news people on all the lists in a short time.

MSNBC and the Democratic National Committee planned to sponsor a debate among the Democratic presidential candidates in Des Moines, Iowa, on Monday, November 24th. Since Des Moines was within my traveling range, I thought I might attend. This prompted an email message sent on November 17th and 18th, which was titled: "10th candidate for President at Des

Moines debate." The message tried to put a positive spin on the fact that I was a political outsider (who would be standing outside the Polk County Convention Center) by pointing out some of the interesting, unconventional things that I had done in my life.

Next, I read a column by the Boston Globe reporter Jeff Jacoby chiding the media for criticizing Howard Dean's remark about "white guys with confederate flags on the pickup trucks" while they gave a pass to that black race-monger Al Sharpton. My position was that both Dean and Sharpton should be allowed to speak their minds freely. "Let Al Sharpton (and Howard Dean) speak," was the subject title of that email message sent on November 12th. The voters, not political pundits, should be the ones to judge politicians' racial positions.

As the 40th anniversary of the Kennedy assassination approached, I watched the History Channel series on "The Men Who Killed Kennedy". I had met the author of a book about the Kennedy assassination at the taping of "Jesse Ventura's America" a month earlier. On November 19th and 20th, I sent an email, "journalist, pursue Kennedy assassination story," to the media lists suggesting that the U.S. news media had gone limp on the story. (This may not have won me any new friends.)

The presidential debate took place in Des Moines on November 24th. Along with John Kerry's campaign staff and supporters, I watched the television broadcast in a sports bar near the convention center. What struck me most was Wesley Clark's response to Tom Brokaw's statement that, by 2010, India would have more computer-software professionals than the United States. He had said: " Let them do the software in India. We'll do other things in this country." I was appalled by Clark's cavalier attitude that America could continue to lose jobs to other countries trusting that better "high tech" jobs would take their place. I titled my protest, dispatched on November 25th and 26th, "Wesley Clark's Gaffe in Monday's Presidential Debate."

On November 27th, Thanksgiving Day, I watched the television news reports of George W. Bush serving turkey dinners to our soldiers in Baghdad. OK, I thought, the President finally did something right. Caught up in the emotion as well as wanting to show I was not a Bush hater, I sent an email, "President Bush hits a home run," later that day.

After reacting to the Thanksgiving dinner, it was back to jobs. Jobs were, in my estimation, the most important campaign issue but the nine candidates had yet to discuss it in a meaningful way. On December 3rd, I sent an email to the political list posing this question: "When are we going to discuss job strategy?" The question was posed in the context of news reports that the economy was showing a strong recovery although the federal budget appeared to be out of control. To pull us through the ballooning debt, we would need a foundation of many taxable, high-paying jobs. Instead, the jobs were going overseas. Let's talk about this, I suggested.

The next email, "why there's a 'jobless recovery' and what to do about it", was a comprehensive statement of my position on the employment issue. In light of rapid advances in labor productivity and historically high levels of overtime, reduced work hours were one of the prongs in my two-pronged jobs proposal. The other was a new system of tariffs, tailored to the individual business firm, which would offset the cost advantage of outsourcing jobs to low-wage countries. A major concern was the debt problem, both federal debt and mounting consumer debt, now caused primarily by borrowing against the increased equity in homes. If housing prices ever came down, it might cause problems in both the housing and credit markets. That's why job growth was so important. This message went out on December 9th.

On December 10th, following Al Gore's endorsement of Howard Dean, I sent another email message titled "a bone to pick with Howard Dean." My statement began: "Actually, I like Howard Dean." Then it took Dean to task for his muddleheaded belief that including workers rights in trade agreements would solve the outsourcing problem. "The sad fact is," I wrote, "it is no violation of any interna-

tionally recognized labor standard for wages in India, Sri Lanka, or China to be so much lower than in the United States." Stop moralizing about these "evil people" stealing our jobs and simply slap tariffs on products imported from low-wage countries. Wages are low in India or China because the process of industrialization is less advanced. No one needs to be blamed.

Even so, the Democratic presidential candidates continued to view our country's trade deficit as a result of "unfair trade practices" by our trading partners, especially the Chinese. Many believed that the Chinese were competing unfairly through "currency manipulation". After disclosing the fact that I was married to a Chinese woman, I blasted politicians' tendency to blame the Chinese government for preferring its own peoples' interest to ours. It was American business executives, not the Chinese government, who decided to close down U.S. factories and open up ones in China to take advantage of cheap labor.

But "the real culprits," I wrote, "are the U.S. Government officials who have a responsibility to protect the interests of the American people but who are actually loyal to their campaign contributors." I also

blamed "the academic hired guns, the think-tank people and talking heads, and the journalists who played up their side of the story while ridiculing or minimizing the other side. You bums! Watch your own country go down as a result." This message was delivered on December 15th and 16th.

One journalist, though, did get the picture. That was Lou Dobbs, host of an evening news program on CNN. Dobbs had made a point of highlighting what he called "the exporting of America" and of naming U.S. companies which outsource production. On December 20th, I sent an email titled "Lou Dobbs for President (or Vice President)" in which I pledged to end my own presidential campaign and support Dobbs if he became a candidate. Lou Dobbs, I said, would make an ideal candidate for the Democrats, because he could bring along many middle-class Americans, worried about job loss, to vote for the ticket.

Again hitting upon jobs, I analyzed the Democratic presidential candidates' proposals in the areas of employment, trade, and worker protection, comparing their approaches to mine. That email, titled "Some of the Democratic Presidential Candidates' Proposals in the Area of Employment and Trade," was sent on December 22nd. While the other candidates spoke of tax incentives to stay in the country, job-retraining programs, health-care reform, increased research spending, and extended unemployment benefits, my proposals were targeted to the particular causes of employment loss.

Finally, on December 29th, I sent what was intended to be my last email to the list of political reporters. I picked what I thought was a cute title: "campaign sitting at a red light (our last email to you)." "Sitting at a red light" was a phrase appearing in a song by Jonny Lang which was frequently played on radio stations during this period. The idea here was that my campaign for President had been "sitting at a red light" - i.e., was stalled in traffic - for a long time now while I was confined to Minneapolis because of the duplex project. But now the light was about to change. Within a week, I would be off and running - first to South

Carolina and then to Louisiana - to campaign in the presidential primaries. Adios, amigos in the press.

Whether my months-long barrage of journalists by email was useful to them is unclear. With each email, two or three persons asked to be taken off the list. A columnist in Missouri did contact me by email about my campaign but we never managed to reach each other by phone. Otherwise, there was a vast, deep silence. It was obvious that mine would not be a winning campaign so long as it consisted of issuing position statements from a distance.

CHAPTER TWELVE

At Last, Personal Contact

It was unnerving to send out plainly worded emails on important topics of the day to 1,500 to 2,000 media people and not receive a single response except from those who wanted to be taken off the list. What were these people thinking? Did they delete my messages without looking at them? I needed more contact with people to have real communication. I desperately needed feedback. Even the email response which said in large bright-red lettering, "THIS IS SPAM!", was better than nothing at all.

There were a few exceptions: notably, Andrew Griffin of the *Daily Town Talk* newspaper in Alexandria, Louisiana, who wrote a column about my book; and Brian Madigan, producer of an afternoon program called "Viewpoint University" on radio station KSOO-AM in Sioux Falls, South Dakota. Ten years earlier he had lived in the uptown area of Minneapolis. Twice I was invited to be a guest on the show as a presidential candidate and once as an ex-candidate - prematurely, as it turned out. The interviewers, Rick Knobe and Randy McDaniel, who seemed intrigued by my advocacy of a shorter workweek, remarked that it was good to be talking with an ordinary person, not just a candidate who delivered the standard canned remarks.

This was in pleasant contrast with my experience in late October when the manager of a radio station in northeastern Pennsylvania responded to my email in support of "Take Back Your Time Day": "Never email me again. I am (a) registered Republican and do not believe any of this garbage. It is all communist fertilizer." Despite having a treasurer in that state, Pennsylvania might not have been a hotbed of support for my campaign. Shortly after I emailed an announcement of the Des Moines event to reporters, a column about me appeared in the *Pittsburgh Tribune-Review* web site. "Meet Bill McGaughey, Dreamer," was the title of this article written by Bill Steigerwald.

The article began: "Some goof with too much money and time to waste is seeking the Democrats' nomination for president in 2004. Not Joe Lieberman, Dick Gephardt, John Edwards, John Kerry ... Try Bill McGaughey of Minneapolis. Never heard of him? Too bad. According to his nifty packet of campaign literature, which somehow found its way to Pittsburgh, he's overqualified. He's a 1964 graduate of Yale. He's written six books on trade and labor topics. He's a former inner-city landlord ... McGaughey's photo looks OK. No antennae are visible. If you'd like to join his presidential crusade, he'll be marching in downtown Des Moines, Iowa, today."

Mercifully, Steigerwald's article then backed off from ridiculing me to point out several of the even more outrageous candidates who were entered in the race: "It's really not fair to single out citizen McGaughey for ridicule," he wrote. "Hundreds of even more hopeless, harmless dreamers and weirdos will officially declare themselves independent or write-in candidates for 2004, just as they did in 2000. Many will make McGaughey look as normal as Al Gore. Clifford Catton, a New Yorker, made the White House (race) in 2000 after discovering 'U.S. Postal employees had been stealing my mail since 1981.' Mike Strauss, an MIT grad who, making a smart career move, ran in Y2K 'because I can, it looks good on my resume and it causes no harm.' And Jack Grimes, the self-crowned leader and director of the United Fascist union, has already officially announced for 2004. The Pennsylvania resident hopes to restore a New World Order based upon the governmental style of imperial Rome."

For months, Steigerwald's column was the top item listed by search engines on the Internet under my name. This was fair game: I was not an elected official. I was not a Hollywood celebrity. My vote-getting prowess was evidenced by the fact that I won 31% of the Independence Party vote for U.S. Senate in 2002, a total of 8,482 votes (which was a vast improvement over what I had received as a mayoral candidate.) And now I was running for President!? My claim to serious consideration was that I had something to say on issues of importance to voters. I had published books on employment and on trade which, despite modest sales, had influence among persons interested in these subjects.

First and foremost, I was a supporter of federal legislation to shorten the workweek who had coauthored a book on this topic with former U.S. Senator Eugene McCarthy, chairman of the 1959 Senate Select Committee on Unemployment. An earlier such book had a foreword by Congressman John Conyers, author of a bill to shorten the workweek in 1979 and the early '80s. My 1992 book on international trade helped shape the fight against NAFTA.

It was, however, another book, *Five Epochs of Civilization*, which might have been most relevant to my campaign. This turn-of-the-millennium book advanced the theory that there had been four "civilizations" to date in world history, with a fifth on the way. While our political values remain planted in the print culture associated with the third civilization, the society itself has moved into a fourth civilization focused on entertainment. Among the concepts presented in this book was the idea that successful political leaders in each epoch had talents in synch with the culture of their age. Thomas Jefferson, Abraham Lincoln, and Winston Churchill had highly developed writing skills. In the fourth epoch, where good writing was not so valued, successful politicians needed the

skills of an entertainer. Ronald Reagan had this, of course. So did Jesse Ventura and Arnold Schwarzenegger.

What about me? I'm more a writer than a man who puts on a good performance before the cameras. Even so, I could try to adapt my campaign to the requirements of campaigning in the entertainment age. This would involve a recognition that issues may be less important than personalities. The best attitude would be to "go with the flow" of this culture rather than complain. Instead of working myself up into a huff about the fact that the media did not pay enough attention to my "issues", I would try to work the issues into a pleasant or amusing routine. I would try to make myself more appealing, entertainment-wise, and think how my campaign might fit in better with what the media are trying to do these days.

That's why it was such an astonishing piece of good luck when, on the very first day of the campaign, Alexandra Pelosi expressed interest in accompanying me to Iowa. My campaign efforts would be directed toward creating colorful events which Pelosi would tape for HBO. (This assumes, of course, that her documentary would air before the primary elections.) Cable-television audiences would be the public to whom I directed my appeal. It would be the entertainment sector rather than news sector of the television industry which would drive me forward as a candidate. Entertaining coverage of the campaign would put wind in my sails. But Pelosi suddenly canceled. I was left dead in the water.

Bill Steigerwald's observation that "no antennae (were) visible" gave me an idea for my next entertainment-inspired move. If the media people expected candidates like me to have "antennae" on their heads as if to pick up messages from outer space, I would give them what they wanted. By coincidence, I discovered that, when a person typed the words "predict the future" in leading search engines, my book's web site, www.worldhistorysite.com, came up Number 2 on the list. (It has since taken the top spot.) That is because *Five Epochs of*

Civilization suggests a strategy for predicting the future course of our own civilization based on looking at past ones. The "prediction" page of the web site contained a discussion of analogies between past and present civilizations that could point to future developments in our own culture.

Doing what any good impresario would do, I hyped myself as a candidate with recognized powers of prediction. Recipients of this email might imagine that the "antennae" on my head were fairly glowing with prophetic pulsations. The "subject" field of my email to more than a thousand political reporters was phrased as a question: "Clairvoyant President?"

The text read: "What would you think of electing a President with the ability to predict the future? One of the lesser-known Democratic candidates has recognized talents in this area. He is Bill McGaughey, a scholar of wide-ranging interests which include finding significant patterns in world history. You can find a web site describing one of McGaughey's books under the category of "paranormal phenomena/prophecies and predictions" on the Internet. If you type the words 'predict the future' in the Yahoo or Google search engine, the page from WorldHistorySite.com which explains how world history can be used to predict the future comes up #2 on the list. Yes, whatever you think of his campaign platform, this candidate does get the big picture." Some recipients of this message seemed to lack a sense of humor. I started getting more responses from people to take them off my email list. (Maybe our culture has not fully transitioned to entertainment.)

Almost as an afterthought, I sent copies of my Independence Party book to two well-known Minnesotans, Garrison Keillor and former Governor Jesse Ventura. What a surprise and a treat it was one day to receive a handwritten letter from Keillor, multi-talented host of public radio's "Prairie Home Companion", acknowledging recipient of my book and enclosing an inscribed copy of his own newly published book, "Love Me". The inscription read: "To William McGaughey, who would make a better senator than the guy who got elected."

Keillor had well-publicized misgivings about Republican Senator, Norm Coleman, the ultimate winner of the 2002 Senate race in which I had been involved. The incumbent Senator, Paul Wellstone, had lost his life in a plane crash a week before the general election. Keillor wrote in an enclosed letter to me that he was a Democrat rather than a third-party supporter. Even so, I knew that he had an eye for exotic political developments, having published a book about Jesse Ventura in 1999. This book, titled "Me", was a fictionalized action story of Ventura's life history, making him out to be a cartoon-like character. Keillor applied the same treatment to himself in "Love Me".

I thought, if I were lucky, my own salvation as a presidential candidate lay in Keillor's converting me into an action figure who did battle against political giants or other quixotic deeds. Garrison Keillor is America's foremost story teller - the Mark Twain of our generation. He would be the one, I hoped, to turn my otherwise pathetic campaign into something to amuse radio audiences. I quickly read, "Love Me" and wrote a letter to Keillor saying that I had read and enjoyed his book and I was now running for President as a Democrat. I imagined that Keillor, having invited me to have coffee with him, would ask diplomatically whether I would mind if he distorted my character somewhat to fit me into the Lake Wobegon scene?

The invitation never came. I was, of course, trying to capitalize on Keillor's graciousness in receiving my book by hopeful expectations that he would propel me upwards in the entertainment culture. Realistically, however, I knew that desperados who hype themselves to run for President are not the types of people who inhabit Lake Wobegon. Also, the racial theme could be a problem. Even a man of Keillor's stature would not be immune to criticism if he treated a "white racist" with anything other than utter contempt. It was hard to reconcile my politically incorrect candidacy with Keillor's routine of appealing to sophisticated audiences with dialogues that exhibited a light touch.

Jesse Ventura was the other entertainment-related person, then, who might elevate my candidacy into the realm of big-time politics. After retiring as Minnesota's Governor, Ventura had landed a job with MSNBC as host of a new show called "Jesse Ventura's America". It was produced at the public-television studio in St. Paul. This national show began broadcasting in early October. I expressed interest in being an audience member and was accepted along with a friend, Charlie Disney, for the October 24th taping session.

In the studio building, we rode up the elevator with a well-dressed Texan who said he was a guest on the show. "Jesse Ventura's America" that week featured rock star Ted Nugent for the first half hour and our elevator companion, Barr McClellan, for the second half hour. McClellan had recently published a book, "Blood, Money & Power", which claimed that Lyndon Johnson was involved in the Kennedy assassination. He himself had been a partner in the Texas law firm which handled Lyndon Johnson's legal work and, in that capacity, had been given certain information to suggest that the Kennedy assassination had been coordinated out of that office. He was also the father of President Bush's press secretary, Scott McClellan.

After the taping, my friend and I talked in the studio both with McClellan and with Jesse Ventura. I was carrying a copy of my Independence Party book in case the previous copy had not reached Ventura personally. The former governor quickly remarked that he already had a copy of this book. He said he had not yet begun to read it because of other obligations but would do so soon. Meanwhile, I signed up to be a member of the show's "talking section" (audience members seated immediately in front of Ventura who might engage in personal interaction with him) in a future session but was never called. "Jesse Ventura's America" suspended operations during the Christmas holiday and then was canceled. Instead, Ventura took a teaching assignment at Harvard.

However, my attendance at this show and the chance encounter with Barr McClellan turned me on to alternative explanations of the Kennedy assassination. I watched all the History Channel shows preceding the November 22nd anniversary and found critics of the Warren Commission report quite convincing. Besides Barr McClellan, insider testimony came from Lee Harvey Oswald's mistress, Lyndon Johnson's mistress, a bystander on the "grassy knoll", emergency-room doctors at the Parkland Hospital, and many others. The evidence was too overwhelming that Oswald was not the killer or had not done it alone.

Yet, the news media contemptuously dismissed all such suggestions. The *Star Tribune* handled the matter by deferring to an "expert" who supposedly had examined all the evidence and accepted the "lone gunman" theory. The article then went on to speculate why Americans were so prone to believe "conspiracy theories". I was totally disgusted. There had been not one response to any of the numerous pieces of evidence conflicting with the Warren Commission report but, instead, a judgment based on authority. Even a man of evident high standing in the community, Barr McClellan, who had stepped forward to offer personal testimony to the contrary, was ignored. That being the case, resistance to the truth about the Kennedy assassination must be impenetrable. Whose testimony would it take to convince these Brahman journalists, God's?

I should mention two other experiences during this time. The Roman Catholic archbishop of the Archdiocese of St. Paul and Minneapolis, Harry J. Flynn, issued a "Pastoral Letter on Race" which received much attention in the press. Archbishop Flynn had been assigned to service in Lafayette, Louisiana, before he came to Minnesota. In the Pastoral Letter, he observed that white racism in Minnesota was as bad as what he had seen in Louisiana despite Minnesotans' greater tendency to hide their thoughts. (This is sometimes called "Minnesota nice.") The archbishop explained his views before a predominantly black audience in north Minneapolis which included several Protestant clergy. There was broad and vocal approval of his anti-racist initiative.

During the question-and-answer period, I stood up to challenge remarks expressed at this forum. The gist of my statement was that one-sided discussions of race such as this merely drove white sentiments further underground. Though one minister called me "insane" for saying such a thing, I hung around to talk with people after the event and managed to part on reasonably friendly terms with most participants including the Archbishop. I typed up my remarks, paraphrased and condensed, along with a narrative description of the event, and mailed copies to the Archbishop and numerous other people. There was a follow-up discussion with his representative. While I doubt that my dissenting statement persuaded anyone, it did allow me to exercise my personal commitment to speaking out. Silence ensued.

As previously mentioned, there was a debate among the Democratic candidates for President on Monday, November 24th in Des Moines, Iowa. I wrote executives of MSNBC (who were cosponsoring the debate jointly with the Democratic National Committee) asking that I be included. Failing that, I wanted the debate moderator, Tom Brokaw, to mention at the outset that there were other Democratic candidates running for President besides the ones participating in the debate.

My letter brought no response. I telephoned a contact person for MSNBC to repeat the request. Someone would get back to me, I was told. This happened twice. No one called me back either time. It was evident to me that MSNBC, a partnership between two of the nation's largest corporations, had assumed the role of deciding who were acceptable candidates for President of the United States and who were not. Neither was there a need to be polite about it any more. They and their friends ran the country.

I decided to drive down to Des Moines to carry on my campaign outside the convention center. So I made another sign whose message read: "Ask the Right Questions!" My handout sheet contained a list of questions which I thought Tom Brokaw should ask. It was a cold afternoon in Des Moines that day. I paraded with my sign on the sidewalk in front of the Polk County Convention Center along with other political gadflies and supporters of the various major candidates among whom John Kerry seemed to have the edge.

Two or three newspaper reporters interviewed me along with a man from a Des Moines television station. There was also a man gathering materials for a cable-access show. There was a female reporter from the *Des Moines Register* and a young man from a college newspaper in northern Iowa who said he'd call me in a few days. A woman from Democracycaravan.org recorded my statement about being excluded from the debate. She suggested that I watch this event with Kerry supporters and staff in a sports bar kitty corner to the convention center. By the back entrance stood a man dressed as Uncle Sam who supported President Bush's reelection. I enjoyed being part of the scene. As a candidate, this was the closest I came to participating in a presidential debate.

CHAPTER THIRTEEN

To South Carolina and Home Again

I was planning to visit my father and brother on the east coast during the Christmas holiday. Then I caught a virus which kept me in bed. Two primary filing deadlines had to be met: The deadline to file for the South Carolina Democratic presidential primary was 5 p.m. on Friday, January 2, 2004. For the Louisiana primary, the filing papers and fee payment had to be received in Baton Rouge between January 28th and 30th. My goal was to establish myself as a respectable candidate in the South Carolina primary and then, using that momentum, do much better in Louisiana. It was a two-part plan.

On December 23, 2003, I wrote a personal check for $2,500.00 in payment for the South Carolina primary and mailed it to the Democratic party chair, Joe Erwin. On the afternoon of Monday the 29th, I received a telephone call from Monica Bell of the South Carolina Democratic Party reporting that, while my check had been received, I also needed to fill out an application form. She would email the form as an attachment. The completed form could be returned by fax to meet the deadline but I should also mail the original.

I was still feeling ill and was in bed when, right after the call from South Carolina, a man called who I thought was from the same office. I did not write down his name. Aware that I had filed for the South Carolina Democratic primary, he was checking my qualifications to be President. Was I at least 35 years of age and an American citizen? Was I born in the United States? I qualified on all counts. Then he asked me if I was a Democrat. I replied that, no, I was actually a member of the Independence Party of Minnesota. Would you be willing to become a Democrat this year, he asked? I said that I would. I added that, as a practical matter, party affiliation in Minnesota was determined by which party's precinct caucus one attended. The caucuses were held every two years. This year's would be on March 2nd. My preference would be, however, to skip the caucus since, after South Carolina, I planned to campaign continuously in Louisiana until the primary on March 9th. The man asked no more questions. I went back to sleep.

I had wanted to leave Minneapolis on December 23rd to see my brother and father, stay for several days, and then return home shortly after New Year's Day. The trip would involve 2,500 miles of driving. I would then pack my bags for a much longer trip to South Carolina to participate in its primary and then, after February 3rd, drive from South Carolina directly to Louisiana for the primary held on March 9th. Hopefully, most of the work would be completed on the condemned duplex, the inspectors would sign off, the city would lift the condemnation and then issue the rental license so that my new tenant could move in. Before my planned departure, I filled out certain forms and signed my name so that required paperwork could be handled in my absence by my former brother-in-law, Alan Morrison, and the apartment building's caretaker, Keith Baker. My illness forced a change in plans.

I was in no condition to travel until after the new year. Reluctantly I saw a doctor at the emergency clinic who prescribed antibiotics. This helped. On Saturday morning, January 3rd, I was ready to leave Minneapolis for my great southern adventure. I would visit my father and brother first, using the house in Milford, Pennsylvania, as a base of operations, and then drive down to South Carolina passing through Washington, D.C. That arrangement would give me the opportunity to visit Kevin Diaz in the Washington offices of McClatchy Newspapers, parent of the *Star Tribune*. We had become acquainted when he was the City Hall reporter for that newspaper and I a landlord activist. When I had first announced my candidacy for President, Diaz had emailed me to visit him if I came to Washington.

First I had to go through the difficult process of gathering all the papers, clothing, and campaign equipment and accessories that I thought I might need in South Carolina and Louisiana. Whether to take a large Mexican hat was a particular issue, resolved in the affirmative. I bought a small tent for possible use in state parks. To avoid late charges on my bills and credit cards, I prepared a list of account numbers and mailing addresses for making prompt payments while on the road. My new cell phone would have many uses on this trip. My wife helped me sort through my belongings and pack. She, too, would be gone between January 24th and March 14th while she visited China. My stepdaughter would remain in Northfield, attending college. We had to worry only about feeding the cat.

Well rested when I departed around 8 a.m., I took the route past Rochester (Minnesota) and La Crosse (Wisconsin) before joining I-94 through central Wisconsin down to Chicago. As night fell, I was in northern Indiana, circling the tall Civil War monument in Angola, and then going east through northern Ohio, first passing Toledo and then heading toward Cleveland, along U.S. Highway 2. Finally, I stopped to sleep on the reclining seat of my car at the Ohio rest area just before the junction with Interstate 90. Having an inflatable neck rest and a blanket, I fell promptly asleep and did not awaken until dawn.

Then I continued my trip through Cleveland and Youngstown, Ohio, and into Pennsylvania on Interstate 80 which traverses the state west to east. I went by Stroudsburg, Pennsylvania, rather than Scranton, because this southern route

along the Delaware river would save a few miles if I first visited my father at a nursing home near Newton, New Jersey. I had a short visit with him and then drove the remaining 25 miles to Milford, arriving at my house on the evening of Sunday, January 3rd.

I had planned to stay in Milford for only two days. On Tuesday afternoon, January 6th, I made preparations to leave for South Carolina. The first order of business was to call political reporters and editors at several of South Carolina's large daily newspapers. I called the *Aiken Standard*, the *Anderson Independent-Mail*, the (Charleston) *Post and Courier*, *The State* in Columbia, and the *Florence Morning News*. Contact persons at these newspapers said that they would welcome a visit from me. Then I called the *Greenville News* and spoke with its political editor, Dan Hoover. Did I know that my name had been removed from the primary ballot, Hoover asked? He added, "I think you'd better call the South Carolina Democratic Party."

I did call the party. The telephone receptionist did not confirm or deny Hoover's report but said I would need to speak with the party's executive director, Nu Wexler. He was not available then. I left my number for the return call. This receptionist, Nancy, thought he might return the call later that afternoon. Wexler did not return my call, either that day or the next, or the day after that. I was intending to leave Milford on Wednesday, January 7th, but stayed there an extra day in case he tried to call. I myself called the party's office two or three times. Wexler was either in a meeting, or he was gone; in any event, he never returned my calls.

If I was to have lunch with Kevin Diaz in Washington, I needed to leave Milford early in the morning. It was a six-hour drive. Departing just before 7 a.m., I drove to Scranton and down past Harrisburg in a light Pennsylvania snow. The snow eased as I entered Maryland. After taking a wrong turn off the interstate, I called Diaz by cell phone to confirm my time of arrival at the National Press Building where he worked. Luckily, I found a free four-hour parking space on the Capitol Mall. Then I walked back to the press building, located the McClatchy offices, and waited for Kevin to finish a phone conversation for a story.

Kevin Diaz suggested that we have lunch at a food place on the second floor. As we rode down an escalator, he pointed ahead and asked: "Isn't that Al Sharpton?" It certainly looked like him. The smartly dressed presidential candidate was seated on a stand having his shoes shined. I went up to Sharpton and introduced myself as a rival candidate for President. I told him I was from Minnesota. Sharpton seemed amused by this. He asked my name. In a good-natured way, he pretended to be worried about the competition from me. We shook hands. Then Kevin Diaz introduced himself to Sharpton and they shook hands. Walking to the food court, Diaz said he was hesitant to approach Sharpton in case it had been someone else. I responded, "I have no reputation to protect." He smiled. There was a story about my encounter with Al Sharpton in Sunday's *Star Tribune*.

Together at a small table, we talked first of his forthcoming trip to Brazil where he would assess the impact of trade upon agriculture, especially sugar production. We talked, of course, about national politics. Howard Dean was then the front runner. Diaz had read parts of my Independence Party book. He was interested in my exchange of correspondence with his boss about the lack of coverage for my Senate campaign. He said he thought that top editors at the paper were sensitive to complaints of "liberal bias" and might be open to discussions. As a fringe candidate for President, he said, I could not expect much coverage; at most, something might be done in the Variety Section. We also talked about race. Diaz said it had been his policy to stay away from this subject ever since he had drawn flak, both from the black community and the police, for a series of articles on the gang problem that he wrote in 1991. He had even received death threats.

As it approached 3 p.m., Kevin Diaz had to go back to work. He first gave me directions for driving south out of Washington.

Rejoining I-95, I drove through Virginia at a moderately fast rate of speed. South of Richmond, I pulled into a rest area to check my motel reservation in South Carolina. I also thought of calling the *Greenville News* reporter, Dan Hoover, who, to date, was my only source of information about being kicked off the South Carolina ballot. I was curious to know how he had learned of this.

Hoover read me an email from the Democratic state party chair, Joe Erwin. It was in the form of a letter to me, stating that I could not be on the ballot because I was ineligible to receive ballots at the Democratic National Convention. The DNC chair had made that determination. Mulling it over in the car, I thought I might salvage the situation by waiving my right to delegates.

There was a long stretch of road through North Carolina and into South Carolina. At Florence, I picked up Interstate 20 for a short trip to Columbia, arriving at the Motel 6 in West Columbia just after midnight.

The following morning, Friday, around 9:30 a.m., I left the motel dressed in my best suit, brief case in hand. I drove into Columbia to pay a call at the offices of the South Carolina Democratic Party, located at 1517 Blanding Street. For the first time, I met Nancy the receptionist. A burning issue in South Carolina, she told me, was whether ketchup or mustard should be used on

barbecued ribs. My business was, of course, to know why I had been kicked off the South Carolina primary ballot. A young man named Wyeth Ruthven, who was a legal expert, appeared from a side room. I learned that he had stayed overnight at a motel near Milford on a recent trip to Boston.

Meanwhile Nancy ran off a copy of Joe Erwin's letter to me, the one which Hoover had read over the phone. This letter referred to "the South Carolina Delegate Selection Rules (Section VI.A.1)" and "Section 11.K.(1)(b) of the Delegate Selection Rules for the 2004 Democratic National Convention." I said that I did not know what those citations meant. Could I please see the text? In time, Ruthven produced a 20-page printout of the South Carolina rules. He also gave me a copy of a two-page letter which Terence R. McAuliffe, DNC chair, had written to Erwin. This is what I wanted. I took several minutes to study the text.

Essentially, McAuliffe had decided that I could not have delegates at the Democratic National Convention because I was not a good Democrat. And South Carolina party rules stated that I could not be on the presidential primary ballot unless I was "entitled to obtain delegates" at the convention. McAuliffe's objections to me were that I had run for Mayor of Minneapolis as a member of the "Affordable Housing Preservation Party" against a Democratic incumbent, had "sought the nomination of the Independence Party as a candidate for the U.S. Senate", and had "publicly stated (that I remained) a member of the Independence Party ... and (had) reservations about joining the current Democratic Party." Therefore, he wrote, "McGaughey is not a bona fide Democrat and does not possess a record affirmatively demonstrating that he is faithful to, or has at heart, the interests, welfare and success of the Democratic Party."

I asked Nancy if Nu Wexler was in. He was not. Nancy herself was not the person to talk with about this situation. It therefore fell to Wyeth Ruthven to listen to my response. I pointed out, first, that there was no "Affordable Housing Preservation Party." The first three words were just a label to identify my main campaign issue. Also, the Minneapolis mayoral election is a nonpartisan contest. The incumbent mayor's chief opponent, who beat her in the 2001 election, was also a Democrat.

McAuliffe's second allegation, however, was true. Yes, I had run for U.S. Senate in the Independence Party primary. It was also true that officially I remained a member of the Independence Party because I had last caucused with them. However, two weeks earlier, I had also told an unidentified caller, when asked, that I would be willing to join the Democratic Party - changing my position from that when I first announced for President in June. Who this man was I did not know. Was he someone from the South Carolina Democratic Party? Wyeth Ruthven and the others were sure he was not.

I called attention to the paragraph in McAuliffe's letter which quoted Article VI of the Call for the 2004 Democratic National Committee. This passage said a bona fide Democrat was someone "whose record of public service, accomplishments, public writings and/or public statements affirmatively demonstrates that he or she is faithful to the interests, welfare and success of the Democratic Party ... and will participate in the Convention in good faith."

Public writings? From my briefcase, I pulled out copies of several books that I had published. One book had a foreword written by a Democratic member of Congress. Another was co-authored with a former U.S. Senator who was also a Democrat. I wanted Ruthven to see these published books in case someone questioned their existence. Therefore, while my organizational affiliation was somewhat shaky, the views expressed in my writings were well within the scope of what Democrats might advocate. Ruthven said he knew this; but my beef was with the national party, not the one in South Carolina. Go see them. (It did not escape me that, had Nu Wexler returned any of my phone calls, I could easily have called on the DNC when I was in Washington the previous afternoon.)

There was little more for me to do at 1517 Blanding Street. These were all nice people having to front for nefarious actions taken by the higher-ups. I went back to my motel and immediately placed a cell-phone call to Phil McNamara, the DNC's Director of Party Affairs and Delegate Selection, who had been given as a contact person in McAuliffe's letter. I reached McNamara on the second try. He pulled up a copy of McAuliffe's letter from the computer. Urging McAuliffe to reverse his decision, I went through the same points as in my argument with Wyeth Ruthven. The main point at issue was whether I had refused to become a Democrat. No, he, McNamara, was not the person with whom I had spoken on December 23th; he did not know who that might have been.

When I had finished covering most points in the letter, McNamara said that he would pass this information along to Terry McAuliffe. But he had to say that, once McAuliffe made up his mind, he seldom changed it. People at party headquarters were upset that I had run for Senate against Paul Wellstone. Norm Coleman's victory in Minnesota had been a major setback. I argued that my campaign was not directed against Wellstone; I was running in the Independence Party primary. I asked if I might visit the DNC office in Washington, D.C. on Monday to meet in person. McNamara discouraged this. He said he would get back to me by telephone the following week. I urged him to respond sooner rather than later so that, if McAuliffe's decision was favorable, I might return quickly to the campaign trail.

After this telephone conversation, I thought it useful to write a letter to McAuliffe, pleading my case. It was a handwritten letter since I had no typewriter. Then, I drove into Columbia to find a post office and perhaps do some sightseeing. I wound up near the South Carolina State Capitol and decided to visit this place. A well-dressed man was giving a tour to a young couple and their son. I asked if I could tag along.

While we were standing at the threshold of the House chambers, I noticed that seven of the state representatives were named Smith. I said, "I guess, around here you stand a good chance of getting elected if your name is Smith. Where I live, it's Olson or Anderson." Our tour guide asked me where I lived. "Minnesota." Where in Minnesota? It turned out that this man was from Duluth, Minnesota, and had also lived in the Brainerd area. He was an "elected official" - perhaps, comptroller general. This man asked me what I was doing in South Carolina? "Running for President." Unsure whether I was now a celebrity or a freak, I continued to tour the beautiful Capitol building with this man and the young family, who were from Sweden. At length, I excused myself for fear that my parking meter had expired. They wished me good luck in the campaign.

There was little point in remaining in South Carolina much longer. I stopped at Maurice's Barbecue Restaurant in Columbia on my way back to the motel. It seemed a hangout for supporters of the lost Confederacy. I bought booklets about the history of the Confederate flag and about how Abe Lincoln was not so honest. Several inscribed photographs of George W. Bush hung on the wall. On a different wall was a picture of Robert E. Lee. The meal was delicious - it was barbecue with a <u>mustard</u> base. I had a good night's sleep and checked out of the motel around 8 a.m. on the following day.

I was headed immediately for Cincinnati, Ohio. A boyhood friend from Detroit, who now lived there, had once invited me to visit him if I were in the area. Driving up Interstate 26, I was pleased to see a billboard near Spartanburg asking if "your job has been outsourced yet?" I then crossed the border into North Carolina on Interstate 40 and, shortly afterwards, passed into Ten-

nessee through mountainous terrain. Near Knoxville, I left I-40 to take I-75 up through Tennessee and Kentucky to the Ohio River in the north. Gassing up in northern Kentucky, I called my old friend.

The last time I had seen this man, John Court - we called him "Christy" - was at the Pentagon in 1968. He had been a policy analyst there. Later, John moved over to the Nixon White House to work for Henry Kissinger. Yes, he had accompanied Dr. Kissinger to China, but his work focused more on Pakistan and the Soviet Union. After leaving public service, John Court turned down a number of attractive job offers (including publisher of the *Star Tribune*) to become a venture capitalist in Cincinnati.

He was general manager and part owner of a printing company, besides being an investor in real estate. His wife, Georgia, taught creative writing at a university. She had also been a health columnist for the *Cincinnati Enquirer*.

Sipping wine, we caught up on the old days and discussed politics. John was a diehard Republican; Georgia was more liberal. In his day, he had closed down union plants and opened nonunion ones, yet he saw a need for unions. Surprisingly, both John and Georgia were in basic agreement with my arguments that housing debt could bring calamity, that jobs were becoming scarce, and more education would not necessarily save the young. We argued, however, about the shorter workweek. Financially secure, John had retired after suffering a stroke two years earlier. Though his speech was slurred, his mind remained sharp. He had recently toured the Far East. I met their teenage son, Andrew, when he returned home for the evening. Then I went to bed in the attic guest room.

The following morning, John Court gave me a quick sightseeing tour of Cincinnati. The rest of the day, Sunday, January 11th, was spent driving back to Minneapolis, via Indianapolis and Bloomington, Illinois. I reached the Twin Cities around midnight. My wife was sound asleep. The next day's accumulated mail included a Fed-Ex packet containing the same two letters from Erwin and McAuliffe that I had seen in Columbia. My returned check was also enclosed. On my first day home, I typed another letter to Terence McAuliffe.

Phil McNamara's promise to call me next week after McAuliffe had reviewed my case turned out to be hollow. After Wednesday I called McNamara twice a day, and then several more times the following week, only to reach a recorded message. When I tried to reach McAuliffe himself, my call was transferred to the "public comment line." Again, I contacted the South Carolina Democratic Party. Had they heard from McNamara or McAuliffe? Someone there let slip the information that the primary ballots had already been printed. That did it. I was no longer under any illusion that the national party would reconsider. Even if it did, the state party would not bear the expense of reprinting ballots just for my sake.

Despite previous assurances that this was my "last message", I sent another email, "campaign is over", to persons on my email list. But that, too, was premature. Louisiana was still a question mark. If McAuliffe would not let me receive delegates from South Carolina, the same rules ought to apply to any other state. But how about getting on the primary ballot?

I called the Election Section of the Louisiana Secretary of State's office. A woman named Julie took the call. After explaining why I had been disqualified in South Carolina, I asked if the same rules applied to her state. Julie took a minute to check. Then, to my amazement and delight, she told me that the rules were different. "In Louisiana," she said, "we don't care what you've been." Anyone can run for President in that state's primary if they pay the filing fee and file within the qualifying period. However, the application form and the fee must be sent to Baton Rouge so that it arrives between January 28th and January 30th. If a candidate cannot appear at the election counter in person, overnight mail would be the best guarantee of timely delivery.

Therefore, another email message went out to Louisiana media informing them that my presidential "campaign (was) still on in Louisiana." This one had a better claim to finality.

Part

CHAPTER FOURTEEN

In Louisiana, Ready for Combat

Before I left for Louisiana, I received a telephone call from a (New Orleans) Times-Picayune reporter named Ed Anderson who worked out of the paper's Baton Rouge bureau. This call came on the day after the filing deadline. Evidently my name had made it to the ballot along with six other names. Anderson wanted to know if I planned to campaign actively in Louisiana. I said that I would. I asked Anderson if I might contact him when I arrived in the state. He gave permission. This was a good sign. Already, Louisiana's largest newspaper was interested in my campaign.

Minnesota was reeling from a snow storm when I headed south on Highway I-35 in the morning of Monday, February 2nd. Plans to leave the previous afternoon had fallen through when

my car's heat gauge registered extreme temperatures. A friend knowledgeable about cars assured me that the engine fan was working. The neighborhood service station checked the level of water and antifreeze. Ed Eubanks had expressed interest in accompanying me to Louisiana for a week but last-minute obligations kept him from going. As I drove down the highway on slick pavements Monday morning, many a car was in the ditch. Snow continued to fall. This condition lasted through southern Minnesota and into Iowa as far as Des Moines. Beyond that point, it would be a new driving experience for me. I had not been here before.

The icy conditions gradually abated as I continued through southern Iowa and into Missouri. I-35 then headed south in a more westerly direction towards Kansas City. I stopped at Cameron in the late afternoon to have supper at a place called Ma and Pa Kettle's kitchen. Besides the lure of a good home-cooked meal, the name attracted me because my father's first cousin, Marjorie Main, had played the role of Ma Kettle in a series of Hollywood films. After skirting around Kansas City, I picked up U.S. highway 71 for the rest of the trip. It was well after dark when I entered Arkansas and passed by Bentonville, home of Wal-Mart, before encountering a winding, mountainous stretch of road in the Ozark mountains. When I came to a town called Alma, I was too tired to continue. I looked for a place to sleep.

The experience was unsettling. It was my practice on long trips to sleep in the car rather than stay at motels. However, no cars seemed to be parked on the streets of Alma. I feared that the police would harass me if I tried to sleep there in violation of city ordinance. Noticing that cars were parked behind garages in alleys, I pulled into an alley and found a garage which appeared to be abandoned. A dog was barking nearby. I put the seat back and tried to sleep. But I had fears of doing something illegal. Around 1 a.m., a car with headlights blazing pulled into the same alley and then into a garage. Though its driver did not stop to investigate my presence, my anxiety increased. Maybe this garage where I was parked was not abandoned and its owner would soon return? I managed to gain an hour's sleep when, in the predawn hours, I decided to continue driving. (Later I thought this place might have been Mena, where the CIA is alleged to have used an airstrip to smuggle cocaine into this country. No, it was Alma.) The irony was that I found an approved rest area just down the road near Fort Smith and took a nap there.

The drive down U.S. highway 71 through western Arkansas (including Mena) was reasonably pleasant. This part of the country, sparsely populated and hilly, had a western flavor to it. Farther along, I entered Texas and the town of Texarkana where I bought groceries at a supermarket in a poor part of town. Heading back into Arkansas, I noticed that one of the magnetic signs on the side door of my car, marked "Bill McGaughey for President/ SAVE OUR JOBS", had fallen off. Maybe someone had stolen it in the supermarket parking lot? Maybe the magnetic backing was too weak? I entered Louisiana a short time later, stopping to photograph a sign with the Pelican state symbol at the state line. U.S. 71 continued through an area with many small oil wells. My immediate objective was Shreveport.

From a printed list of Motel 6 facilities in Louisiana downloaded from the Internet, I located a motel just east of Shreveport in Bossier City. I gathered maps and brochures about places in Louisiana at a nearby tourist center before checking into

the motel. Then it was time to rest. I had come more than a thousand miles. I watched the results of the South Carolina primary on CNN in my motel room. John Edwards took this state. Wesley Clark later took Oklahoma. John Kerry, however, swept the primaries in Missouri, Arizona, North Dakota, and Delaware. My campaign, in its more active phase, had not yet started.

My car was packed with gear in the trunk and back seat. I had a large suitcase for my clothes, a large plastic container with bags and other specialized items, a folded tent (which was never used), a cardboard carton filled with books and literature, two suits hanging on hooks, a large Mexican hat, several small flags on sticks, food and drink, and other items. My daily routine was to take the suitcase and plastic container, and perhaps some food and reading materials, with me into the motel room, leaving the rest in the car.

Before leaving on this trip, I had tried to prepare myself on issues by collecting newspaper articles and writing down significant information from them. I had also bought a book titled *After the New Economy* which seemed to be a good source of information and analysis about the contemporary U.S. economy. What had interested me in this book was an interview with its author in a Twin Cities alternative newspaper revealing the fact that U.S. consumers were borrowing $400 to $600 billion a year against the increased equity in their homes.

Rising debt was of growing public concern. A news report heard on the car radio mentioned that the federal deficit had reached $521 billion. Administration spokesmen blamed it on the recession and the fight against terrorism. One economist argued that federal deficits were no problem now because of excess capacity in the private economy; but when the economy heated up, the Federal Reserve Board would have to raise interest rates and the deficit would cause pain. This was expected after the election, some time in 2005.

These thoughts helped to clarify my position as a candidate. Up to this time, I included "white-male" advocacy among my political issues. Now, as a Minnesota resident coming south, that position would look too much like pandering to race prejudice among white voters. I would be an outsider meddling in race relations. Besides, as a believer in solving such problems by personal example rather than legislation, I thought that what I hoped to accomplish in that area had already been accomplished to the best of my ability, energy, and time. Employment problems, on the other hand, were a proper object of government action. They had risen to the top of political discussions at that time.

The two areas were related. Following the principle that tyrants first besmirch the reputation of those whom they intend to abuse, I saw the campaign to cast white males as racist and sexist oppressors of other groups as a prelude to stripping them of their economic privilege. White males were still the most numerous group among well-paid employees. They formed the core of union membership. If the economic elite could break the political back of this group of people, it would have free rein in cutting back on their compensation as employees. My speaking openly about race did offer a certain opportunity for North-South healing. On the other hand, this issue was too complicated and emotionally wrenching for me to present effectively in the short time that I would have in Louisiana. My issue was, therefore, employment.

Before leaving Minneapolis, I had run off several hundred copies of a double-sided sheet titled "The Democratic Presidential Candidates' Job Proposals." In this sheet, I analyzed the nation's "jobless recovery" in terms of two problems: (1) increasing labor productivity and high levels of overtime and (2) outsourcing production to low-wage countries. I proposed to address these problems by shorter work hours and by tariffs on the outsourced products applied when they were imported back into the United States. This flier also summarized the other candidates' proposals. Their suggestions ranged from extended unemployment benefits to reduced taxes on companies that stayed in the United States to job-retraining programs to enforcing trade agreements. (See text in the Appendix.) In my view, these proposals were marginally useful.

In a standard pitch, I would say that this leaflet summarized my campaign platform. Housing might lead our country into an economic downturn when interest rates rose next year. Rising interest rates would precipitate more mortgage foreclosures. As more homes were foreclosed, they would go back on the market. The excess supply of houses for sale would put downward pressure on prices. Falling housing prices would put financial pressure on the people who had borrowed against the equity in their homes. What would save us, as interest rates rose and housing prices fell, would be if we had a strong base of wage earners. Someone needed to purchase those excess houses.

Obviously, the base of jobs was not there. That's why it was so important that political candidates presented realistic proposals for job creation. None of the Presidential candidates, Democrat or Republican, were doing that. Even if I lost the primary, my job-centered campaign would force the other Democratic candidates to come up with better proposals in the employment area. A good healthy debate on this subject would get people focused on employment. That would work to the advantage of Democrats in the general election. The U.S. voters were too smart to fall for glib generalities. If the Democrats offered a solid plan to create jobs, they would be more likely to win.

I myself had a credibility problem. As an unknown candidate entered in only one primary, I could not possibly win the Democratic nomination. Why, then, was I running? Why should anyone vote for me? My answer was that I was running not so much to win convention delegates as to advance a certain agenda. It was realistic for me to run in a presidential primary because politics is a game of expectations. People did not expect me to do well. To win, therefore, I would not have to beat John Kerry or even come close. All I would have to do is beat expectations. If my candidacy attracted, say, 10% of the primary vote in Louisiana, that would be a spectacular result. It would get noticed, not just in Louisiana but around the country. An unexpectedly strong showing by me would be interpreted as support for my approach to creating jobs. That was the goal here.

I should therefore run as a single-issue candidate so that the election result could not possibly be misinterpreted. Discard all the other issues that I had raised in the past and just talk about employment. Be unambiguous and clear. That's how my running for President would best promote change. It was not that I was using the primary election as a personal soap box to talk about issues but that I was giving Louisiana voters a chance to be heard. Nobody cared what I thought. People did care what Louisiana voters thought. An election result, reflecting voter preferences, validates the issues advanced by the winning candidates or, in my case, by someone who did unexpectedly well.

Actually, the opportunity for Louisiana voters to influence the Democratic nomination were slim to none. By March 9th, when the state primary would be held, the contest for the Democratic nomination would most likely be decided already. It would be too late for voters in Louisiana to affect the result. On 

the other hand, in voting for me they could affect U.S. employment policy, which was even more important. They would have a chance to tell the national political establishment that they wanted candidates to talk realistically and specifically about employment problems. They would be saying that they were dissatisfied with the answers provided to date. This was a chance for Louisiana to make a difference in the 2004 election campaign. To make a difference, however, I had to receive an unexpectedly large number of votes. I thought it reasonable to shoot for 5% to 10% of the Democratic primary vote. Less than 5% would not get noticed. More than 10% would be a huge victory.

That is how I tried to sell myself as a credible candidate - someone hitching his name to issues. I would be one of seven candidates on the Democratic ballot. Al Sharpton's name would not be there. According to a news report, he had sent a personal check to pay the filing fee. Election regulations in Louisiana required payment by a certified check, postal money order, or another such device. While the state had relatively open ballot access, it was also a stickler for proper procedure. Sharpton had paid for his carelessness. I later learned that, since the ballot listed candidates in alphabetical order by last name, my name would appear last on the ballot. The rules also required that nicknames be placed in quotations. Since I had registered as Bill, the printed ballot would present me as "Bill" McGaughey. I did not like that since quotation marks suggest that something said is allegedly true. However, it was too late to change the listing. I was lucky to be included.

As a practical matter, candidates could expect to receive a few votes just from being listed on the ballot. That level of support would not make it worthwhile for me to run. To get noticed, I needed to beat the odds. The Republican candidate who was opposing George W. Bush could expect some votes because he was the sole alternative to the President. Republicans hating the war might go for him. I, however, was included with six other better known candidates. Five had strong name recognition from the televised debates. Lyndon LaRouche was a veteran campaigner with his own organization and newspaper. As a relatively unknown candidate, I had to stand out by running an effective campaign.

The way to do that, I had learned from my the 2002 Senate race, was to try to outhustle the other candidates. Visit every nook and cranny in the state. Introduce yourself to newspaper editors. Try to get radio interviews. Have a clear and relevant message. I was hoping that people would buy my rationale for being a candidate even if I had no chance of winning the nomination. If that argument was too esoteric, perhaps they would appreciate my forthright stand on employment issues. I knew that jobs were important to Louisiana people.

CHAPTER FIFTEEN

Down the West Side of the State and Over to Baton Rouge

Shreveport, Louisiana's third largest city, was the starting point of my campaign. *The Times* of Shreveport is the area's dominant newspaper. I could not make an appointment to see a reporter there on my first day of campaigning, which was Wednesday, February 4th, but did set something up for the following day. Teddy Allen, a columnist, would see me on the morning of the 5th. In the meanwhile, I set up appointments by cell phone with some of the other newspapers to the east and north of Shreveport: in Minden and in Ruston. The *Springhill Press* in Springhill, near the Arkansas border, discouraged a visit then.

I called first on the *Minden Press-Herald* and met with a young reporter named Teresa Gardner. She took my handout materials and a photo. Then I headed north to the small town of Homer for an unannounced visit to its newspaper. Although it was lunch time, Catherine Graham stayed in the office to talk. She was interested in talking with me about veterans' benefits. Her husband was a Vietnam vet who needed medical care. The government was refusing to help unless they could provide enough documentation of his military record. What to do about this? My only advice was to tell her to keep at it: "The squeaky wheel gets the grease." Graham wanted me to eat lunch at a restaurant in town owned by another relative. I was sidetracked when by chance I ran into another newspaper office, belonging to the *Haynesville Advertiser*, just around the corner. The editor, Kathy Foster, seemed interested in my issues. After talking for awhile, she took my photograph and said she would put something in the paper.

My next stop, Ruston, was more than forty miles away on Louisiana highway 146, a beautiful country road. As I crossed what we would call the "county line" into Lincoln Parish, I was reminded of the different terminology used in Louisiana. "Parish" is, of course, their term for county. This word has a religious flavoring reinforced by all the parishes whose names begin with Saint - St. Mary, St. Tammany, St. Charles, St. John the Baptist, etc. My favorite Louisiana term, however, was "Police Jury" This has nothing to do with a police force but is equivalent to our "County Commission". They are the people who run the parishes. Along highway 146, I saw a crew of young men dressed in prison garb, picking up trash along the road. They put it in black plastic bags for later pickup. Louisiana is not unique in this regard. I have seen the same type of work crew in my own neighborhood.

Arriving at my destination, I had a twenty-minute visit with the editor of the *Ruston Leader*, Tre Bishof, and another man. I was a bit tired by then but got the job done. We talked about economic issues and they took a photograph. These men referred me to Greg Hilburn at the Monroe newspaper, east another twenty-five miles. That visit would have to be postponed. While listening to the car radio, I had heard that State Farm was closing its regional processing center in Monroe to consolidate its southeastern operations elsewhere. The decision would cost 1,300 jobs. This news was still fresh and people were in shock. A long-time agent with State Farm was arguing on the radio that the move would save money and, in the long run, benefit Louisiana people by producing lower insurance rates. After my interview in Ruston, I drove back to the motel in Bossier City which was one hundred miles to the west. If I had been properly prepared, I might also have stopped in Arcadia to visit the newspaper there. Instead, I called it a day.

Next morning, I had an appointment with Teddy Allen at *The Times*. He came out to the front desk to talk for a few minutes. I gave him a photo of myself and left some literature. After that appointment, I visited the office of the *Bossier Press-Tribune* in Bossier City. Reporter Seth Fox and a young woman named Erin talked with me in a conference room for half an hour. We had a thorough discussion of debt and employment issues. I left a packet of literature focusing upon my trade proposals. I forgot to leave a photo but then, recognizing the omission, came back to the front desk with one. A day later, Seth Fox called me on the cell phone to ask permission to use a photo of me with my wife appearing on my campaign web site. He also asked for permission to refer me to a man at *Politics Louisiana* in Baton Rouge. Fox said he wanted to stay in touch about the campaign.

After the interview in Bossier City, I scouted downtown Shreveport for good locations in case I wanted to stage a television event in that city near the end of the campaign. Where was the most pedestrian traffic? I found a public building, later identified as the Caddo Court House, on Texas Street between Market and Marshall. This had been Louisiana's state capitol under the Confederacy. A replica of the last Confederate flag flew in front of a war monument. I jotted down sev-

eral locations in the red-colored spiral notebook which I used to record information for my campaign. Now it was time to head out of town.

All afternoon I visited newspaper offices to the south along U.S. highway 171 after calling ahead on the cell phone. First was the office of the *Enterprise and Interstate Progress* in Mansfield. Cindy Williams, the editor, was a down-to-earth person who talked with me in her office. I had to interrupt our meeting briefly to take a cell phone call from Teddy Allen of *The Times*. It was Williams who let me know of the Governor's Conference on Rural Economic Development taking place next week in Natchitoches (pronounced NACK-ih-tish). This is something, she said, which a political candidate ought to attend. She photocopied a sheet with the pertinent information. Before leaving, I remember Williams saying to me: "Be sure to take time to see something of our beautiful state."

Another forty miles down the road, I came to Many, the seat of Sabine Parish. The receptionist at the *Sabine Index* informed me that the paper's political reporter was out of the office. While we were having a conversation about the campaign, an African American man in his mid 40s joined us, Conway Terrel Jones. He said it was a coincidence that I was from Minnesota because, on that very day, he had been talking with someone about moving to my state. This man was a Christian minister and political activist who worked with a nonprofit organization that provided services to delinquent men. He said he was an assistant to the Speaker of the Louisiana House of Representatives. About that time, the political reporter, Pam Russell, returned to the office. We had a good ten-minute conversation about my issues. She took my photograph and promised to write a story that would appear on the front page.

That was an upbeat visit. The next one, in Leesville, was less so. I arrived at the office of the *Leesville Leader* about 4 p.m. just as the political reporter, Kelly Moore, was leaving to cover an assignment. She did not have time to talk with me then, but gave me her business card. I left a copy of my leaflet about the candidates' employment proposals. There is a large military base just south of Leesville called Fort Polk which has a newspaper with a circulation of 14,000. That was my next stop. A guard at the entrance to the base asked my business. Pulling off to the side of the road, I placed a cell-phone call to the newspaper editor. There was no answer. I therefore did a U-turn and left the premises.

My next stop was Deridder. Hopefully I would arrive there before closing time. The *Beauregard Daily News* in DeRidder had a policy of allowing political candidates to write campaign announcements of up to 400 words which would be run for free. Subsequent publicity would be through paid advertising. I took my time in composing the statement. Then I gave the editor, Elona Weston, a photograph of myself and a copy of my employment flier.

Done for the day, I headed for Baton Rouge. This involved a drive of around 140 miles. Since it was now evening, I could not visit newspaper offices along the way. First I drove southeast on Louisiana highway 26. West of Basile, I picked up a major highway, U.S. 190, which went east to Baton Rouge. I made a reservation by cell phone for a room at the Motel 6 in Port Allen, a city this side of the Mississippi river from  Baton Rouge. The desk clerk, a young Italian woman named Angel, checked me in. She later called my room to ask if everything was OK. This was to be my home away from home for much of the time spent in Louisiana.

I had come to Baton Rouge because I thought it important to get in touch with the state's large newspapers early in the campaign. Ed Anderson of the New Orleans paper, the *Times-Picayune*, was assigned to its state capitol bureau. My top priority was to make contact with him. Since Baton Rouge has Louisiana's second largest population and is the state capitol, its newspaper,

The Advocate, was another priority. I left a message on Anderson's answering machine. He called me back promptly to report that he was sick with the flu and would not be coming to work that day. From a call to *The Advocate*, I learned that this newspaper's political reporter, Marsha Shuler, also worked out of the press office in the Louisiana state capitol. It was imperative, then, to go to the capitol the first thing on Friday morning.

Shuler was in when I visited her office at the state capitol on Friday. We did not talk long. She wrote notes on her pad and took some of my literature. An associate helped pick out the best photograph, opting for the picture of me in suit and tie rather than the more casual plaid shirt. The *Times-Picayune* office was next door. I popped my head in to introduce myself. I said I had already spoken with Ed Anderson who was sick with the flu. A man in the back of the room said: "I'm Ed Anderson." Despite his illness, Anderson had come to the office to work on a deadline story. He said, however, that he might be able to find a few minutes to talk with me. We went to the cafeteria across the hall to grab some coffee and talk.

Anderson's questioning centered on the nuts and bolts of my campaign. He was less interested in hearing my views on economic issues. How much money did I plan to spend in the campaign? I said it would be close to $5,000. Expenditures over that amount required filing with the Federal Election Commission. In the end, I thought, I would probably have to file. How would I campaign? I said that I would be visiting newspaper offices, trying to get on talk-radio shows, and making public appearances in an effort to attract television coverage. Anderson suggested that Mardi Gras might offer some opportunities for public appearances.

Since he was with a New Orleans newspaper, I took advantage of this meeting to ask Ed Anderson which he thought were the best locations in New Orleans to find crowds who might be willing to talk with political candidates. He made two suggestions: (1) Woldenberg Park along the Mississippi River. This was close to Harrah's Casino, the French Quarter, and other tourist attractions. (2) the junction of Veterans Memorial Drive and Causeway Boulevard in Metairie. Studies showed that many people congregated in this area (north of downtown, near Lake Pontchartrain). Regarding my purpose in running for President, I said for the first time that I was hoping to get 5% to 10% of the primary vote. It would be a definite victory if I received 10%.

After Ed Anderson excused himself, I walked along the corridor of the press offices. Down the hall were offices of the Associated Press. A young woman was sitting at a computer terminal near the door. I introduced myself. When I said I was from Minnesota, she remarked that she thought I had a Minnesota accent. Despite some well-publicized humor about "speaking Minnesotan", I did not think there was such a thing as a "Minnesota accent". I responded, however, by saying that I did not think Louisiana residents had accents. I had come here expecting to hear regional dialects but found people - admittedly, often on television - speaking a fairly standard version of Americanized English. She didn't have an accent, for instance.

No, said this woman, whose name was Melinda Deslatte, she was from southern Louisiana. When she first came here, she had an accent; but now she had lost it. There were, indeed, regional accents in Louisiana. People in the northern part of the state had "southern accents". Those in the Lafayette area had another kind of accent. Those in New Orleans had still another. However interesting this discussion was, she had to return to work.

Deslatte gave me her business card and invited me to stay in touch.

After leaving the capitol, I dropped by the headquarters of the Louisiana Democratic Party on Government Street to introduce myself. Emily, a receptionist, and Michelle, sitting at a computer, spoke with me for a short time. If I came back on Monday, some of the bosses would be in. Michelle was able to confirm that my name was on the ballot. Lieberman was not. Sharpton was not. But Howard Dean, Wesley Clark, Dennis Kucinich, Lyndon LaRouche, and John Edwards would still be listed as, of course, would John Kerry.

The Louisiana Election Bureau in the Secretary of State's office was the official source of information about elections. Its office was located on the east side of Baton Rouge several miles from the capitol off I-12 behind the Louisiana Archives building. Not being familiar with this highway, I took a wrong exit which brought me to a largely deserted city park near a lake. There was no entrance ramp back to the highway. Some strange-looking geese were feeding on a beach. I drove south around a larger lake only to discover that I was now on the campus of Louisiana State University (LSU). Taking Stanford Street would get me back to the highway. After more wanderings with the help of a map, I rejoined I-12 and, in time, located the Election Bureau office.

My primary purpose was to inquire if I might obtain a sample copy of the primary ballot (the one you see on the cover of this book). That would be no problem. I filled out a request form. An election official also gave me a printout of the candidates' names,

which confirmed what I had been told at Democratic Party headquarters. Here I learned that my first name would appear in quotes: "Bill" McGaughey. Joe Lieberman's name also appeared this way on the printout but his withdrawal from the presidential race had come in time for him to be removed from the ballot. Sharpton was challenging his exclusion in court. I was apprehensive about being the only candidate on the ballot whose name, besides being listed last, would have quotation marks around it. I was assured this was no big thing. Plenty of other candidates in Louisiana have their first names in quotations, the official said. In any event, it was now too late to make changes. If I had come in the previous day, they might have been able to do something. The order for ballots had already gone to the printer.

Still having some time left in the day, I decided to visit more newspaper offices. I tried to make appointments with the *Baton Rouge Weekly Press*, an African American newspaper, and with the *Port Allen West Side Journal*. It was not a convenient time to call on either. Fifteen miles south of Port Allen was the town of Plaquemine (pronounced PLACK-mon). I called ahead to its weekly newspaper, the *Post South*, to ask for directions. A woman on the phone directed me down Louisiana highway 1 to a fork in the road beyond the city limits. Cross over the railroad tracks. Take a right turn at the "Jack-in-the-box". I did not know what this meant but was too timid to ask. Was "Jack-in-the-box" another unique Louisiana term for a road configuration? In my confusion, I turned off the main highway too soon and crossed over some railroad tracks. It was not the right place. After asking di-

rections, I did find the newspaper office. But I never saw any Jack-in-the-box. (Weeks later, passing through this area again, I spotted it. This is a restaurant franchise. There was a sign on highway 1, maybe forty feet tall, plainly lettered "Jack in the Box".)

The editor of the *Post South*, Steve Colwell, had to finish some business for twenty minutes. We then discussed political issues. It was one of those discussions which, I came to realize, made campaigning so worthwhile. Besides giving my pitch, I was receiving interesting feedback from a man knowledgeable about local issues. Colwell said he was a big fan of the Job Corps to train and discipline youth. This parish had many chemical factories owned by Dow Chemical and other companies which produced plastic. The high cost of natural gas was killing that industry. There was increased competition from abroad. Sugar growers in the area complained of subsidized sugar from Mexico. The crawfish industry was suffering from Chinese competition. Trade issues were much on people's minds.

Additionally, Steve Colwell, who was not a Cajun, worried that Louisiana was losing its culture. The requirement to study French had been dropped from the high-school curriculum ten or fifteen years earlier. Years ago, when the locals wanted to keep a secret from you, they would talk among each other in French. But that generation was dying out. Today's children were facing an uncertain cultureless future - jobless, too, I might have added.

We finished our conversation after 5 o'clock. I was ready to begin my first weekend in the state.

CHAPTER SIXTEEN

My First Weekend in Louisiana

Weekends are down time in my political campaigns. This is when I thought I might go to a state park and pitch a tent. However, it rained much of the first week. Motel life seemed increasingly attractive. I was staying at the Motel 6 in Port Allen on the outskirts of Baton Rouge. Partly this was because of its central location; partly because of the relatively low price. After the AARP discount, I was paying about $30 a night on weekdays with another $5 on the busier weekends. A room at Motel 6 in New Orleans would run $50 a night - less in the neighboring city of Slidell. If I could find motels in the $30 to $40 price range, my lodging for the month would cost slightly more than $1,000, which was bearable.

While other chains such as Days Inn also had competitive rates, I preferred Motel 6 because of its consistently low prices

and its familiarity. I had brought with me a printout from the Internet showing locations and giving phone numbers for all the Motel 6's in Louisiana. It was convenient to call ahead on my cell phone to book a reservation for the evening. Timely cancellations were no problem. Even with an uncertain itinerary, I could expect to find a Motel 6 in a city not far from that day's destination.

I preferred rooms on the lower level, preferably non-smoking and with one bed because that left room for a table which could also be used as a desk. All Motel 6 rooms have basic cable television. They have coin-operated laundry equipment in a room near the front office. Free ice is available. If one requests a wake-up call in the morning, a recorded voice says: "Hello, this is Tom Bodett calling to tell you you've just won $10 million. Just kidding. Actually, it's time to get up." In other words, the Motel 6 has many of the comforts that one would find at home.

My style was to buy groceries at supermarkets instead of eating at restaurants. (Toward the end of the campaign, that pattern began to change.) I did not take full advantage of the ice machine until later. I had brought with me a limited supply of laundry soap, a small number of food containers and kitchen utensils, and, most important, a battery recharger for my cell phone. I also had a few religious books and reading materials relating to the campaign. I ate light meals in my room. There was a shower for bathing. I had packed enough clothes for one week's wearing if a fresh set was worn each day. Weekends would be a time for laundry.

On Friday evening, February 6th, I prepared a load of clothing for the washer at the Port Allen Motel 6. Next to my unit was parked a small truck with a trailer and, on top of the trailer, a motor bike. Its owner struck up a conversation with me. He was a young man from Quebec named François who was returning from a bike trip in the Chiapas district of Mexico. He was driving back to his home in Quebec, about forty miles north of Ottawa. François had supported the Quebec separatist movement and suspected underhanded dealings when this initiative was defeated. He also owned a portable logging mill from which he made a good living. Quebec, he said, was the "Brazil of the North". By that, he did not mean to express mutual admiration but soul-searching regret that some of the earth's last great natural forests were being cut down at such a rapid rate.

François ordered pizza. He invited me to share his meal while we looked at photographs taken on the Chiapas trip. Though he traveled by himself, he did have regular places to stay. While much of his travel followed the Pacific coast line, he also went into the more dangerous places bordering Guatemala where gas was harder to find and strangers were not always welcomed. I thought this quite courageous for a man not fluent in Spanish. Next to his, my adventures in Louisiana were tame. Yet, the two of us did share a certain spirit. I was on an impossible mission to be elected President of the United States. He had courted danger in the jungles and deserts of Mexico. On the other hand, François' trials were behind him - another 1,500 miles and he would be home - while mine were just beginning. We called it a night when I went to remove my wet clothes from the washer and place them in the dryer.

Saturday morning, I organized materials for the campaign. From a directory provided by a public library in Minnesota, I had photocopied pages giving information about Louisiana's radio and television stations. Some seemed more news-oriented than others. Some radio stations featured call-in talk shows or programs which might welcome interviews with political candidates. I had to identify these on the listing and ignore the others. I went through the photocopied sheets writing down the most promising stations in each city including telephone numbers and contact names. Then I started calling some of these.

Because it was Saturday morning, the majority of calls reached an answering machine. That was OK. If the recipient was interested, he or she might call back next week. The only immediate positive response came from Dave Graichen, co-host of a morning show on station KSYL-AM in Alexandria. I planned to be in Alexandria Monday morning for an interview with the *Daily Town Talk* newspaper. Graichen proposed that I be at his radio station at 8:15 a.m. A man at another station told me to call the station manager when I came to town. Another said he was only interested in political candidates if they placed paid ads.

I also used my time on that weekend to organize the campaign literature. Starting then, I delivered a standard packet of literature to newspaper offices that I visited. The top sheet was my double-sided statement on "The Democratic Presidential Candidates' Job Proposals", already mentioned. Next came a one-sided photocopy taken from the handout at the candidates' debate in Des Moines which was titled "HEY - there's a tenth candidate for President seeking the Democratic nomination!" This gave biographical information about me. Then I had another one-sided sheet titled "Second Thoughts on Free Trade", which was an Op-Ed article in the *New York Times* coauthored by New York Senator Charles Schumer and a Reagan Treasury Assistant Secretary, Paul Craig Roberts. I wanted to suggest that opposition to free trade was now in the political mainstream or, at least, had opponents both on the right and left.

The bulkiest items in my campaign packet were photocopies of two articles written by me which appeared in the St. Louis Green Party publication, *Synthesis/Regeneration*, in the 1990s. One was titled "A Labor and Environmentally Oriented Trading System" and the other "A Search for Trade Standards to Protect Labor and the Environment". Here I had spelled out my trade proposals in some detail. I took them off the Internet at www.greens.org/s-r/06toc.html and www.greens.org/s-r/09toc.html. At the bottom of the pile were photocopies of three opinion articles related to the shorter-workweek issue which I published more than twenty years ago: one in the *New York Times* and two in the *Christian Science Monitor*.

Saturday morning, I visited the Kinko's copy shop in downtown Baton Rouge to make sure that I had enough copies of all these materials. It cost me $63 to produce everything in this round of copying. More would come later. I already had several hundred copies of the top sheet. Having neglected to bring biographical materials, I had to search through assorted papers to find the Des Moines handout and then run copies. The most paper was consumed by the two *Synthesis/Regeneration* articles, six and four pages in length respectively. Yet, it was important to have these articles to prove I was not just making my issues up on the fly. My campaign was beginning to focus more on trade to the detriment of other issues. I characterized my main proposal as "employer-specific tariffs".

To combat job loss from outsourcing, I proposed a new type of tariff whose rate reflected an employer's cost differential between producing in a low-wage country and in the United States. Roughly speaking, for each type of product which a company produces abroad, the federal government might develop a tariff

rate which equalizes the cost of production. It would determine the employer's cost savings from outsourcing, apply this savings to total product cost, and determine a rate of tariff which, applied to the product as it entered the United States, would cancel the cost savings from cheap labor. Yes, I was for trade protection; but the tariff should be employer-specific. Nation-specific tariffs invite trade wars. Employer-specific ones are a way for national governments to regulate international business.

Now that I had restocked my supply of campaign literature, it was time for some serious sightseeing. The most interesting attraction for me in Baton Rouge was the Louisiana state capitol. This is one of the few - perhaps, the only - state capitols which does not have a domed roof. Instead, the Louisiana capitol is contained in a 27-story skyscraper which also houses other state-government offices. Huey Long was responsible for this building. His fingerprints are on much of Louisiana politics, especially in Baton Rouge. So a visit to the Louisiana state capitol was also a tour of the legacy of Louisiana's former governor and U.S. Senator whose body is buried in a garden adjoining the capitol building, Huey P. Long.

Visitors to the Louisiana state capitol are told of an exhibit in a lobby behind the main elevators. This is where Senator Long was shot. In September 1935, a disgruntled medical doctor named Carl Weiss fired a bullet into Long at close range. Long died in a hospital several days later. A display cabinet at the site of the

shooting contains the assassin's gun, Long's death certificate, copies of newspapers from the time, and other mementos of this event. There is even a bullet hole in a nearby marble column, most likely fired by one of Long's body guards in the retaliatory round of shooting. Thousands of mourners passed by the Senator's coffin as it lay in state at the capitol. I was surprised to read in the posted newspaper that thousands also attended the assassin's funeral. The state capitol building was Huey Long's monument. As governor, he had rammed legislation through authorizing its construction. Even as U.S. Senator, he micromanaged legislation there and was doing that on the fateful day when he was shot.

As a boy, I had the impression that Huey Long was a colorful but somewhat disreputable figure. Politically, he stood for sharing the wealth. In a gift shop atop the capitol building, I bought a booklet of Long's writing, "Share our Wealth", and later a video documentary of his life produced by Ken Burns. The idea of confiscating superfluous wealth from multimillionaires and giving it to the poor was certainly not new, but Huey Long pushed this proposal with his customary energy and skill. He built a nationwide "Share the Wealth" society which had hundreds of thousands of members. Had he lived, Senator Long might have been a formidable rival to President Roosevelt in the 1936 national election. In fact, Long published a book shortly before his death titled "My First Days in the White House."

Some have compared Huey Long to Mussolini and Hitler who were also flamboyant speakers and ruthless wielders of political power. They have called Long a "dictator". The flip side, however, was that Long was a politician who delivered on his promises. Before his administration, there were only 300 miles of paved road in Louisiana. Long embarked on a massive road-building project. He was first to construct a bridge across the Mississippi river. Governor Long gave free textbooks to Louisiana's school children. He built a new state capitol and a new campus for Louisiana State University. What's more, he made big business pay for much of this.

Standard Oil had oil wells throughout Louisiana and much political influence. When Governor Long proposed a five-cent-per-barrel tax on crude oil refined in the state, it so offended political sensibilities that the state legislature began impeachment proceedings against him. By much arm-twisting, Long beat back this challenge. Determined not to repeat the experience, the governor concentrated even more power in his office. He exacted regular donations from state employees. He used the national guard to intimidate political rivals. He printed his own newspaper.

So colorful and strong was this man and so powerful his legacy that even today people are trying to figure him out. While his opponents concede that Long was an intelligent man who did some good for the state, they insist that the political excesses outweigh his positive record. Many others revere his memory. Myself, I am among those who believe that Huey Long was a great man. I am also willing to suppose that the good he did outweighed the bad. To think that one man could accomplish all that Long accomplished, when the powerful forces in society were stacked against him, is quite remarkable. Yet, undeniably, Long's administration of government also brought many abuses of power and was a threat to the democratic process.

A college professor of mine, Robert Penn Warren, wrote a prize-winning fictional biography of Long titled "All the King's Men." We remember Huey Long today through works such as this. As the sun is too bright to gaze at it directly, so Long's im-

age may be too powerful to be held in our national mind. We tend to blot him out of our memory. A way of comprehending this situation may be, first, to acknowledge that the United States is more a plutocracy than it is a democracy; and, then, to recognize that one cannot remain a loyal member of a plutocratic society while holding a balanced opinion of Huey Long. Long was the arch antagonist of this type of society. He was the purest representative of a thought which runs through our politics even today that a society should be run for the benefit of its people rather than just the wealthy. For many, this is a dangerous idea which must be suppressed. But it was impossible for me not to think of Long and his bold ideas while sitting on a bench in the beautiful, fragrant garden near the massive statute which also serves as a marker for his tomb.

Sunday was a quiet day. No activities were planned for the morning except to place a few long-distance telephone calls. My wife in China had caught the flu. She was planning to take sev-eral short trips outside Beijing. I myself had to buy a tooth brush and leave film to be developed in Baton Rouge. In the afternoon, I left that city and traveled to Alexandria where several appointments were scheduled

for the following morning. The most direct route to Alexandria was along U.S. highway 190 - reversing my course of last Thursday - and then, at Krotz Springs, up U.S. highway 71 through Bunkie. The trip would be about 120 miles. I could save time by taking interstate I-49, but was in no hurry that day. I saw a sign advertising Cajun food on highway 190 but did not stop.

An hour later, in Bunkie, I did stop at a restaurant that had Cajun specialties and wanted to order something. For some rea-son, this restaurant was not open for busi-ness. A crew of workmen was hosing down the floor. So I continued on to Alexandria looking for its Motel 6. I was coming up MacArthur Boulevard from the south. The recorded directions assumed arrival from another direction. Along the way, I spot-ted a retail store specializing in Cajun foods. I ordered a wurst-like sausage called Boudin and a crispy, tasty chicken snack called Spracklin.

The Motel 6 was just beyond Super One foods across the highway from a strip mall. The clerk at the desk helpfully gave me directions to the two places I would visit the next day. Radio station KSYL-AM was not far away. Just cross U.S. highway 71, go a block to Texas Avenue, turn right, and go several more blocks. The *Daily Town Talk* newspaper was located in downtown Alexandria. In this case it was necessary to take Monroe to Bolton, turn right, and then take a left at Jackson and follow it for a dozen more blocks. I spent the late afternoon orienting myself to Alexandria, reading historical markers, and walking about the downtown area. It was the end of a full weekend.

CHAPTER SEVENTEEN

In Alexandria and Natchitoches

I was up bright and early on Monday morning to make my 8:15 a.m. appointment at radio station KSYL-AM on Texas Avenue. The show was already in progress as a woman in the upstairs reception area invited me to take a seat on the sofa. Fifteen minutes later, Dave Graichen came out of the studio to greet me. I followed him back to meet his co-host, Bob Madison. When I showed these men my leaflet about the Democratic candidates' positions on employment, Madison advised I should not make negative comments about the other candidates but offer my own proposals. So I started with trade.

Standing at the mike, I went through my economic arguments. The first caller was - surprise! - Andrew Griffin of the Alexandria *Daily Town Talk* newspaper. He was the journalist who had written a column last October about my Independence Party book. Griffin wanted me to talk about the shorter workweek. I responded by saying that I was not stressing a reduction of the standard workweek in the current campaign because it was more important first to address overtime and bring weekly work hours down to forty. The next caller was a conservative man who said I sounded just like George McGovern. This man went on at length with arguments that I could easily have refuted. However, we had to take a break and,

afterwards, were on to another subject. I was able to say only that, while I realized that McGovern symbolized a political loser to many people, my politics were different. Actually I was closer to Eugene McCarthy. I also thought I had something useful to say about employment.

This radio interview lasted about twenty minutes. Upon leaving the KSYL-AM studio, I tried to find the office of Alexandria's African-American newspaper, the *Alexandria News Weekly*, located on Mason street. The office was closed when I found it. I dropped a piece of literature and a note into the mail slot. Then I drove to the offices of the *Daily Town Talk* for my 10:30 a.m. appointment. William Taylor was the reporter assigned to interview me. First, however, I stopped by the desk of Andrew Griffin to introduce myself. We talked briefly about Paul Wellstone - Had there been foul play in the Senator's plane crash? - and other subjects. With Taylor, I went through my economic arguments, campaign strategy, and some personal history. A photographer snapped some shots of me in the conference room. The article which appeared in the paper was reasonably sympathetic. However, I noticed that it also referred to my "beige leisure suit and a wrinkled pale green shirt". I would need to pay more attention to my wardrobe.

Andrew Griffin took me to lunch at a buffet following the interview. The young female cashier was thrilled to have a presidential candidate in their midst. Griffin said he had been at the *Daily Town Talk* for several years, starting as a news reporter and now working as a columnist concerned with culture and entertainment. He had a personal interest in politics including underdog candidates like me. In 2002, he had interviewed a man from New Orleans named Patrick "Live Wire" Landry, who was a libertarian and gun enthusiast, in a local coffee house. He was pleased to report that "Live Wire" had received a higher percentage of the votes in Rapides Parish (Alexandria) than anywhere else in the state. Griffin had moved quite often while growing up because his father was a city planner with changing work assignments. Career wise, he was not sure where he would be in five or ten years. He had once applied for a job with a newspaper in Rochester, Minnesota.

I had to be in Natchitoches for an evening reception starting at 5 p.m. This would kick off the Governor's Conference on Rural Economic Development, held at Northwest State University. My chief concern was where I would spend the night. Natchitoches did not have a Motel 6. It was a good sixty miles from Alexandria, and seventy miles from Shreveport. I thought I would keep an eye open for closer motel locations during my drive up Louisiana highway 1. A woman in the Tourist Information Center said it was unlikely that I would find anything. Best Western was advertising a $45 daily rate on a limited basis; that might be my best bet. The conference literature had assured guests that Natchitoches lodging places would cap their rates for conference attendees at $75 per night - way out of my price range. As luck would have it, I found a motel in Natchitoches itself which charged $33 per night. Bathroom cleanliness and carpet condition were not up to Motel 6 standards but the place would do. I booked a reservation for two nights. A nearby camp ground would have let me stay there for $15 a night; however rain was expected.

Pulling into Natchitoches on highway 1, I spotted the office of the *Natchitoches Times*, the local newspaper. A reporter named Stephanie Masson, who might also have been involved with editorials, talked with me while sitting in front of a computer screen. She expected that business groups would press for lower taxes to bring Louisiana in line with neighboring states. This might be an important "economic development" issue at the forthcoming conference. I went through my routine and left literature and a photo. It was not a long interview.

The preconference reception took place in the student union of the Northwest State University. I wore a purple-colored plastic badge identifying me as "BILL McGAUGHEY, Presidential Candidate." This badge was part of my standard uniform. Munching hors d'oeuvres off a paper plate, I first sat at a table with an investment banker from Thibodaux who was checking out the scene. He gave me some useful information about Mardi Gras festivities in New Orleans. Most of the remaining time was spent talking with an elderly Italian man, Joe B., who was a World War II veteran.

This man had strong, hawkish views about the U.S. mission in Iraq which did not coincide with mine. He was also a Louisiana history buff. He knew that Hubert Humphrey had studied at LSU. He knew and admired Archbishop Harry Flynn, formerly of Lafayette. He was proud of the fact that so many famous generals had lived on military bases in Louisiana. He said he had run for mayor of Jonesville and nearly won. I enjoyed talking with this opinionated man, Joe, who might have been in the consumer-finance business. Not having a business card on him, he said he

would give me one at the conference on the following day. We did not make contact again.

The conference itself was held in the college gymnasium. Several hundred persons participated. Most seemed to be local

government officials or employees of non-profits concerned with economic-development and employment problems. The opening speaker informed us that Governor (Kathleen Babineaux) Blanco would not be attending this conference as promised. She was in Baghdad visiting with Louisiana troops. Utmost secrecy had surrounded her change of plans. The Governor very much wanted to be here, though. She had sent her husband, Raymond, and her top staff aide, Andrew Kopplin, to represent her at the conference.

That out of the way, the speaker told us that the Governor did not agree with those who said that Louisiana was not a good tourism state. She wanted the state to do more to attract tourists and also to attract business generally, especially in the rural areas. What did business look for? They wanted good education, adequate infrastructure, a business-friendly environment, and low taxes. We should try to save the businesses already here before recruiting new ones.

A parade of speakers that day presented business-development ideas for rural Louisiana. Areas officially classified as "rural" had 95% of Louisiana's territory but only 25% of its population. At 19.6%, the state's poverty rate was higher than in most other states; and rural poverty was higher still. Some of the strategies for revitalizing the rural economy in Louisiana included wiring rural communities for access to the Internet, improving business-related courses at community colleges, informing business of support services in the community, making capital more readily available, encouraging business mentoring, and fostering a culture of entrepreneurship.

The trouble, said one speaker, is that young people today think of "taking" a job rather than "making" one for themselves. We know that small business creates most of America's new jobs, and entrepreneurs are the spark plug which makes this happen. Business-development strategy begins with creating a climate conducive to entrepreneurial activities. Who are these entrepreneurs? What do they want? What would it take to make them locate in our community? Communities would be well advised to do asset assessments. Who are the service providers and what are the cultural factors attractive to business?

Role models are also important. An African-American woman in Vanceboro, North Carolina, created a successful business when her employer, after considering whether to close it down, instead offered the business to her. Knowing the operation inside and out, she managed to revive the company. A Caucasian man in Shenandoah, Iowa, practiced what he calls the "front porch" model of entrepreneurship. Every Friday morning, he invites business people to hold informal discussions on his front porch; out of these discussions have come a new convenience

store and a car wash. A druggist in Ord, Nebraska, facing competition from the big chains, survived by specializing in veterinary services and continuing care. A woman in Adams County, Ohio, helped community residents to develop business plans in the area of historical and eco-tourism. In Surry County, North Carolina, they make a practice of "celebrating success" - telling stories of successful entrepreneurs. Any community can do this sort of thing. Invite successful entrepreneurs to address the local chamber of commerce. Visit their businesses. Map community assets.

The day was filled with bullet-point presentations of various kinds. A consultant from Washington, D.C. said that successful strategies for economic growth were: (1) community based, (2) regionally oriented, (3) entrepreneur-focused, and (4) learning based. Recruiting new business was expensive. Many stay for five years or so and then move on, often to places overseas. Business retention strategies are more effective. Communities need to invest in "anchor institutions" like technical schools, provide networks where business people can learn from their peers, stress entrepreneurial education, nurture the homegrown firms, and fund start-up capital. A developmental report card for the state showed that Louisiana did not perform up to par.

Another speaker specialized in business motivation. He had failed in two businesses before achieving impressive success in his current one (motivational speaking). Business people should try to maintain a positive tone. Don't complain about how bad business is. Surround yourself with positive people. Listen to people - don't "make them wrong". Three ways to grow a business are: (1) increase the number of customers, (2) Increase the number of sales, and (3) increase the size of each sale. It was possible, he said, to get your property tax reduced but you must do your homework and give good reasons. Don't accept professional fees as gospel; they can always be negotiated. Try to get lower interest rates. Here's a tip: Ask the magic question, "Is that the best you can do?," and then say nothing for a few seconds while looking the other person in the face.

Reward your employees for making suggestions. Keep them informed - they appreciate being in the know. Don't neglect employee development. Have accurate job descriptions, good training and cross training, and clear accountability. Consider giving employees bonuses rather than salary increases because bonuses suggest that pay is tied to company performance. Exercise each day to increase your energy level - but also take time for nature. Slow down and relax. If your customers are slow in paying bills, get to know the key people in their accounting departments. Maybe even take some of them out to lunch. Businesses either expand or die. Have a strategic action plan consisting of several different options. But don't go too far: "Pigs get fat but hogs get slaughtered." Audit your own beliefs. What do you believe in? What's important to you? Value family and friends. Take time to pray together.

There was one break in the mid-morning and then a break for lunch. During the first, I talked with a man who made brick-like concrete. He was facing competition from Australia. This man felt his competitors were cheating on trade classifications and the U.S. Government was letting them get away with it. A woman in the hallway who worked for the city of Many was related to Jim Taylor, former rusher for the Green Bay Packers who is now in the Football Hall of Fame. She was interested in business development that might take advantage of a large lake in her area.

The main luncheon speaker was Andrew Kopplin, the Governor's assistant. Fighting for jobs was the Governor's top priority, he said. He referred to the State Farm closing in Monroe and the loss of Fruit-of-the-Loom in Arcadia. Kopplin noted that the State of Louisiana had provided grants for infrastructure im-

provements and tax incentives for distressed areas. There were CD block grants and training programs. Unfortunately, rural areas had too few health clinics. The Governor would be convening a "Health Care summit" in New Orleans on March 3rd. Louisiana ranked Number One in the country in school accountability. Yet, there was a problem in finding qualified teachers for Advanced Placement. There were deficiencies in teaching algebra - considered the gateway to college.

The state needed to pay more attention to community and technical colleges which would train tomorrow's work force. It needed to finish the I-49 north-south highway and, indeed, all rural highways. Admittedly, the sales tax on manufacturing equipment and the franchise tax on debt were too high. The Governor would convene a special session of the legislature on March 7th to deal with these problems. She had met with President Bush privately for fifteen minutes and given him a list of things to help Louisiana including trade protection for agricultural products: sugar cane, shrimp, cotton, soybeans. It was important for the state to develop better "value added" industries from its forestry resources.

Along with many others, I rushed up to the stage after the luncheon speech. I shook hands with Kopplin, the Governor's husband, and House Speaker Joe Salter. Kopplin had read about my candidacy in the newspaper - probably, the *Times-Picayune*. He took a copy of my campaign handout. I also gave my pitch and my literature to Joe Salter who seemed genuinely interested. He knew Conway Terrel Jones whom I had met in Many. "Yes, he's been quite active politically," Salter said. On the conference floor, I spoke with a female aide to U.S. Senator Mary Landrieu. She took my handout but was not interested in talking.

The first afternoon session had to do with assessing broadband capacity in rural areas. Louisiana had to be competitive in this respect, and rural areas needed to attract their fair share. Costs were higher in rural Louisiana, but there were strategies for dealing with that problem. I thought this one of the best parts of the conference from an information standpoint.

Then came a presentation on rural education. The presenter had gone to school with Junior Samples of Hee Haw fame. As a school superintendent, he had taken a failing school in South

Carolina and turned it into one of the state's best performers. The key, he said, was raising the level of expectations. Set clear goals. Communicate regularly with the teachers. Hire a "literacy coach" for the school and also pay special attention to mathematics. Schools also need to provide extra help to the worst-performing students. While providing a solid academic core, they also need to sell students on the idea that all this work will lead to real, high-quality jobs.

In the second part of the afternoon, conference participants were invited to attend break-out sessions on topics of interest. I picked the one on strategies for economic development. A representative of the state's department of economic development spoke first, saying many of the same things as previous presenters. Then, rather uniquely, a representative of the business community spoke. He worked for Weyerhaeuser, the wood-products company, which he said had been in Louisiana since 1996. High taxes and excessive state regulations were of concern to business, he said. An inferior educational system discouraged executives from locating in the state. A business-friendly atmosphere was important. Labor strife and an "us-vs-them" attitude were big turnoffs to business. In the end, he said, business decisions were driven largely by cost. Become a low-cost place to do business, he said, and business will gravitate to your state.

During the question-and-answer session, someone asked if any industry was safe from going offshore? If an industry was

highly automated, that afforded some protection. However, excessive environmental regulation in the United States hastened the flight of jobs to foreign countries.

Then I spoke up for the first and only time at the conference. I began by saying that the Weyerhaeuser Company was an important part of the economic heritage of my state, Minnesota. I had come to Louisiana, I said, to participate as a candidate in the Democratic presidential primary. My main issue was trade. I thought it unrealistic, if cost was the main consideration for business, to expect business firms to stay in the United States with its high-priced labor. It was fine for states like Louisiana to develop local strategies for retaining business but the solution really lay at the federal level. We needed to impose tariffs to equalize the cost of production between ourselves and low-wage countries. The best strategy, then, to revitalize Louisiana's rural economy would be to pressure federal officials to end the damage being done by free trade.

There was no immediate response to my remarks. The presenter took someone else's question. However, my comments began sneaking into some of the subsequent discussion. A bit later, a man who identified himself as an economics professor at Grambling State University said he disagreed with my analysis. Trade protection was not the answer. Instead, he said, U.S. firms could save jobs by automating and becoming more efficient. Privately, I pointed out to this professor, who was from Africa, that automating production destroys jobs rather than creating them. His "solution" wouldn't work. The professor was polite but unyielding. I was equally convinced of my views. I also spoke with several other people following this session. My statement had captured their attention but none would admit to sharing my views on trade.

Later that day, I roamed the downtown section of Natchitoches in the rain. Founded by the French in 1714, this city was the oldest settlement in the Louisiana Purchase. It was a beautiful, historic town on a river bank. I walked through the streets of Natchitoches, protected from the rain by a large umbrella with a *Daily Town Talk* logo which Andrew Griffin had given me. I was both walking and thinking.

On the whole, this had been a worthwhile conference. However, its theme of encouraging entrepreneurship seemed a cop-out to me. Here state government was saying to Louisiana's laid-off workers: There's little we can do for you. Create your own job. Become an entrepreneur. So these fearful, economically distressed individuals who have lost their jobs were supposed to pull their chin up and, with mortgages to pay and hungry mouths to feed, go start their own business, presumably competing with all the highly capitalized businesses that had fled to low-wage countries to earn even more money.

The politicians knew they could do more. Some even knew we needed trade protection. But they were afraid to put their own jobs on the line by showing any sympathy for what they knew would anger business - the T-word, tariffs. Instead, the little guy had to be heroic.

CHAPTER EIGHTEEN

Covering the Northeastern Part of the State

The Governor's Rural Economic Development conference continued through Wednesday morning, February 11th, but I decided to resume campaigning. The northeastern part of Louisiana still had to be covered. After spending the night in Natchitoches, I stopped by the conference for early-morning coffee and rolls. I spoke briefly with yesterday's business-motivation speaker and with another man who worked for the state. Then it was time to visit Coushatta twenty-five miles north of Natchitoches before coming back part way and then taking U.S. highway 84 west and north toward Monroe. At Coushatta, a re-

porter for the *Coushatta Citizen* named Joe Jones listened to my pitch and took a photo. He said he would write something up from my handout.

The drive from Coushatta to Winnfield, my next stop, was more than fifty miles. Part of the journey went through a forested area. The address of the *Winn Parish Enterprise* had changed. I searched for the old address on the edge of town before asking for directions. The newspaper's new location was on Main Street. The editor, Bob Holeman, greeted me warmly. Although he was in a hurry to make a regular luncheon meeting of the Rotary Club, he spent ten minutes talking with me. Then he invited me to be his guest at the luncheon. I could not give a campaign speech - there would be another speaker for the event - but at least I could

meet some people and see what was happening in this town. Holeman also mentioned that the Louisiana Political Museum was just across the street from his office. Depending on how much time I had to spend, I might be interested in visiting the museum before or after lunch.

Winnfield was the boyhood home of Huey Long. The Museum had an exhibit containing a life-sized statue of Huey in his study and, in the adjoining one, a statue of his brother Earl K. Long, speaking at a microphone. Earl Long had been governor of Louisiana in the 1940s and 1950s. There were also mementos of other politicians with Louisiana connections including John F. Kennedy. After visiting this museum for fifteen minutes or so, I drove to Linda's Country Kitchen in the Economy Inn, following Bob Holeman's directions. The Earl Long park, along the way, was the site of the Long family home. In a back room, Holeman and the guest speaker, George Harrel, were sitting by themselves at the head table while a dozen or so others sat at flanking tables on both sides. I seated myself in the corner next to Holeman.

George Harrel, owner of an insurance agency, gave a short, entertaining talk on several topics. First, he told how a certain judge had recently been inducted into the Louisiana political hall of fame. This judge had two interesting aspects: (1) He had been convicted of a crime. (2) He was Senator Ted Kennedy's father-in-law. Harrel wryly noted that criminal convictions were not that unusual for Louisiana politicians and, therefore, should not bar them from being recognized for political fame. Senator Kennedy had called the event organizer asking to be allowed to introduce his father-in-law at the induction ceremonies. The woman in charge, a stickler for the rules, had refused that request despite Kennedy's persistent pleading. Nevertheless, the Massachusetts Senator had attended the ceremony and enjoyed himself immensely. Everyone thought he was a great guy.

Harrel also spoke of his own long-standing effort to secure government funds to continue the I-84 highway through Winnfield. He asked for my opinion. I said that I-84 passed by Milford, Pennsylvania, where I owned a house, and it had done much to help the economy there. Harrel said that was a good answer. Later, he offered to contact Moon Griffon, a popular radio talk-show host broadcasting from Monroe, to see if he could get me on the show. He gave me his business card. I introduced myself to the others at this luncheon and to Linda, our hostess.

The stop in Winnfield had been unexpectedly fruitful. Even so, I had to continue traveling north. My cell phone rang before I left town. The call was from Brittany Shay, producer of a talk show on Baton Rouge radio station WJBO-AM. I had left a message for her on her answering machine the previous Saturday. They wanted me on the show later that afternoon. I thought I might have a conflict, having previously agreed to be on a New Orleans call-in show between 4 p.m. and 5 p.m. Shay thought her people could interview me at a different time.

The next place to visit was the office of Jonesboro's *Jackson Independent*. No editor was there when I called, so I left literature and departed. While stepping into the car, I was approached by one of the paper's employees, Jay, who had  read about me. He urged me to return another day. Then I drove north to Ruston and east along I-20 to Arcadia, arriving around 4 p.m. I had hoped to visit the office of Dring Publishing in Arcadia but, because of the scheduled radio show, time would not allow this. Ordering a soft drink at the McDonald's near the interstate highway, I waited for the New Orleans radio interview to begin. The host, Christopher Tidmore, was a political columnist with the *Louisiana Weekly*, a community newspaper for minorities. Andrew Griffin had referred him to me by email. Tidmore's radio show was broadcast on station WVOG-AM in Metairie (New

Orleans area) and also on a station in Thibodaux. An hour was allotted for my interview.

Tidmore was a tough questioner. He wanted to know all about my trade proposals. Wouldn't they lead to trade wars? Wouldn't they result in higher prices for the consumer? I responded that, no, employer-specific tariffs need not spark trade wars; the situation today was quite different from that in the 1930s. Today's "trade" is often intracorporate trade, intended to cut out high-priced American labor. Yes, there might be an increase in prices but, remember, the company does not pass all its cost savings along to the consumer. Tariffs would cut into profit margins before they affected consumer prices. At one point, Tidmore sprang on me the results of a study purporting to show that the number of U.S. jobs had increased under NAFTA. I said I had not heard of that study. Whose was it? Tidmore admitted that his numbers had come from the U.S. Chamber of Commerce. There were also several questions about my position on the shorter workweek and a number of short ones about abortion and other hot topics.

After the interview, I hurried over to Dring Publishing but its offices were closed for the day. Also, the Baton Rouge interview had fallen through. Brittany Shay said they would try to have me on some time closer to the election. Call her when I was in town. Since it was now after 5 o'clock and too late for more visits, I drove east on I-20 to Monroe, the largest city in northeastern Louisiana, and booked a room at the Motel 6 near the junction of I-20 and U.S. highway 165. I also thought that I should make reservations now to stay somewhere near New Orleans during the Mardi Gras period ending Tuesday, February 24th. New Orleans motels were booked solid from Friday before the Mardi Gras weekend through Tuesday. The Motel 6 in Slidell, twenty miles northeast of New Orleans, had a few vacancies for Thursday, February 19th. I thought I had better take what was available.

The next day, Thursday, February 12th, was jam-packed with campaign activities. First, I planned my day. Greg Hilburn turned out not to be the man I wanted to see at the *News-Star* in Monroe. He was a business editor. The managing editor assigned a reporter named Chuck Cannon to interview me at their office around 10:30 a.m. Cannon talked with me for about twenty minutes and took a photo. He confirmed that the loss of the State Farm jobs had been devastating for the community. No, this loss was said not to be trade related; but one does not know whether to believe company representatives who explained it was a simple consolidation of operations.

After this interview, I thought that I would again try to visit the offices of Dring Publishing in Arcadia, which published the *Bienville Democrat*, before returning to Monroe for a 1:00 p.m. appointment with the West Monroe newspaper. This was an hour's drive west on I-20. Just before reaching Ruston, I called the Arcadia newspaper. The editor, Wayne Dring, said that they closed the office at noon and would not reopen until 1: 30 p.m. I said I would try to make it. After asking my location, Dring said, "Well, you'll have to break the speed limit to be here by noon." But I did pull into a parking spot in front of his building with three minutes to spare.

The gruff-speaking editor, in farmer's overalls, was actually receptive to my message. Job loss had hit hard in his area and he agreed that tough measures needed to be taken. Dring liked President Bush personally for his straight-talking ways but was not sure about the policies. A female assistant nearby shook her head vigorously in dissent when she heard her boss's favorable comments about George W. Bush. However, I had kept them in the office past the start of the lunch period. I left my literature and departed.

I then raced back to West Monroe for an early-afternoon appointment at the *Ouachita Citizen*. Mark Rainwater, the news editor, ushered me into his office. He remembered having received email from me. Was I trying to be humorous? He said that these messages, far from being spam, were refreshingly direct. He had enjoyed reading them. That out of the way, I went through my pitch about trade and employment. We had a good conversation about that. In a reflective mood, Rainwater then started telling me about the area.

For many years, West Monroe had played second fiddle to Monroe. The tables had now started to turn. West Monroe, the growth area across the Ouachita river, had the more solid job base. Like many large cities, Monroe had become a magnet for poor people. Once northeastern Louisiana was sitting on huge reserves of oil and gas but those resources were gone. Only the infrastructure of pipelines remained. The pipelines could themselves become an economic asset, though. The area had become a major storage location for financial documents of large eastern banks. Chances are that the original copy of your mortgage is there.

This used to be cotton-growing country but now the textile mills were gone. The parishes of northeastern Louisiana were some of the poorest in the nation. Racial tensions were also a problem. The school system was segregated by virtue of the fact that white children were in the Ouachita Parish school district while black children were in a district affiliated with the City of Monroe, one of two city-run school districts in the state.

While pondering the situation in northeastern Louisiana, Rainwater suddenly remembered that he had another appointment and excused himself. I was enjoying the conversation but, at the same time, starting to get a headache from the day's stress. Bastrop, Louisiana's 26th largest city, was 26 miles north of Monroe up U.S. highway 165. I fought the afternoon traffic on the way to that city. A reporter for the *Bastrop Enterprise* named Lydia gave me a brief interview. Then, after buying a large soft drink to ease my headache, I headed east on Louisiana highway 2 toward three smaller newspapers not far from the state line. The first, forty-five miles away, was in West Carroll Parish in the

town of Oak Grove. The other two were in East Carroll Parish and in Madison Parish, south of there. I was not sure I could reach all three by closing time but would give it a shot.

Johney Turner was the editor of the *West Carroll Gazette* in Oak Grove. Again, my focus on employment problems seemed a fortunate choice. These northeastern parishes were mired in poverty. Once dependent on cotton, the local economy had benefited from the presence of small-manufacturing facilities. Farm wives could supplement the family income by working at such places. However, a number of them had closed down in recent years because it was cheaper to produce in Mexico. No one knew where the replacement jobs might be found. The owner of one plant had been strongly anti-NAFTA but the local Congressman, now retired, argued that free trade would be good for the economy. Few people believe that these days. Turner had seen me drive up to the office. He wanted a photograph of me standing next to the sign on my car door which read: "McGaughey for President 2004/ SAVE OUR JOBS."

It was well after 5:00 p.m. when I next reached the newspaper office in Lake Providence, which was across the river from Mississippi. The office was closed for the day. I slipped a leaflet under the door with a "sorry I missed you" note. Another thirty miles south on U.S. highway 65 was the larger town of Tallulah. Here again, I slipped my campaign literature with a personal note under the door. I was gambling that these after-hours visits might result in a short statement in the paper that presidential candidate Bill McGaughey had been in town, especially if I followed them up next morning with a phone call. I doubt if that happened. However, it was even less likely that I would be in that area again during the campaign. Then I drove fifty miles back to Monroe west along I-20 where I had another night's reservation at the Motel 6.

CHAPTER NINETEEN

From Monroe Back to Alexandria

Friday morning, February 13th, it was time to visit places in northeastern Louisiana south of the parishes covered on the preceding day. As always, I planned the day's itinerary by plotting a route on Louisiana's official highway map. I had circled the names of cities and towns which had a newspaper. That made it easy to determine a route that would allow me to visit the maximum number of newspaper offices in the nine-hour period (8 a.m. to 5 p.m.) when I thought they might be open for business. This day's travels, I hoped, would take me to Rayville, Winnsboro, St. Joseph, Ferriday, Jonesville, and Jena. Normally, three or four visits per day constituted a full day's work. To start each day, I wrote down the names, addresses, and telephone numbers of the newspaper offices, along with the name of a contact person, in my spiral notebook.

First, however, I had a radio interview in Monroe. This would be an in-studio interview at station KEDM-FM located at Louisiana State University - Monroe. I should be there at 8:15 a.m. for an interview to take place between 8:30 and 8:45 a.m. Sunny Meriwether, news director for this public-radio station, would be interviewing me. She had given me directions to the station located on campus in Stubbs hall. Meriwether was on the air when I arrived. While sitting on a sofa in the waiting room, another woman approached me and gave me her business card. Her name was Bernadette Cahill. She had a program on the same radio station about people's memories of music. Could I think of a particular song or piece of music which reminded me of an unusual experience? If I could, she invited me to tell of this experience on her radio show. Never one to turn down an opportunity to be on the radio, I immediately accepted. I put her card in my wallet.

My interview with Sunny Meriwether lasted about seven minutes. We first talked for a few minutes off the air. When the live portion began, Meriwether asked me about myself and my campaign issues. I launched into a monologue about employment and trade, not giving Meriwether enough time to ask follow-up questions. Afterwards, I chided myself for misusing the opportunity. The goal of a radio interview was not to try to pack as many arguments as possible into the available time but to connect with the listeners. I should have been more laid back and interacted more with the interviewer. A little humor goes a long way. I thought I needed to prepare a list of key points that might be included in interviews. In future interviews, I should try to cover a few of these points while carrying on a more lighthearted conversation with the host. I later wrote a script for an ideal radio interview, summarizing some of the key points. (See Appendix.)

After leaving the studio, I drove east to Rayville along I-20, covering the same stretch of highway that I had driven yesterday evening in the other direction. Amanda Smith, editor of the *Delhi Dispatch* and the *Richland Beacon News*, interviewed me for about ten minutes. I stressed the point that the purpose of my campaign was not to win the nomination but do well enough that the political establishment would take my employment proposals seriously. Smith said that approach made perfect sense. (We were, after all, in a part of the state heavily hit by job loss.) She took a picture of me. I was happy about this visit.

Then, after gassing up in Rayville, I headed south on Louisiana highways 137 and 15 to the town of Winnsboro (not to be confused with Winnfield) in Franklin Parish. I was interviewed by Rod Elrod, a reporter for the *Franklin Sun*. Like Mark Rainwater in West Monroe, Elrod said he knew about me from the email messages sent out during the past several months. I made a short presentation of my campaign issues and passed out literature. Already having a good idea of me as a candidate, Elrod said he would write something up for the newspaper. His article would also appear in the Ferriday paper since the two newspapers were owned by the same person. Afterwards, someone took a photograph. Then Rod Elrod remembered a labor activist named Roger Beale, who lived in Winnsboro. I should try to get in touch with him. Elrod looked up the man's name and number in the telephone directory and wrote this information for me on a slip of paper. I did try to call Beale later but the number had been disconnected.

Still thinking about radio interviews, I called several stations in the area. Radio station KMAR-FM was located two miles outside of Winnsboro. The man who took my cell-phone call had a program in the morning. It was too late to be on that show. He suggested that I might stop by the station to record a short interview or, if I had time, wait for the live program starting at noon which was hosted by Regnal Wallace.

Wallace talked with me in his office after I arrived at the station. We were killing time until the live broadcast but having a good discussion. Wallace had once been a sportscaster with a large radio station. He had interviewed some big-name baseball players in his day. Sportscasters, he said, are either grossly overpaid or underpaid. A "star" system governs this occupation. The little guys put up with their low wages waiting for an opportunity to become a star.

Sports broadcasting was his first love but he had not been able to make a living from it. Wallace later became public-affairs director for the Louisiana Farm Bureau, an organization which provides insurance and marketing services for farmers. He told me about the state's farm economy. Commodity imports were threatening price levels. People in Louisiana were interested in tariffs to help fight competition from Mexico and other low-cost areas. Wallace also favored a strong system of subsidies to help farmers stay in business. They want to compete, he said.

I spent a good hour and a half with Regnal Wallace waiting for the live broadcast to begin at 12:20 p.m. He would give me perhaps five minutes to make my pitch on the show. First the chairman of the Franklin Parish Police Jury talked for five or ten minutes about issues affecting the community. Then it was my turn to talk. My presentation, mostly on trade and employment, went more smoothly than it had earlier in the day. What worried me, though, was that the midday wait had put me behind schedule for my newspaper visits in the area. The conversation had been interesting but I really needed to make my afternoon calls because I might not be by here again during the campaign.

Relatively long distances were involved. I had planned to stop next in St. Joseph near the Mississippi river. This was about fifty minutes east and south of Winnsboro. About ten miles this side of St. Joseph, I received a cell phone call from Robin Meyers, editor of the *Tensas Gazette* in that city. She said she had left a message for me on my cell phone that it was not necessary to visit in person. The *Tensas Gazette* had a sister relationship with the paper in Oak Grove. They would use what Johney Turner had written. If I had known about her message, I might have saved myself thirty miles of driving to Ferriday. I had not checked the messages, though. I was a novice with respect to cell-phone features.

The Ferriday paper, the *Concordia Sentinel*, did not have to be visited because Rod Elrod in Winnsboro had said that his article would suffice for both newspapers. Though I could easily have paid a courtesy call in Ferriday while passing through town, I decided against that in the interests of time. I then made another wrong decision. Looking at the map, I noticed that Vidalia seemed to be a good-sized city yet I had not circled it on the map as having a newspaper. That was probably an oversight on my part, I supposed.

Therefore, instead of turning right for Jonesboro, I turned left for Vidalia which was ten miles to the east on U.S. highway 84. It was across the river from the larger city of Natchez, Mississippi. I stopped at a Tourist Information Center in town to ask directions to the Vidalia newspaper. Another customer kept the staff person tied up for a long time. Instead of waiting for her questioning to end, I thought I would drive across the Mississippi river to Natchez to be able to say that I had been there and take a

few photographs. This consumed another twenty minutes. When I returned, the Tourist Center employee told me that Vidalia did not have its own newspaper. That community's news was handled out of Ferriday.

As the clock ticked, I raced back to Ferriday and then headed for Jonesville, fifteen miles west of Ferriday on U.S. highway 84. An iron bridge built during the Long administration marked the entrance to town. I had a hard time finding the office of the *Jonesville Catahoula News Booster*. Once located, I learned that this newspaper office was closed for the day. It was several minutes before 4 p.m. Maybe the paper closed early on Fridays.

I then placed a cell phone call to the *Jena Times Olla-Tullos Signal* in Jena, another twenty-three miles up the road. A woman in that office reported that the Jena newspaper closed at 4 p.m. and the editor had already left for home. So, all my delays and detours earlier in the day had made a difference. They had cost me two newspaper visits. There was nothing left to do but drive to the place where I would spend the night. Comparing weekend prices and locations for the Motel 6 facilities in Alexandria and Port Allen, I chose Alexandria, which was forty miles southwest of Jonesville on Louisiana highway 28.

Another weekend in Louisiana meant another day for laundry and chores. It rained on Saturday, the 14th, St. Valentine's Day. I placed a telephone call to my wife with the calling card. No longer ill, she was traveling in Fujian province across from Taiwan. The people in Minnesota were also doing all right. It was time to make sure that my monthly bills were paid. I wrote personal checks to certain vendors utilizing information on a prepared sheet. I also found that I was running out of certain pieces of literature in my packet of campaign materials. These I replenished at the Kinko's a mile down U.S. highway 71 from the motel.

I was also worried about the car. Had I checked the oil and transmission fluid lately? The brakes were starting to screech. The drums might be wearing out. I bought a tire gauge and checked the pressure. A Phillips 66 station near the motel did not do brake work but referred me to the Sears Auto Center about two miles down Texas Avenue. Yes, this service center could check the brakes before the Saturday closing time. The brake drums were indeed worn out, but I would have to come back on the

following day, Sunday, to have the work done. The brake job, a tune-up, two new tires, and an alignment cost me $650, charged to my credit card. For a car with 135,000 miles on the odometer, such expenses were perhaps inevitable.

While sitting in the Sears waiting room, I read through literature from Verizon Wireless, my cell-phone provider, seeking to learn how some of the features worked. I also checked the time used in the current month. I was on a calling plan which allowed my stepdaughter and me to use 400 minutes per month between our two phones before extra charges were applied at $.46 per minute. I found that we had already used 426 minutes. I had been planning to switch to a plan that would allow more time, expecting that my cell-phone minutes during the campaign would be unusually high. Before incurring further charges, I placed an order with a Verizon Wireless customer service representative to switch to a plan allowing 1,200 minutes per month, assured that I could switch back to the previous plan after the campaign was over. Had we incurred $11.96 in extra charges? No, the figure actually came to $52.00. That's because Verizon Wireless prorates the time if a customer switches plans in the middle of a billing cycle. We did not have 400 minutes to cover the time already spent, but only 310 minutes.

I later discovered that the same trick applied when I switched back in March after the campaign. Verizon Wireless wound up charging me $243.95 for the first month, despite my switching to a plan with significantly more minutes, and then $136.13 for the following month. (The normal monthly charge had been around $75.00.) The billing statement did not explain how these charges were calculated although a customer service representative could explain them over the phone. It was totally baffling. What was a stupid person like me doing in running for President? Additionally, because I had switched from one "type of plan" to another, Verizon Wireless was making me start a new two-year contract, with heavy early-termination penalties.

That weekend I went to the Alexandria public library to see if I could find newspaper articles written about my campaign. I did find William Taylor's story in the *Daily Town Talk*. The library had back issues each day for both the Alexandria and Baton Rouge papers but only Sunday papers for the *Times-Picayune*. I thought that the New Orleans paper must have run Ed Anderson's story but could not find it.

Even so, this limited search of Louisiana newspapers inspired me to think about advertising. A notice in *The Advocate* said that for $250 one could place a 25-word classified ad in ninety newspapers around the state through the Louisiana Press Association. That would be an ideal opportunity for me. I also thought about placing retail ads in several large-circulation newspapers. The back issues at the library allowed me to look for positions in the paper that I might request, both for weekdays and Sundays. The first section, devoted to national news, seemed best. Preferably, the ad should appear in the upper right hand corner. The most I could afford would be an ad running one column inch. Since newspaper offices were closed on Sunday, I would have to wait until a week day to confirm rates.

CHAPTER TWENTY

The Southern Tier of Cities on Interstate 10

Monday morning I delayed my departure from the motel in Alexandria to check with the advertising departments of several large Louisiana newspapers. For each paper, I calculated the cost of running a one-inch retail ad on the day of the primary, March 9th, and on the two previous days including Sunday. Most papers gave discounts for multiple insertions on consecutive days. I already had circulation figures and ad rates for these publications. I had made a preliminary assessment of advertising costs per reader and had ranked the newspapers by cost effectiveness.

These rankings changed as I called the advertising departments and obtained more current numbers. The following cities' newspapers ranked in descending order of effectiveness: (1) Lafayette, (2) New Orleans, (3) Lake Charles, (4) Baton Rouge, (5) Alexandria, and (6) Shreveport. Monroe's newspaper was even more expensive than Shreveport's in advertising costs per reader. In addition, I checked with the Baton Rouge paper to see if political ads were accepted for the ninety-paper deal offered by the Louisiana Press Association. While this had not been done before, a staff person agreed to check association policies. My ad was accepted.

I had already composed copy for both the classified and retail ads. For the classified ad, the text read: "Vote Bill McGaughey for President in Democratic Presidential primary March 9th. He's

for tariffs to stop employment loss to low-wage countries. Straight talk on jobs!" For the retail ads, the text read: "Vote Bill McGaughey for President in Democratic primary March 9th. Straight talk on jobs - tariffs on imports from foreign sweatshops." Before the second ad ran, I had softened "foreign sweatshops" to "low-wage countries" and made other alterations. This text should fit within one column inch of space. A thick black border would set it apart and draw attention, I was sure.

In the late morning, I departed Alexandria to make another swing through Leesville, fifty miles to the west. Reporter Kelly Moore of the *Leesville Leader* had been on her way out the door when I called last time. Today would be an unusual time for Leesville, though, since President Bush would be visiting the troops at Fort Polk on the following day. I thought of contacting radio stations in the area. A call made to station KVVP-FM while on the highway was suddenly disconnected when the cell phone went dead. Perhaps I was out of range of the Verizon Wireless network.

Once again, no one was available to talk with me when I arrived at the newspaper office. Everyone was preparing for the Bush visit. I also called the base newspaper at Fort Polk and reached a recording. Since I had already visited the two papers immediately south of Leesville on U.S. highway 171, my plan for the day was to visit two other papers in the extreme southwestern part of the state: in Sulphur and Lake Charles. This would be the start of a swing through southern Louisiana where the bulk of the state's population lived.

First, I thought I would follow up on the call to KVVP-FM, the station reached on the road. Radio stations KVVP-FM and KROK-FM were housed in a building just off highway 171 a mile from the turnoff to Fort Polk. When

I walked in to introduce myself, I was referred to the owner and manager, Doug Stannard. We had a short but wide-ranging conversation. Stannard was a career military officer who had lived in several other bases before coming to Fort Polk. He liked living here and had stayed in the area following his discharge from military service. We discussed economic issues. "Are you a socialist?', he asked when I presented my views on work hours and trade. I assured him that I did not favor government ownership of productive enterprise but did believe in government regulation of business to promote certain ends.

Stannard believed in the democratic process and was happy to have a presidential candidate visit his station. He brought me into the studio to see the news director, Jim Alexander. Alexander was fiddling with knobs on a computerized control panel. Once he had finished this task, he recorded a statement from me. I talked for five to ten minutes. Alexander said he would edit this down to a suitable length and play the edited recording several times during the next few days. (I had fantasies of President Bush listening to this as his motorcade traveled to Fort Polk.) I bade farewell to Alexander and to Stannard in his office and continued my travels south.

It was 65 miles from here to Lake Charles. I tried calling the *Southwest Daily News* in Sulphur but the number had been disconnected; or perhaps I misdialed. In any event, my destination for this day was the *Lake Charles American Press*. The managing editor, Bobby Dower, gave me directions to the newspaper's office. He was in a meeting when I arrived. I decided to talk with the advertising department during the wait. I placed an order for a one-inch ad, paying by credit card. Dower was still meeting when I finished my business with the sales representative. I asked a reporter if he would notify Dower that I had arrived. He appeared shortly, assigning reporter Mike Jones to talk with me. We had a good interview focusing on economic issues. Since Mardi Gras week was approach-

ing, I asked Jones about events in Lake Charles. He photocopied a page from the newspaper telling about a "lighted boat parade" on the lake Sunday, February 22nd, starting at 7 p.m.

Lake Charles has one of the most striking vistas in the state of Louisiana, situated as it is on the edge of a large lake. A boardwalk along the lake connects the Civic Center in the downtown area to Harrah's Casino and points beyond. Coming from the west on I-10, I stopped first at the Tourist Information Center which has an alligator pond. The Motel 6, where I spent the night, is several miles to the east. That evening, I visited the casino dropping $2.00 on the video slot-machine games. The gambling rooms are located in two large boats moored to the dock - for legal reasons, I suppose. The whir of electronic machinery is quite hypnotic. I could see how a customer might spend himself silly before realizing what time it was. I also searched the area near

the Civic Center for good locations for campaign appearances when I returned for the Mardi Gras boat parade. I would need to let the television stations know where to find me if they chose to cover my activities.

Early next morning, Tuesday, February 17th, I drove west and then north about 25 miles to meet with Jerry Wise, editor of the Wise newspapers in Dequincy. After briefly discussing my campaign issues, Wise had a photographer take a picture of us together. He suggested that I also call upon the *Southwest Daily*

News in Sulphur. An article in that paper might also appear in the *Leesville Leader*. Wise gave me directions to their office. I dropped by unannounced at the *Southwest Daily News* only to learn that no reporters were available to inter-

view me. They would be in the office starting at noon. That was hours away. I left a copy of my campaign leaflet and a photo with the receptionist and then drove east on U.S. highway 90.

The Lake Charles paper had already been covered. My next stop was in the town of Welsh. The editor of the *Welsh Citizen* was a Swedish immigrant named Bengt Lindell - someone I might have expected to meet in Minnesota rather than Louisiana. He had taken this job after marrying an American. We talked about Sweden, the United States, and cultural topics, besides trade and employment issues. I told Lindell that Robert Bly, a Norwegian-American, had jokingly proposed to bomb Sweden if he became Secretary of Defense in my administration.

Then, I continued down the highway to the larger town of Jennings. A young reporter named Rebecca Chaisson interviewed me for the *Jennings Daily News*. After running through my set of issues, I asked Chaisson about political attitudes in her community. Jennings is mostly Republican, she told me. Republican organizations were quite active there.

My visits to towns along I-10 were settling into a routine. I would call ahead to the next place after finishing an interview. The editor or receptionist would give me directions to the news-

paper office. I am used to going by street names. In Louisiana, however, it seems that people prefer to give directions by naming landmarks. In this case, it was always

something like: "Take exit 64 off the interstate, go straight ahead and over the railroad tracks, then turn left at the first stop light. Our office is two blocks down the street on the left."

I had street addresses for all the newspaper offices. Once I spotted the street name on a sign, I was comfortable that I could find the office. Confusion was possible, though, where two or three turns had to be made before reaching the street.

After Jennings came Crowley, another good-sized town. The editor of the *Crowley Post-Signal*, who handles its political reporting, is Harold Gonzales. He was not in when I arrived at the office. An assistant told me that the plumbing had backed up in

his home and water was all over the floor. He was waiting for a plumber to arrive. As a landlord, I could appreciate that situation. Reached by cell phone, Gonzales was not able to say when he would come into the office. I could wait for him if I wished or go on to my next appointment.

I decided to drive to Rayne, which was six miles east of Crowley. There were two newspapers in that town. The editor of the *Rayne Acadian Tribune* said it was not a good time to come calling since his weekly paper was being printed on the next day. The publisher and sports editor of the town's other paper, the *Rayne Independent*, was willing to see me. He was Walter Cart. His wife, Jo, was listed in my directory as the editor. Mr. Cart talked with me for a minute or two at the counter and took literature and a photo. Then I drove back to Crowley. Harold Gonzales was sitting in his office among stacks of reading material. He thanked me for returning to Crowley and then talked for ten minutes or so and took a photograph.

The dominant newspaper in the area was the *Daily Advertiser* in Lafayette, Louisiana's fourth largest city. Here I was not so lucky. I first had trouble finding the right contact person. A man in the editorial department gave me directions to the office. He said I should turn off Interstate 10 at the "Evangeline Thruway", then take this road a mile or so until I reached Jefferson Street, where I should turn right and take the underpass. Unfortunately, there was no exit marked "Evangeline Thruway". I drove past Lafayette as far as Breaux Bridge where I realized I had gone too far. Placing another cell-phone call, I learned that the Evangeline Thruway was also Interstate 49 going south. The name, familiar from a Longfellow poem, reminded me that I was in the heart of Cajun country. The real Evangeline had waited for her lover to return under a tree still standing in St. Martinville, ten miles east of town.

I found a parking place two blocks off Jefferson and walked to the office of the *Daily Advertiser*. The receptionist contacted an assignment editor who, after a brief investigation, informed me that there were no reporters on hand to interview me. A young reporter named Arnessa Garrett came to the counter to meet me and take literature. She would make sure that my literature reached the right person. While at the newspaper office, I decided to talk with the sales representative, Mary Abrams, about placing my ad. I followed Abrams to her upstairs office, showed her text of the proposed ad, and discussed how the art work might be done. She took my credit-card payment.

That was all for the day. I would need to return to Lafayette to seek coverage in the *Daily Advertiser* and also in *The Times of Acadiana*, a free-circulation weekly whose offices were in the

same building. Mary Abrams had urged me to pick up a copy of that publication saying that it occasionally runs stories on political subjects. However, there was no point in spending the night here. Some important business remained to be done in Baton Rouge. That city, Louisiana's second largest, was 52 miles to the east on Interstate 10.

One would think that the stretch of highway between these two major cities would be dotted with cities and towns. In fact, it ran through a swamp associated with the Atchafalaya river. More than ten miles of highway sat on a concrete platform above this swamp, alleged to be North America's largest. Joining a heavy stream of traffic, I navigated the scenic highway until I reached Port Allen. I then took the Lobdell exit and booked a night's stay at the Motel 6, my lodging place of ten days earlier.

CHAPTER TWENTY-ONE

On the Road from Baton Rouge to Thibodaux

It was Wednesday, February 18th, and I was back in Baton Rouge. The Mardi Gras period was fast approaching. It would end abruptly at midnight next Tuesday when the police would chase all the party goers away. This would not be a time when I could do normal campaigning. Tuesday, February 24th, would be a holiday - "Fat Tuesday". That day would be as dead for my campaign as any weekend day. Even Monday was a question mark. So, I had to make the most of the next three days before this long holiday began.

I called George Harrel. No, Moon Griffon had not yet responded to his emails. Therefore, I called Griffon myself and left a message. I also called Bernadette Cahill, the woman in Monroe who had a radio program on KEDM-FM about musical memories. My memory from the 1960s consisted of walking down a street in Princeton, New Jersey, while a song by Manfred Mann blared in the background. It reminded me of an unsettled time in my life, when I had dropped out of college, but otherwise I did not know its significance. Cahill knew the tune - she hummed it - and said that type of experience was what she wanted. She would put something together based on my story and play it on the morning of the primary election.

Another item on my list was to visit the press room again in the Louisiana state capitol. Neither Ed Anderson nor Marsha Shuler were in the office. I talked with one of Shuler's colleague with the Baton Rouge paper. Melinda Deslatte of the Associated Press was again at her desk. She said only to keep her informed as the campaign progressed. In a cell-phone conversation, Brittany Shay of radio station WJBO-AM in Baton Rouge said likewise to call her again.

Another task remaining to be done in Baton Rouge was to place an order for the one-inch ad in *The Advocate*. Its office was located several blocks down from the state capitol on Lafayette street. I met with Karen Marchand, the national advertising representative. She suggested putting a star border around the text and placing this ad in the "A" section near the news makers section. I asked her about Mardi Gras events in Baton Rouge. The main event, she said, would be the parade through "Spanish Town" next Saturday. The parade would go down North Street and by the newspaper office, too. With that information, I drove around the downtown area scouting locations. The intersection of North and St. Louis streets seemed a good place for me to stand. Later I put that location in a press release.

I returned to the Democratic state party headquarters on Government street. As I pulled up in the car, I could see some men talking in a parking area behind the building. One of the men was standing near the front door when, having parked my car, I approached to enter the building. I asked him if he was with the state Democratic party. He was. Inside, this man said he had to finish several items of business but then could talk with me for a few minutes before driving to Lafayette for an afternoon meeting. This was Mike Skinner, the state party chairman. I gave him my packet of campaign literature. He gave me his business card.

I mentioned that my name had been removed from the South Carolina ballot and I appreciated the opportunity to participate in the primary here. He responded that there was no interest in taking my name off the Louisiana ballot. It was good that I had stopped by since the state party sometimes receives requests for

contact information for the different candidates. I pointed out that my cell-phone number was on several pieces of literature. I also said that, regardless of the primary's outcome, I was personally committed to a Democratic victory in November. Skinner said he appreciated that comment. If anyone wants to "steal" my campaign issues, I said, they're welcome to do so.

It was noon and time to leave town again. During the rest of the day I would try to cover the newspapers south of Baton Rouge towards Houma. Houma itself was not on my itinerary. The editor of *The Courier*, Keith Magill, had discouraged a visit at this time. He asked me to mail him copies of my campaign literature and then call on Monday after he had a chance to look over this material.

My first stop, then, was at the office of the *Gonzales Weekly*. A person in the office said that I should take the "Tanger Mall" exit from I-10, drive a mile to the Duplessis car dealership, turn left, and go another mile to Worthy street and turn left again. This was one of those places where, instead of an interview, candidates were invited to write short statements of their candidacy and submit a photo. I composed my statement at the counter as editor Arlene Bishop worked quietly at a nearby desk.

The next place to visit was Donaldsonville, twenty miles distant by a circuitous route. I had to take the Route 70 exit from I-10, drive about ten miles on this country road until I crossed the Mississippi river on an old steel bridge. Highway 70 intersected

with another highway two miles later. I then had to turn right toward Donaldsonville while route 70 went on toward Thibodaux. The offices of the *Donaldsonville Chief* were in the heart of town on Railroad Avenue.

Two women in the office talked with me. They were Monica Dubois and Cheryl Jacob. The jobs issue seemed to resonate with them. This was a big sugar-growing area. Jacob said she lived in a house in the center of a large sugar field. The sugar industry there was under severe pressure from foreign competition which, people believed, was subsidized by the government. Louisiana Congressmen favored protecting sugar producers. I left this office pumped up. On the way out of town, I stopped at a dime store to buy a large manila envelope to mail my campaign literature to the editor of the Houma paper.

Now I had to drive back to the junction with highway 70 and, this time, take the Thibodaux turn. Seven miles down the road, I would cross Louisiana highway 1 or perhaps highway 308 - they looked the same on the map - and follow it to Thibodaux. Because my instructions had been to stay on highway 308, I stuck to it religiously. This was a narrow, winding country road, admittedly scenic but also potentially dangerous.

Built upon wet soil, Louisiana highways are elevated well above the ground with ditches on either side. Frequent crosses mark the spot where cars have run off the road killing the passengers. So it was here.

On my way to Thibodaux, I went through a small town where school buses blocked the highway for several minutes, putting me behind schedule. I drove as far as Lafourche on highway 308 before realizing that something was wrong. The map told me that I had gone too far. Thibodaux was several miles back in the other direction. Later I noticed that highway 1, then close by, paralleled highway 308. This was a faster, straighter road. Eventually,

I made my way into Thibodaux on highway 1 and found the offices of the *Daily Comet*.

This arduous trip was worthwhile. The managing editor, Jeffrey Zeringue, assigned an intelligent young reporter named Emilie Bahr to interview me. She gave me two cups of ice water before we began. Seated at a conference table, Bahr spent half an hour with me asking questions about my campaign. She wanted to know how shortening work time would help employment. Would trade protection be beneficial? In the course of the interview, she asked me about books that I had written, especially *Five Epochs of Civilization*. I went through some of its concepts with her. Since she seemed interested, I promised to send her a copy of the book when I returned home. Bahr herself had grown up in Texas and, in fact, had attended school with President Bush's two daughters in Dallas.

I also talked with city editor, Mike Gorman, and with Zeringue himself. The *Daily Comet* was a sister paper of Houma's *The Courier*. This was Cajun country. It was also a center of Louisiana's sugar-growing industry. If I drove through nearby Raceland, they said, I could not escape the peculiar odor of a sugar refinery in that town.

Before leaving Thibodaux, I tried to mail my literature to the Houma *Courier*. However, I was a few minutes too late. The post office had closed at 4:30 p.m. A decision now had to be made. Should I return to Port Allen or should I - looking at the map - instead go to Lafayette, one hundred miles to the west? I chose Lafayette because that set me up for visits to cities along I-49 in the extreme southern part of the state.

The roads out of Thibodaux were confusing. A gas station clerk gave me directions to I-49 near the Chacahoula exit, ten miles away. Under the cover of darkness, I drove west on the interstate all the way to Lafayette and to the Motel 6 on the north edge of town, passing places that I would visit on the next day.

CHAPTER TWENTY-TWO

Finally, New Orleans

Thursday, February 19th, would be another busy day. To this point, I had not yet visited New Orleans, Louisiana's largest and best-known city, capital of the Mardi Gras celebrations. I had a long-standing reservation for the night at the Motel 6 in Slidell. That city was east of New Orleans not far from the Mississippi border. My starting point was Lafayette. The first order of business was to mail the envelope with my campaign literature to Keith Magill of *The Courier*. He should have enough time to look at it by Monday when I called. There was a post office not far from the motel on a road paralleling I-49. After mailing the packet of materials to Houma, I entered the interstate.

South of Lafayette about twenty miles is a town called Abbeville. A young man named Steve, who was a sports editor, received me and then introduced me to Kathy, who was the boss at the *Abbeville Meridional*. She had me write a one-page statement about my campaign. I also gave her a photo. Steve made a point of telling me that he was a liberal Democrat, which I took to mean that his views were in the minority around there.

I needed directions to the highway leading toward my next stop, New Iberia, which was twenty miles to the east. Instead of retracing my previous route, someone told me of a short cut in the other direction. That worked despite construction detours in town. I found Louisiana highway 14 which went straight to New Iberia, Louisiana's tenth largest city. Editor Steve Bandy of the

Daily Iberian talked with me in his office for about ten minutes. We stuck to economic issues. It was a good interview. Bandy took one of my photos and said he would put a story in the paper that weekend.

The town of St. Martinville was seven miles north of New Iberia. I placed a cell-phone call to the *St. Martinville Teche News* which, together with the *Breaux Bridge Banner*, belong to Louisiana State Newspapers. I was told that the editor, Henri Bienvenu, was out of the office but was expected back in perhaps an hour. That was too long to wait.

Instead, I decided to take Louisiana highway 182 southeast toward several of my other planned visits. In Jeanerette, I stopped for lunch at a roadside place which advertised Cajun chicken. I bought several pieces and ate them in the car. The cashier told me that the offices of the *Jeanerette Enterprise* were straight down the same highway. I should pass through three stop lights and look for T-Bob's seafood restaurant on the left. However, the front door of the newspaper office was locked. I wrote a note for the editor on my campaign leaflet and stuck it under the door. Then I drove out of town heading east.

Four miles up the road, my cell phone rang. It was the receptionist at the *St. Martinville Teche News*. Mr. Bienvenu was back in the office. This required a quick decision. Should I head back towards New Iberia and St. Martinville or continue traveling east?

Being the politician eager to please, I said I would turn around and come to St. Martinville. The journey required some close work with a map. After driving back on highway 182 for ten miles, I needed to turn right on highway  320, turn right again on highway 86, and then, shortly after Loreauville, take highway 345 north which would lead straight into St. Martinville. All the while, I was skirting New Iberia on the east.

I did find the newspaper office in St. Martinville. Henri Bienvenu, the editor, talked with me for awhile at the counter. He was interested in my arguments concerning employment. St. Martinville had been home to the mother plant of Fruit-of-the-Loom, which had once been the town's main employer. However, its production had gone to Honduras after the local factory closed down. Unlike many other places in Louisiana, St. Martin Parish had a solid majority of Democrats - perhaps 70 percent. Bienville said he could not promise me much coverage but might mention my visit in his column.

The trip back to highway 182 by a combination of routes was easier this time. I rejoined the highway to Jeanerette and again stopped at the town's newspaper office next to T-Bob's seafood. The door was still locked; this must have been the editor's day off. Then I drove to the next large town, Franklin, twelve miles down the road. Here I talked with the editor of the *Franklin Banner-Tribune*, Allan Von Werder.

After listening to me for several minutes, Von Werder said that the main problem in Franklin was finding qualified people to work in the aluminum-boat factories. The companies could hire many people today if they could find the skilled labor. Was this a problem with the school system? Partly it was, but there was also a problem of young people's attitudes toward work. Even so, Von Werder said he agreed with much of what I said. He was

pleased that I was visiting Franklin. The last presidential candidate to visit this city was Pat Buchanan. In 1996, Buchanan had unexpectedly won the GOP primary in Louisiana after stumping the state.

After the visit with Von Werder, I placed a cell-phone call to what I had hoped would be my last stop of the day: offices of the *Daily Review* in Morgan City. It was too late in the day. Most reporters had already left the office. The man who answered the phone said that the newspaper office would be closed tomorrow, Friday. It would open again on Monday for part of the day. Then it would be closed on Tuesday, the final day of Mardi Gras. My best bet would be to stop by on Monday morning but be sure to call ahead. Also, I should consider attending Sunday's Mardi Gras parade in Morgan City. I was then beginning to formulate my plans for Mardi Gras and was not sure then what I would do.

There was nothing left to do that day other than to head for the Motel 6 in Slidell. The trip required another 132 miles of travel. Much of it was fast interstate driving. I passed the Thibodaux exit, and then Houma and Raceland, en route to New Orleans on U.S. highway 90. The town of Boutte marked the beginning of metro traffic. There were stop lights for the first time in many miles. Struck in traffic, I saw a bumper sticker that read: "My money and my daughter go to Tulane." Here was a man after my heart, making a not too subtle political statement.

There was a chance to avoid a toll bridge and downtown New Orleans traffic by turning off on Interstate 310 and then taking I-10 through the northern part of the city and then east and across the causeway to Slidell. I chose to take the business route for I-10. I'm glad I did. The toll bridge crossing the Mississippi river from the south offered a beautiful view of New Orleans at night. As my car climbed up the ramp on one side of the bridge, I could see the glistening lights of the city spread out in front of me. New Orleans must be a larger city than Minneapolis, I thought, although I had always considered them to be comparably sized.

The traffic moved quickly through the city on the elevated portion of I-10 downtown. It stalled twenty miles later on the causeway crossing the eastern section of Lake Pontchartrain. Slidell was on the other side of the bay. Eventually the cars moved again. My motel was near the intersection of I-10 and U.S. highway 190. It was the closest I would get to lodging in New Orleans during Mardi Gras.

Friday morning, February 20th, I was scheduled to do a radio interview with station KNOC-AM in Natchitoches starting at 9:10 a.m. I handled it from my room at the Motel 6. The interview with George Sluppick lasted twelve minutes and, I think, went quite well.

Then I set up my appointments for the day. As the state's thirteenth largest city, Slidell was itself a prime location for campaigning. However, the editor of the *Slidell Sentry-News* asked me to postpone my visit until Monday, February 23rd. The whole part of the state north of Lake Pontchartrain but below Mississippi remained unvisited. Some of the major cities were Bogalusa, Hammond, Ponchatoula, and Covington. I thought I might start with the tier of cities along the eastern border with Mississippi and work my way west. Friday's visits, starting in Bogalusa, would also include Franklinton and Amite.

I also wanted to place an ad with the *Times-Picayune*, New Orleans' daily newspaper. The paper had a satellite office in Slidell a mile down from the Motel 6 on U.S. highway 190 (also known as Gauss Boulevard). I spoke with Janice Parker in the advertising department. We discussed art work and positioning. The text was the same as for the other newspapers.

While in the office, I thought I might ask someone in the editorial department about the possibility of news coverage during Mardi Gras. Carol Wolfrum, a reporter, said that the *Times-Picayune* had a section called "carnival gems". She would pass the information along to an editor that I would be joining the Mardi Gras crowd wearing a large purple Mexican hat. In what location? Ed Anderson's suggestions of Woldenberg Park and a busy intersection in Metairie came to mind although I had not yet had a chance to inspect either site.

To begin the day's travels, I drove north on I-59 to Pearl River and then exited to Louisiana highway 41. After traveling this road for some distance, I took Louisiana highway 21 the rest of the way to Bogalusa. The distance between Slidell and Bogalusa was 44 miles. A young reporter named Eleanor Evans interviewed me at the *Daily News* as she sat in front of a computer. I was impressed by how she seemed to be writing up the story even as we spoke. Evans' story, now posted on the Internet, said that I was hoping for 10 percent of the vote to "send a strong message" on trade to the other candidates. It mentioned my twin proposals, "employer-specific tariffs" and shorter work time; I characterized increasing leisure as "another definition of freedom". She also took a photograph of me.

It was hard to find the road to the next town, Franklinton, after I left Bogalusa's newspaper office. An African-American man from whom I asked directions led me to the right intersection in his car. The 20-mile drive west to Franklinton took me through beautiful countryside. The editor of the *Franklinton Era-Leader*, Moggie Bickham, was out of the office when I arrived. During her absence, a woman with the unusual name of Ettine Sue kept me entertained. Louisiana, she said, was a state with much rain but little snow. In fact, it had only snowed three times since her 20-year-old daughter was a child; and they were light dusters.

I excused myself to go to the car parked in back so I could make some more cell-phone calls and plan the rest of the day. I thought I might drive next to Covington, due south, but the editor of the *Covington News-Banner* told me his paper did not cover national politics. Then I thought I would visit the newspaper in Kentwood. It had a small circulation and was located in an out-of-the-way place up north that I might never visit again. The answering machine contained a message that this office was open Monday through Wednesday before noon. Today was Friday.

By this time, the editor of the Franklinton paper had returned. She was a pleasant, older woman, much involved in community life. She said that, while she was personally a Republican, she had many friends who were Democrats. One was a man named Brad (Orman) who worked a few doors down at the H&R Block office. He was quite active with the local Democratic party. They often had friendly arguments about politics. Perhaps I could drop by to introduce myself once we were done.

I introduced myself to a group of perhaps six women when I entered the H&R Block office. Brad Orman was not there but his wife was. It caused a minor stir to have a presidential candidate in the office. Orman's wife made a telephone call to her husband and put me on the line. Orman said he was on the Democratic Party executive committee, not the parish "leader". But he would be happy to circulate some of the literature left with his wife to the other party members.

I then drove east into Tangipahoa Parish on Louisiana highway 16, bound for Amite. Along the way from Franklinton, I saw some David Duke campaign signs nailed high up on trees. The former Ku Klux Klan official had been the Republican candidate for Governor a decade earlier, running against Edwin Edwards, the Democrat, who was elected but is now serving a prison sentence for corruption. This type of race gave Louisiana a reputation for wild, wide-open politics, some people said.

Amite was a town about the size of Franklinton, having a rather more industrial appearance. Carol Brook, editor of the *Amite Tangi-Digest* talked with me in her office. I gave her a photograph. She said she might mention my visit in her column. Brook then invited me to introduce myself to others in the office. It was my last stop of the day.

As previously noted, motel rooms in New Orleans were booked solid for the Mardi Gras period. My best bet was the Motel 6 in Port Allen. Not only were rooms available there, but Baton Rouge would have its own Mardi Gras parade on Saturday. This was the Spanish Town parade. Pushing my luck, I called an organizer of this event to see if I might participate in the parade as a political candidate. I was told that the entrants had already been determined. Having never been to a Mardi Gras parade before, I could not have been expected to know that a solitary marcher with a sign displaying a serious message but a colorful hat would not be enough to sustain crowd interest. Mardi Gras is something else.

I still had some time left in the day. This gave me an opportunity to scout the downtown area of New Orleans. I expected to be there both for Mardi Gras and in the closing days of my campaign. I drove down I-55 west of Lake Pontchartrain toward the

city. It was an unsettling experience to pull off I-10 at the Claiborne exit, wind around the New Orleans Superdome, and be driving on unfamiliar city streets with little idea where to go. Fortunately, there was an empty parking space on Tulane Avenue. Wearing my purple Mexican hat and carrying a campaign sign, I walked down Tulane for several blocks and then back to my car. No one paid the slightest attention to me. This was enough exploration for one day.

I was happy to discover that Poydras street going north had an entrance ramp to I-10. A sign pointed to Baton Rouge. I took this ramp, of course. Several miles up the road, I exited I-10 to take a look at the intersection of Causeway Boulevard and Veterans Memorial Boulevard in Metairie. Yes, there were many cars but I could not imagine where the pedestrian traffic might be. Entering I-10 once more, I drove back to Baton Rouge.

CHAPTER TWENTY-THREE

Mardi Gras In Baton Rouge, Lafayette, and Lake Charles

It was Saturday, February 21, 2004, and my 63rd birthday. Now my mother was gone for almost three years and I was here by myself in Louisiana campaigning for President. My father was alive in a New Jersey nursing home. The day's first order of business was to buy Mardi Gras beads at a party-favor store. A friend in Minneapolis had told me that everyone who celebrates Mardi Gras needs these. He did not tell me that I might soon have a superabundance of beads from attending the parades. Another Mardi Gras tradition was to have gumbo. I drove to the Party Time store on Airline Highway and waited for the store to open at 9:30 a.m. There I purchased a small bag of beads and a fancy chain with larger beads that cost more.

On the previous day, after my stop in Amite, I had worked the cell phone lining up potential newspaper and television coverage for my Mardi Gras appearances on the weekend. I would be attending the Baton Rouge parade starting at noon and a parade in Lafayette organized by the "Krewe of Bonaparte" starting at 6:30 p.m. It was an hour's drive between the two cities. I told someone at Baton Rouge station WBRZ-TV that I would be standing at the corner of North and St. Louis wearing a large purple sombrero. The same message went to a man at station WAFB-TV. They both said they would be looking for me. I left messages with two or three other Baton Rouge stations and either left messages on the answering machine or received busy signals. I also called *The Advocate* newspaper. They, too, would be covering the parade.

With respect to Lafayette, I had a booklet listing all the Mardi Gras events in that city. It even showed maps of the parade routes, which made it easy to pick a location. I told persons at stations KADN-TV and KATC-TV that I would be standing at the corner of West Congress and Lafayette streets, again wearing a purple sombrero. I could also be identified by a sign. This was the sign, anchored in a brass stand, which was prepared for my June 20th campaign announcement last year. It read on one side: "Meet Bill McGaughey, another candidate for President seeking the Democratic nomination." That would be the side exposed to the television cameras. I also spoke with Jim Bradshaw, an editor of the *Daily Advertiser*, about my Mardi Gras appearance.

While Mardi Gras would prevent my daily visits to newspapers, it was not down time so much as a shifting of gears. This was an opportunity to seek free television coverage. Television was the most powerful medium used in political campaigns. The other advantage of Mardi Gras was that it gave me a chance to wear the Mexican hat. This had been a burning question for me ever since I decided to pack the hat in the trunk of my car. The flamboyant Mexican hat would certainly attract attention, but was it the right kind of attention? There was a chance that it would offend Hispanic voters if they felt I was making fun of them. Also, I might come off as a clown wearing this hat; and people don't vote for clowns. Mardi

Gras made it acceptable to wear outlandish costumes of all varieties. For my part, I liked the hat. It liked it as a wild and colorful head adornment which oddly suited the grandiose purpose of someone running for President. I was aching for a chance to wear that unique hat, and Mardi Gras gave it to me.

Mardi Gras also forced me to think about where to campaign. I needed to mingle with people in an appropriate place. There were two problems. First, the place to campaign should have a sufficient number of people. Second, it should be an acceptable place for campaigning. It should be a place where the police or security guards would not evict a person for trespassing. Even if legal, it should be a place where people welcome or at least tolerate solicitations by political candidates.

On most big-city streets candidates are allowed to shake hands or pass out literature. The problem is usually that not enough people walk by to make the activity worthwhile. On the other hand, congested suburban areas may have the people but lack appropriate places to approach them personally. These places are designed for the automobile, not for pedestrian traffic. I would not be advised to roam mall parking lots engaging customers in political conversations as they stepped out of their cars. Mardi Gras does bring crowds of people to big-city streets. The problem here is that people are expecting to enjoy the Mardi Gras parades, not to be approached by a political candidate. Maybe this is why media coverage has become so critical to political campaigning. The opportunities for personal contact and interaction have dried up.

The crowds were obvious as I drove into the downtown area of Baton Rouge shortly before noon, Saturday, the 21st, and parked my car in a lot off Convention street. I had promised the news media to stand at the corner of North and St. Louis. Where was that? I followed the crowds. I had driven by North and St. Louis a week earlier but could not find the place now. I thought it might be closer to the river. Huge crowds filled North Street as I walked toward the smaller numbered streets. Where was St. Louis? Finally, I asked a police officer. North and St. Louis was still blocks away, he said. Did the parade go past this intersection? No, it did not.

After I had a chance to look at the map in the car, I realized what had happened. Downtown Baton Rouge has two streets named "North". One is North Street and one is North Boulevard. They parallel each other five blocks apart. Also, I could not find St. Louis Street because it stops at North Boulevard. North of the boulevard, the same street is called North Third Street. No wonder I could not find the desired intersection as I walked west on North Street. There was no St. Louis Street intersecting here. That's the problem with old cities like Baton Rouge whose streets were laid out before there were city planners. I should have known.

This meant that my first Mardi Gras event was a bust. All I could do now was to find a place to put my sign as the parade went down North Street. I found a big tree near the northeast corner of North Street and North Sixth Street. Here my sign would not block someone's view of the parade. I leaned the sign and the stand against the tree. Because of the noise, I then walked behind a house to call the media with information about my new location. No one answered the phones. Maybe it was because I could not hear. I walked back to my position near the tree and waited for the parade to pass by this spot.

The "Spanish Town" Mardi Gras parade in Baton Rouge must have had seventy floats, each colorfully decorated. On each float, a "krewe" would toss Mardi Gras beads and other items off into the crowd. We in the crowd would jump for the beads as they were tossed our way. It was like children jumping for candy. This was not a good environment for political campaigning. Giving up hope of television coverage, I, too, became caught up in the spirit of catching as many beads as possible. By the end of the parade, I had caught at least as many beads tossed from the parade floats as I had bought that morning at the Party Time store.

During lulls in the parade, I talked with some of the other spectators. There was a middle-aged couple from Baton Rouge who had been to this parade many times. The man taught world history in high school. I told him about my book and promised to send him a copy. Many adults were aggressively helping their kids catch beads. The kids were perched on their shoulders in front of us. There were, however, no news reporters or television crews.

Right after the parade, I drove to Lafayette. It was late in the afternoon. I thought I knew the streets in downtown Lafayette but now found the layout confusing even with a map. Police barricades lined the parade route, adding to my difficulty in finding a parking space near West Congress and Lafayette. I parked around the corner from Lee Street, a block from West Vermilion, which intersected with Lafayette Street four blocks away. Right at the corner, it was another long block to West Congress. The crowds in Lafayette were not as thick as they had been in Baton Rouge. The parade route turned at my corner. There were mostly African Americans standing at that spot. Early on, two white girls asked if they could take a picture of me in my Mexican hat. My sign

was leaning against a lamp post, virtually unnoticed. Then the parade began.

The parade in Lafayette had a greater police presence than the one in Baton Rouge. As officers stood in the parade route to control the crowds, teams of police on motorcycles zoomed in circles, doing "high fives" with spectators. There were not as many floats as in the Baton Rouge parade although the Mardi Gras beads were tossed with equal abandon. Toward the end of the parade, a television reporter and cameraman from KATC-TV, Channel 3, unexpectedly appeared. "Are you Bill McGaughey?," the reporter asked. I was. In this noisy place, it was hard to hear the questions asked in the three-minute interview. I did my best to respond. Afterwards, some spectators nearby struck up conversations with me, among them a woman from New Orleans. I asked her what was the best New Orleans Mardi Gras parade. She said, "Endymion", her own neighborhood's parade.

Walking back towards my car, I had several offers to buy my Mexican hat. Most were from young white men with their girl friends who had been drinking. I tried to explain in good humor that the hat was not for sale. Loud music was coming from a night club just off the street. I walked in and sat down at the bar. I asked what was a good local beer. "Purple haze" was the

bartender's answer. It was bottled by the Abita Brewing Company of Abita Springs, Louisiana, in that part of the state north of Lake Pontchartrain. I struck up a conversation with a young lady seated next to me. Then her friends appeared, and I was ignored for the rest of the evening. Humiliated, I placed a few cell phone calls to people in Minnesota. Then I drove to the Motel 6 in Lafayette, and watched the Channel 3 news, hoping that my interview would be aired. If it was, I missed the segment. I called it a night. That's how I spent my 63rd birthday.

Sunday morning, the 22nd of February, I thought I might attend the 11 a.m. Mardi Gras parade in Carencro, a suburban neighborhood northwest of Lafayette. My only other plan for that day was to attend the "boat parade" in Lake Charles, starting at 7 p.m. From the Motel 6, I drove west to the next major north-south highway. Already cars were parked on the shoulders of the highway. Groups of people were passing by on foot. With my gear, I, too, started walking. After several hundred yards, I asked someone how far it was to the parade site. Half a mile, at least. At that point, I decided that the event was not worth the trouble. The deciding factor was that the media had not been notified that I would be attending the Carencro event. I would be stuck in a place far from my car. Maybe it would be better to spend the time in Lake Charles. I returned to the car.

North on the same highway, I approached the entrance ramp to I-10 which would take me to Lake Charles. A hitchhiker was standing near the ramp. I decided to pick him up. The man's name was Michael. He was 35 years old, of French ancestry, and originally from Ville Platte. He had just split up with his girl friend in

Lafayette and was leaving town for an unknown destination. He just wanted to leave town. Michael said he had not worked since 2000. He had worked for a

construction firm in Baton Rouge but he was injured on the job and had been awarded a cash settlement. His girl friend had squandered it. He thought she might have been using cocaine. She always denied it. Their relationship was hopeless. He wanted to move on and start a new life. Who was the greater desperado, I asked myself, this man or me running for President?

Down the road, I pulled off the interstate to buy Michael a pack of cigarettes. Cheap cigarettes, he said, would be OK. He just needed to smoke. We passed an oil rig at the side of the highway which was like one he had worked in his younger days. I was going as far as Lake Charles. He said he would accompany me to that city. I could see that Michael was having second thoughts about leaving Lafayette. He asked for my opinion about relationships. I'm generally in favor of renewed attempts to communicate. I told him that I would attend Mardi Gras activities in

Lake Charles for several hours and then be returning on the same highway to Baton Rouge. If he changed his mind about leaving, he was welcome to ride back with me to Lafayette.

Michael and I hung out together for several hours in Lake Charles. We went to the Tourist Information Center and looked at the alligators. He knew how to catch them in the wild. Their meat was delicious. Michael said he thought Britney Spears had grown up in the Jennings area which we had passed that after-

noon on the highway. (Actually she's from Kentwood.) We had coffee and a bite to eat along the route of the children's Mardi Gras parade. This was an event which featured children tossing beads to us adults. Having already parked, I found another parking spot closer to the Civic Center. I thought I might repark the car here.

About that time, Michael decided that he wanted to return to Lafayette. There was still more than an hour before the boat parade began and he was getting restless. I therefore drove Michael to the entrance ramp of I-10. He planned to hitchhike back home. I promised to look out for him when I came that way several hours later in case he had failed to catch a ride.

Now by myself, I reparked the car and had a light meal at Wendy's. The period following the children's parade was, in fact, quite productive, although no television crews or newspaper reporters appeared. I talked with a number of people in the parking lot while passing out literature. Most were interested in my campaign for President. Most agreed with me on employment and were receptive to my proposals on trade. There were, however, a few Republicans who could not be swayed, I admit. There were also some who were concerned mainly about immigration or the war in Iraq.

Promptly at 7 p.m. lighted boats began cruising past spectators who stood along the rail of the board walk. Like other Mardi Gras parades, this one included tossing of beads. Standing along

the dimly lit harbor, we caught what we could. The first part of the parade lasted perhaps 20 minutes. Then the line of boats headed out into the lake for another pass. I decided to leave.

In retrospect, I should have remained for the second round of parading boats in case news reporters from Lake Charles were looking for me. After all, the television crew in Lafayette had found me after the parade. But I was tired and did not think clearly. I had a long drive ahead of me that evening before I reached Port Allen. Michael must have found a ride for I did not see him anywhere along the highway. It was shortly before 10:00 p.m. when I checked in at the Motel 6. These Mardi Gras events had been impressive but the big ones would come in New Orleans during the next two days.

CHAPTER TWENTY-FOUR

Mardi Gras in New Orleans

The Mardi Gras celebrations still had two days to run when the weekend was over. "Fat Tuesday" (which is the English translation of "Mardi Gras") is a legal holiday in Louisiana. Monday, February 23rd, also fell within the period of festivities although not to the same degree as Tuesday. As most people know, Mardi Gras is a time forty days before Easter, immediately preceding Lent. Devout Christians celebrate Lent by practicing personal sacrifice. Some who may be less religious presumably want to get wild revelry out of their system before crossing this desert of self-deprivation. So they engage in every kind of sensual excess in the Mardi Gras orgies preceding Lent. It says something about our culture that tourists flock to New Orleans for the exhibitions of debauchery and leave as soon as religion is more strictly practiced.

When I mentioned to people that I would be attending my first Mardi Gras event in New Orleans, they would often respond:

You'll see things you never saw before. With a knowing wink, they would refer to the wild women who roam the streets on those days. Specifically, I think they meant that the women would pull up their blouses and expose their breasts. Some wanted to be rewarded for this exciting act by being given beads. The woman with the most beads around her neck would be the wildest, baddest girl in town. I was rather looking forward to that, especially if the right person came along.

To tell the truth, no woman exposed her breasts to me. Light rains this year kept the crowds down and might also have dampened people's spirits. The closest that I got to nudity in New Orleans was when, while waiting for the Orpheus Krewe parade in the company of several people, a woman changed her baby's diapers. She chided me when I recorded this event, among others, with my video camera.

I might not have experienced any Mardi Gras flashing because I did not participate in the late-night partying. I was in town for business, needing to be sober and rested on the following day. For an entire week, beginning February 22nd, I spent the night at the Motel 6 in Port Allen. That meant that I would have to drive 85 miles to New Orleans before I could do anything in that city, and then drive back another 85 miles before spending the night. I became quite familiar with the section of I-10 between those two cities.

In the previous week, the editor of the *Slidell Sentry-News* had asked me to return Monday morning for an interview. I had an appointment at 10:30 a.m. A young reporter named Chad Hebert interviewed me in an upstairs conference room. He let me talk for several minutes and then started asking questions. Our conversation focused on my trade proposals and the idea that cutting work time in response to productivity improvements might increase employment. I stressed that tariffs could be used "harmoniously" with other nations as a development tool.

The main theme of his article was that I, a "virtual unknown", was stumping Slidell in pursuit of the Democratic nomination for President. "Bill McGaughey is a fern in a forest of redwoods," Hebert wrote.

I could continue my hopeless quest in a reasonably cheerful spirit, he said, because my candidacy would serve to highlight employment issues even if someone else was nominated. After the interview, I told Hebert that I planned to attend several parades later in the day. He said that the Orpheus Krewe parade, organized by singer Harry Connick, Jr., was New Orleans' premier Mardi Gras event. I should try not to miss it.

Monday's Mardi Gras parades were in the late afternoon. I thought that I should try to attend the Zeus Krewe parade in Metairie which began at 6:30 p.m. This parade would pass by the busy intersection of Causeway Boulevard and Veterans Memorial Boulevard which Ed Anderson had mentioned. Unfortunately, the Orpheus Krewe parade would take place at the same time. I had to make a choice. There would be an opportunity to attend four different parades in the "Uptown" area (along St. Charles Street) on Tuesday morning. By attending the Metairie parade today, I could cover both parts of town.

Before the day's event began, I had several hours to spend in New Orleans scouting locations. I was worried about parking. On such a busy day, street parking near the parade routes would probably be taken. The paid lots would be expensive. By chance, I found some empty spots in metered parking spaces on Perdido Street just north of Rampart. I drove around and found St. Charles street. The famed French Quarter was nearby. I spent some time driving around Metairie as well. Now I had a plan of action.

I called several New Orleans radio and television stations as well as the *Times-Picayune*. A man at a television station told me that Mardi Gras was a family event. It was not for political campaigns. Rather foolishly, I asked him how to pronounce Metairie. "You're a candidate and you don't know that?," he asked. He said he would help me out this time. It was pronounced MEH-ta-ree. Most of the other media people took the news of my New Orleans campaign appearances more politely. There was light rain.

I had another idea. Editorial boards typically endorse candidates for election to public office. Certainly they would be interested in the race for President. Maybe, even, some would be willing to talk with me as an aspiring nominee. A woman in the editorial department of *The Advocate* said that the Baton Rouge newspaper does not endorse candidates. The *Times-Picayune* did endorsements for the general election but not the primary. I received a similar reaction from the Shreveport paper. Never mind, it was just an idea. Not everything works.

I had a snack at the Wendy's on Causeway Boulevard and then parked in a residential area several blocks away from the intersection of Causeway and Veterans Memorial boulevards. Police barriers lined Veterans Memorial. In spite of this, few people seemed to be walking around the area. What had happened? I asked a store clerk about tonight's parade. He had no information. Then I asked two Mexican guys. "Haven't you heard?" one of them said. "The parade has been postponed because of rain. Come back tomorrow." However, the media had been informed that I would be at this parade on this day. It was another Baton Rouge-type media fiasco for my presidential campaign.

The silver lining was that tonight's cancellation of the Metairie parade freed me up to attend the one in Uptown. Harry Connick Jr. and his Krewe were probably finishing up to adoring cheers. Surprisingly, the crowds were light. The same parking spaces on Perdido Street were available; and, because it was after 6 p.m., the meters did not need to be fed. I walked the six blocks to St. Charles and Poydras streets, where I was scheduled to be tomor-

row, and found that the Orpheus Krewe parade hadn't even started. More accurately, it had not yet reached that spot. I stood behind the police barricade in front of a set of bleachers. People needed tickets to sit there. Eventually, the police asked ticketless persons like me to leave the area. We could stand on the corner of Poydras and St. Charles - the northwest corner - to watch the parade.

I spent the next three hours with a small group of people standing at that corner. To my left was a young black couple. Right in front of me was a heavy-set white woman with a baby. All stood by silently until an outgoing white man behind me asked about the Mexican hat. It was not that this hat blocked his view. The hat was a conversation piece that led to further personal disclosures.

The man said he worked for a large bank in Atlanta, Georgia. His job was to line up retail firms to issue credit cards to their customers through this bank. I knew about that type of arrangement as a customer of Home Depot. The man was a Republican. Son of a general, he was strongly pro-military. He liked President Bush. There was a conflict here in that he was also gay. He was a gay Republican which, in today's political world, involves many contradictions. For the time being, however, his separate identities were intact.

He mentioned some ugly things that people had said about him. I responded that he had only one customer to please: himself. He was happy that I had said that. Of particular interest to me, this man said that his life was quite stressful. He was working 60-hour workweeks with 95% travel. When the bank gave him the job, they had promised less travel but "they lied." He wanted something different but did not see any alternative to keeping his current job.

Some others joined in the conversation including the woman who had changed her son's diapers. To this group, I disclosed my presidential ambition. The time passed more quickly than it otherwise might have done. After a good hour and a half of waiting, the parade reached our spot. These floats were larger and more

elaborately decorated than the Mardi Gras floats I had seen before. Harry Connick, Jr., famed singer and son of a former New Orleans district attorney, was on one of them. Otherwise, it was much the same routine of tossing beads and other Mardi Gras trinkets from the floats while persons in the crowd scrambled to catch whatever was thrown their way. I added to my immense collection of loot. Then there was another long drive back to Baton Rouge.

After a night's rest in Port Allen, I turned around the next morning and drove right back to New Orleans. In fact, my destination was the same street corner, Poydras and St. Charles. Driving down I-10, I wished I had a camera ready when I saw a man

by an open truck door standing on the shoulder of the highway with a fishing rod in his hand - right in front of a sign that said: "Emergency Parking Only." That's the spirit - emergency fishing! But it was a holiday, after all. Another man was also fishing several miles farther down the road. A public holiday after a good spring rain creates an irresistible desire to do this kind of thing.

A radio commercial also caught my attention. "Fire your landlord," it began. This commercial was sponsored by an outfit called Consumer Resource Network promising to get you into your own house with little or no money down. Bad credit was not a problem. You, too, can own your own home. "Fire your landlord today." As a landlord, I was not bothered so much by the harsh rhetoric concerning my own occupation as by the fact the persons of limited financial capacity were being given a hard sell to buy houses that they could not realistically afford. What does this say about today's housing market? I knew that I, too, was vulnerable should there be a jolting round of foreclosures and a drop in housing prices.

Before entering New Orleans, I stopped at a restaurant near the interstate to have a bowl of gumbo. It was cheaper here than in the city. Once downtown, I found my favorite parking space on Perdido Street. This time I did not have to feed the meter because it was a holiday - Fat Tuesday, Mardi Gras day. A parade was already passing down the street when I arrived at the street corner where I had promised the media I would be standing for the day's events.

Today, I had to stand behind the rails on Poydras street some distance from the parade route. An attractive older woman was standing next to me. She said she was from Paris, France. She was touring several cities in North America. A male companion, perhaps her husband, arrived more than an hour later. The two walked together up Poydras street and vanished in the crowd.

I stayed at this spot for another half hour. A television reporter was working the crowd on the other side of St. Charles street. He never crossed over to my side. I confined myself to the pursuit of beads. I caught a package of medallions that were highly prized. A woman suggested diplomatically that I give one to a small boy who was standing on top of a fire hydrant next to his mother. I walked east on St. Charles until I was on the opposite side of a viewing standing for Mardi Gras dignitaries. A middle-aged woman there told me that a well-dressed young

woman in the stands across the street from us had a major role to play in the pageantry surrounding this annual event. Rex, king of the carnival, would shortly arrive here and claim her as his queen.

As parades followed each other, all the Mardi Gras loot made us a bit punch drunk. People on opposite sides of the street began hurling strings of beads at each other over the floats. There was so much stuff, on the sidewalks, on the streets, in our bags, that we were losing interest. I tried to talk with people about politics. Few were receptive. Winning more approval was my large Mexican hat. In the late afternoon, I drove back to Baton Rouge. Mardi Gras was over for me.

CHAPTER TWENTY-FIVE

Back to Campaigning: Ponchatoula and Port Allen

With Mardi Gras over, the final phase of the campaign began. I still had not visited a number of newspapers in the state. Circling the names of cities and towns where these were located, I prepared regional itineraries to hit the remaining places. Wednesday, February 25th, was a day to complete my campaigning in the area north of Lake Pontchartrain. Also, I had to get back to Keith Magill of the Houma paper by telephone; he hadn't been available on Monday. There was also a large-circulation weekly newspaper in Denham Springs, east of Baton Rouge. If I drove east on Interstate 12, I could stop in Denham Springs first and then continue to places north of the lake such as Hammond, Ponchatoula, and Covington.

The *Livingston Parish News* in Denham Springs was hard to find coming from I-12 but a receptionist gave me good directions: Turn left at the Denham Springs exit, right at the next red light just beyond the McDonald's, then drive along a curvy road for half a mile to the first stop light, turn left onto Pete's Highway which after several miles becomes Florida Boulevard, and then take a left at Hatchell Lane where the office is located. When I arrived, the editor was not in. I said I would return later in the day.

After half an hour I arrived in Hammond and received directions to the office of the *Daily Star*. The traffic was unexpectedly heavy. I then made an appointment by cell phone to visit the office of the *Ponchatoula Times*, located just south of Hammond on I-55. The editor, Bryan McMahon, said he was about to leave for the city (New Orleans) but would wait for me. In the newspaper's second-floor office, he interviewed me while seated at his desk.

My talk of a shorter workweek rang a bell with him. McMahon was originally from Michigan. He had gone to college at Oakland Community College north of Detroit and had attended high school with one of UAW President Walter Reuther's daughters. (My younger brother went to school in Vermont with another.) Detroit's industrial culture was a matter of pride for him, as it was for me also. We both knew that Henry Ford had been the one most responsible for creating America's consumer society. McMahon had formerly been a reporter for the *Detroit Free Press* who had been active in union organizing. Fired from the *Free Press*, he got his job back after a difficult battle in court but had then decided to seek employment elsewhere. On the wall of the office was a framed letter informing him that he had won his court case.

This was the amazing thing about political campaigns. One never knew who would be the next interesting person to meet. Down here in Louisiana was a man from my old home town. Earlier in my life, I had lived both in Detroit and in a suburban community north of there. My partner in a dancing class was the daughter of a wealthy couple who had donated the land on which the main campus of Oakland Community College sits. At that time, when Walter Reuther lived, labor and management were much at odds. My parents were part of the business community. After business ceased to be managed by inspired tinkerers of Henry Ford's ilk and instead became dominated by Wall Street financial managers and graduates of business schools, I gained increasing sympathy for labor's objectives. And it all came together again in talking with Bryan McMahon. For many Americans, this is a forgotten era.

After the meeting in Ponchatoula, I drove north again on I-55 toward the newspaper office in Hammond. Because I was coming from a different direction, I missed the exit and continued to the next one. I knew I had come too far. Trusting my sense of direction, I gambled that the next highway over would take me to the right place. Sure enough, I spotted South Morrison Boulevard where the Daily Star's offices were located. Lillian Mirando, editor of the paper, did not have time to talk with me but she did send a message for me to leave my literature and a photo at the front desk.

There were two newspapers in Covington, another twenty miles east on I-12. On Friday of the previous week, the editor of the *News-Banner*, a weekly newspaper, had told me that his paper did not cover national political campaigns. However, I was welcome to drop off my literature at the office. Covington's other weekly newspaper, *St. Tammany Farmer*, did cover national politics. Unfortunately, its office was closed that day and would reopen Thursday at 8:00 a.m. I left literature and a photo at the *News-Banner*.

Having free time, I now made a list of Louisiana's minority-owned newspapers and called some of them. I reached the editor of the *Baton Rouge Weekly Press*, an African-American newspaper, who talked with me about my campaign. This editor, Ivory Payne, proposed having me meet a number of people from the community at an agreeable time and place. He later called back to say that there had not been sufficient interest in such a meeting. People had not heard of me. How could I run for President with so little reputation or support? Payne did agree to look at my campaign literature. He gave me directions to his office in a northern suburb of Baton Rouge. Early the next day, I drove to this place and slipped literature under the door.

I also called the *Louisiana Weekly*. My list of community newspapers said this was a paper which served the Hispanic community. The receptionist gave me the phone number of an editor. It happened to be Christopher Tidmore, the same man who had interviewed me two weeks earlier on the New Orleans talk show. I did not recognize his name in this context but he remembered me. Tidmore said that he had written a column about my campaign in the *Louisiana Weekly*, which was being distributed on news stands throughout the city. Had I seen it yet? I had not. The column was also posted on the Internet. Tidmore also said that a young colleague named Jayson Lee, who hosted a call-in show on station KTIB-AM in Thibodaux, had been trying to contact me. He gave me Lee's number to call. He would also like to have me back again on his own show, perhaps the Monday before the primary. I was delighted at this turn of events.

Several other African-American newspapers needed to be called. At the *Alexandria News Weekly*, a woman told me that this was a small, understaffed newspaper which did not keep regular business hours. The reporters mostly worked out of their own homes. It would be best for me to call ahead when I was coming to Alexandria and try to set up a meeting. At the *Gambit Weekly*, I was told that this paper would not be covering the Democratic primary. They already had my literature. A third newspaper was the *New Orleans Data News Weekly*. A woman named Katrice answered the phone. She said she would check with the publisher, Mr. Jones, to see if there was any interest in covering my campaign. I also spoke with Keith Magill in Houma. Yes, he had received my envelope but had not yet had a chance to look at the contents. He would call me back if he had any questions.

After talking on the cell phone, I took Interstate 12 back toward Baton Rouge. I called the office of *Livingston Parish News* in Denham Springs. The editor was now back in the office. Might I stop by for a short visit? The editor asked me where I was from. Minnesota. After a pause, he said that he did not feel like giving out-of-state candidates free publicity. I asked if I might simply drop off some literature. "It's a free country," he replied, but I'd be wasting both his time and mine. Even though I had the directions to the newspaper office down pat, I bypassed Denham Springs.

There was time for a mid-afternoon visit to the press room at the Louisiana state capitol. Ed Anderson was sitting at his desk. He said he had been sick for four days and was busy catching up on work. Contact him again soon, Anderson said. Marsha Shuler of *The Advocate* was again away from her desk. I also spoke with Melinda Deslatte and gave her my most recent packet of materials. She said to let her know if I had plans to do anything in Baton Rouge. The Associated Press had already produced a short

announcement of my candidacy based on the *Times-Picayune* story. What about the other candidates? Deslatte did not think that any of the Democrats had campaigned yet in Louisiana except for Wesley Clark who was in the state a month ago.

Another newspaper that remained to be visited was the weekly in Port Allen where the Motel 6 was located. Chris Chatelain, editor of the *Port Allen West Side Journal*, had time to talk with me that afternoon. Another man was sitting at a table in the office whom I mistook for Chatelain. After he straightened me out, we had a short interview sitting at the same table. Chatelain was well-versed in local economic conditions and interested in what I had to say.

That evening, I broke down and had my first full-scale restaurant meal. I could not resist the temptation to indulge in the prime-rib dinner at Shoney's restaurant in Port Allen, just down the road from my motel. The prime rib was incidental to a sumptuous buffet including many of my favorite foods. Previously, I had eaten a few meals at Wendy's after discovering that the 99-cent hamburger was almost as filling as hamburger meals elsewhere costing much more money. The Shoney's dinner showed me that a larger life was available to me gastronomically if I chose to take advantage of it. On the other hand, my skimpy eating had brought my weight down. That's another advantage of an active political campaign - quite effective if you're an underdog candidate.

I should also mention that long evenings in motel rooms offered a continuing window on the world through cable television. The Motel 6 service included more than a dozen channels such as CNN, HBO, public television, and the local news. The most important programming for me was election-night coverage of the Democratic presidential primary which took place on successive Tuesdays. On Tuesday, February 3rd, I had watched reporting of South Carolina's, Missouri's, Oklahoma's and several other states' primary results. Next week, in my Natchitoches motel room, I watched the results come in from Tennessee and Virginia. Clark and Edwards had each won a primary on the 3rd. Everything else went to Kerry. Edwards' South Carolina victory was marred by his failure to win the two southern states on February 10th.

The Wisconsin primary on February 17th was Howard Dean's do-or-die. He had promised to drop out if he did not win that primary but had then waffled a bit. The Wisconsin primary gave a boost to John Edwards, not expected to do well here. Edwards had pushed the trade issue and finished second, five percentage points from first place. He delivered the quip of the night directed at Kerry: "Warning, the object behind you is closer than it looks."

After losing Wisconsin, Dean did formally withdraw. The race was narrowing down to Edwards and Kerry. While another primary took place in three small western states on February 24th, the pundits were biding their time until the real contest on "Super Tuesday", March 2nd. That would be the day when New York, California, Ohio, Massachusetts, Georgia, and four other states would hold primaries. There would also be a caucus in my own state, Minnesota.

Lou Dobbs had several interesting guests on his evening-news program during this period. One was the business guru, Tom Peters, who embraced Schumpeter's theory that capitalism advanced through "creative destruction". We should not mourn the demise of the buggy-whip industry, the argument went, if a new automobile industry was around the corner. Business is never static as progress relentlessly takes place. What of today's loss of jobs to outsourcing? Well, that's just another bump in the road to

business progress. Surprisingly, Peters said he doubted that the Fortune 500 companies would create *any* net jobs. The new jobs could have to come from small businesses created by entrepreneurs. It was the same line of argument that I had heard at the Rural Economic Development Conference in Natchitoches. Now America's foremost business guru was saying that creative destruction would take place simultaneously in the largest business firms in *all* sectors of industry, not just in buggy whips. Somewhere, a new Bill Gates was being born to take up the slack.

Peters, who travels widely in Asia, provided another explanation for job loss. In the *Strait Times* of Singapore, he had read that business people in that city were worried about the loss of jobs to microprocessors. More jobs in the United States, as well, have been lost to microprocessors than to trade with foreign countries.

Peters was restating the old trade-union argument that automation costs jobs. Trade unionists of yesteryear would have known the response: cut work hours. Even if labor-saving equipment is introduced, the resulting job loss can be offset by shrinking the general schedule of hours. Then work will be needed from everyone. Peters and other business spokespersons know, however, that today's union people will not use that argument. Organized labor is today more interested in getting overtime pay for its members than reducing work hours. Labor has, as I said, "lost its way". Business can cite increased productivity as an excuse for job loss because everyone knows that productivity improvements are "good". No one remembers the rest.

On the evening of February 24th, the Dobbs news hour presented its usual potpourri of discussion related to employment and trade. Professor Ron Hira of the Rochester Institute of Technology was opposed to free trade. Dr. Katherine Mann favored exporting American jobs. Senator Christopher Dodd of Connecticut had introduced a bill to withhold federal funding from government entities that outsource work. Rep. Dan Burton of Indiana agreed that outsourcing was the problem.

Meanwhile, Chairman Alan Greenspan of the Federal Reserve Bank was warning that Fanny Mae's and Freddy Mac's exposure to bad home mortgages had grown to the point that the stability of the entire economy was at risk. That's what I was telling people every day when I traveled the state of Louisiana. It was good to find confirmation on national television.

I should also mention a program that I saw on Louisiana public television about Emmett Till. A documentary told the story of his 1955 murder in Mississippi. Emmett Till was the only son of a well educated black woman in Chicago, a 14-year-old boy with a teenager's normal high spirits. His uncle in Mississippi had invited him to visit. Till whistled at a white woman while leaving a movie theater. Several days later, he disappeared. Till's body was found at the bottom of a river. The authorities arrested two white men and put them on trial for murder but an all-white jury acquitted these men.

Till's badly decomposed body was sent back to Chicago for burial. At the visitation, Till's mother decided to open the casket so that people could see what had happened to her son. Tens of thousands of mostly black mourners with scarcely concealed anger filed past the open casket. Months later, a national magazine published an article in which the acquitted men told how they had committed the murder.

I had heard Emmett Till's name before but was unfamiliar with the story. Events of the 1950s and 1960s now made more sense. Even more than when Rosa Parks refused to give up her bus seat to a white man in Montgomery, Emmett Till's murder a year earlier is what sparked the Civil Rights movement. Anyway, that's how it struck me.

CHAPTER TWENTY-SIX

Finishing up the Week in the South

The town of Larose is located at the southern end of Louisiana highway 1 in Lafourche Parish - bayou country. While isolated, the *Lafourche Gazette* in Larose has a weekly circulation too large to be ignored. I liked to plan daily itineraries that allowed me to travel in a circle visiting different cities along the way. In this case, having a single destination, I would drive forty miles to Larose and then return by the same highway. The dead time did not matter so much if the driving took place after business hours - or before. Therefore, my strategy for Thursday, February 26th, was to rise before dawn, drive from Baton Rouge to Larose, and arrive at the newspaper office close to the time when it opened for the day.

The editor of the *Lafourche Gazette*, Vicki Chaisson, had told me Wednesday afternoon that, while her newspaper probably would not do much about my campaign, the office opened at 8:00 a.m. I was there around 8:30. There was not much conversation. I left a photo and some literature. Then I returned north on highway 1, passing through Raceland, and joined Interstate 49 heading west. My next stop was Morgan City which I had planned to visit a week earlier. The office of the *Daily Review* was on Front street, across town from the interstate exit. I was told to look for a green awning.

Ted McManus, the editor, greeted me when I arrived. He conducted a short interview and then told me about the local economy. It was another of those educational experiences which added so much to the campaign. Morgan City was the center of the offshore oil drilling industry. Factories in the area fabricated sections of platform. Other facilities trained the deep-sea divers who worked on platforms in the Gulf of Mexico. Morgan City was also a center of boat fabrication and shrimp fishing. A problem, said McManus, was finding skilled labor to work in these jobs. He encouraged me to talk with economic-development people at City Hall. McManus also suggested that I talk with people in his office. As a photographer snapped pictures, I had a lively conversation with two women at a table in the other room who were counting money from subscription receipts. One had a husband who was a diver.

This was an invitation to be more outgoing as a candidate than I usually was during these visits. I located Morgan City's municipal offices which were across the street from the post of fice. (I needed to mail campaign literature to the editor of the *Pointe Coupee Banner* in New Roads.) The mayor was not in but I did meet with the city's chief administrative officer, Michael Loupe. He said that a number of businesses were interested in locating in Morgan City if the right facilities were available. There

was a Chinese trading company, for example. It needed a 30-foot channel and a larger dock. The U.S. Army Corps of Engineers was legally obligated to maintain a 20-foot channel but did not always comply because of competing priorities.

Leapfrogging past Franklin on U.S. 90, I next visited the office of the *Jeanerette Enterprise* which had been closed a week earlier. This time, the editor was in. She was Karma Champagne (pronounced sham-PINE). She had looked at my campaign leaflet slid under the door and was interested in the subject. Trade-related job loss had hit the town hard - "emptied out main street" was the way she put it. Champagne suggested that I call upon Jeanerette's mayor just a few blocks away. The mayor, an older man, was in a meeting but he came out to talk with me for a few minutes. Presidential candidates did not come here that often. Following the discussion I bought several items at a supermarket across the street, including bananas and tangerines.

I rejoined U.S. highway 90 after driving a mile down the road which met highway 182 near the *Jeanerette Enterprise* office (and T-Bob's restaurant). Next, I wanted to give the *Daily Advertiser* in Lafayette another try. I had left messages with Arnessa Garrett but not been interviewed yet. The managing editor, Mark Gilbert,

introduced himself at the front counter. Gilbert said he had assigned reporter Lou Rom to interview me. It could not be done today; Rom would call me next week. While in the office, I also met with Mary Abrams in the advertising department and with Judy Johnson, editor of *The Times of Acadiana,* a free-circulation weekly. When I returned next week for the interview, I picked up a copy of Johnson's paper and found an announcement of my candidacy along with a photograph.

A number of smaller newspapers west of Lafayette remained to be visited. The most efficient use of my time, I felt, would be to drive west on I-10 to Rayne, stop at the office of the *Acadian Tribune*, and then head north to Church Point, Eunice, and Basile. The editor of the *Acadian Tribune* in Rayne was out of the office when I approached that town. He was expected to return in an hour. After then driving north on Louisiana highway 35, I talked with two women at the *Church Point News*. I left literature and a photograph there. Eunice would have been my next destination except that a woman who answered the phone in that city's newspaper office said it was not a good day to visit. So I turned around and drove back toward Rayne. At that point, I received a cell

phone call from Juan Carlos of *La Prensa* in New Orleans. I explained that I was a presidential candidate who wanted to visit their office. Carlos said he would make some inquiries and get back to me.

Approaching I-10, I had a sudden thought. It was around 3:45 p.m. If I hurried, I might have enough time to reach Sulphur in the western part of the state before the offices of the *Southwest Daily News* closed at 5:00 p.m. This might be my last opportunity to visit that important newspaper before the primary. I raced west along Interstate 10 past Lake Charles to Sulphur. Then I made a big mistake. From a previous visit, I remembered that the *Southwest Daily News* was located on a major east-west highway. I assumed it was this one. However, the newspaper office was actually on U.S. highway 90 which paralleled I-10 two miles north. The problem now was that, having failed to exit I-10 at Sulphur, I had to drive to the next exit which was fifteen miles down the road - eight miles from the Texas border - with a half hour left before the newspaper office closed. There were dirt roads along the way where authorized vehicles might turn around but I dared not use them.

I called the editor, Diane Regan, to explain the situation. Her response was disheartening. She explained that the *Southwest Daily News* was a small local newspaper which did not do much coverage of national politics. They already had my campaign sheet and a photo and would go with that. Even so, I decided to drop by the office to talk with anyone still there. It was two minutes before 5:00 p.m. when I arrived. Regan herself had left for the day but another woman took some of my other materials. Deflated by my failed gamble, I turned back toward Baton Rouge, a good two hours' drive east.

Like so many others feeling down on their luck, I stopped at Harrah's casino in Lake Charles for emotional solace. After dropping my usual $2.00 at the electronic slot machines, I sat down at a cocktail bar in the lobby and ordered a dish of fresh oysters. The man next to me was finishing a huge plate of crawfish. We struck up a conversation. I was running for President and he was on his way to Florida to seek construction work at a military base. He had done that kind of work in California. However, California was an economic basket case, he said. Businesses were leaving the state in droves because of high taxes, workers compensation, and other problems. The main beneficiaries were its neighboring states. This man was enjoying himself as he drove across the wide-open spaces of Arizona, New Mexico, Texas, and Louisiana toward Florida. I told him of the Motel 6 in Port Allen where I would be spending the night.

I did spend the night in Port Allen and early the next morning, Friday, February 27, had a bright idea. Melinda Deslatte had asked me to inform her of campaign events in Baton Rouge. What campaign events did I have planned for the capital city? As yet, there were none. My idea was to see if I could arrange a discussion of trade policy with faculty or students at Louisiana State University in Baton Rouge. My advocacy of tariffs to combat job loss should be of interest to persons in the field of economics. I would approach the Department of Economics at LSU to suggest a public event.

A secretary talked with me in the departmental office. She said she would pass my literature (including copies of my two articles in *Synthesis/Regeneration*) to the department chair. The students had a monthly economic forum which sometimes brought in outside speakers. That was one possibility. I thanked her and went on my way.

The day's mission was to complete my visits to newspaper offices in New Orleans or adjoining communities. Laplace and Boutte were on the west side of the metro area, *La Prensa* was on the north (Metairie), Arabi was on the east, and the *New Orleans Data News Weekly* was near downtown.

I had a pleasant and engaging conversation with the managing editor of *L'Observateur* in Laplace, Leonard Gray, and sat down for a length interview and photos. My trade proposals were of particular interest. The visit resulted in a front-page article on my candidacy which outlined my stands on issues. The article also described my books and articles on economic subjects at some length. Outsourcing, I said, was "the preferred (corporate) strategy for breaking unions." I was running for President because "the leading voices in the parties are not really addressing these issues." Gray introduced me to Ellen Ishmael, the publisher, prior to my departure.

After leaving Laplace, I crossed the Huey Long bridge to Boutte where I had been a week earlier, passing through that community on my way to New Orleans. Blake Petit, editor of the *St. Charles Herald-Guide*, did not have much time to talk but he took my literature and a photo. Around lunch time, I drove to Metairie and the offices of *La Prensa*. Although Juan Carlos had not yet called me back, his call on the previous day had given me a contact person. Street parking was hard to find. I parked on a side street blocks away and walked to the multistory office building at 111 Veterans Memorial Boulevard. La Prensa's offices were on the 18th floor, along with a Hispanic radio station. The receptionist located Juan Carlos. He took my literature but made no promises.

The day's only scheduled appointment was at the office of the *New Orleans Data News Weekly* at 3:00 p.m. Katrice called to remind me that Mr. Jones, the publisher, would see me then. Perhaps I had time for one more newspaper visit. I chose the *St. Bernard Voice* in Arabi. This decision precipitated a time squeeze and mid-afternoon panic. From the map it appeared that to reach Arabi I had to take I-10 east toward Slidell and then head south on I-510 which turns into highway 47, and finally turn right on Judge Perez Drive. I might save some time by taking U.S. highway 90 through the city and then joining I-510. Either way, it was a trip of perhaps 25 miles through a congested urban area. I had to call several times for directions but finally arrived at the office.

The *St. Bernard Voice* was run by an elderly brother and sister. The brother, Edwin Roy, was the editor. The sister, Mazie Roy Doody, was the advertising sales manager, doubling as receptionist. They were nice people. We talked for awhile about several things. The Roys believed that personal visits were important to political candidates. The father of the state's current secretary of state had been elected Governor of Louisiana by traveling the state just as I was doing. They were not sure about my economic proposals but agreed the times were troubled.

Meanwhile, I was nervous about the time. I was due at another newspaper in half an hour and it had taken me the better part of an hour to get here. Not to worry: My hosts assured me that from Arabi I could be in downtown New Orleans in less than twenty minutes. Just drive to the end of the street, turn left on St. Claude Avenue and cross the river. St. Claude Avenue becomes Rampart Street near downtown. Mazie sketched the route for me on a sheet of paper. And they were right. Despite city traffic, I did reach downtown in less than twenty minutes and was at my next appointment right on time. This was the stuff of dreams.

The office of the *New Orleans Data News Weekly* is located in a converted mansion on Napoleon Avenue just off the downtown loop. Finally I met Katrice. She took me into the private office of Terry Jones, the publisher, who appeared several minutes later. We spoke mainly about employment and the need for more leisure for working people. Jones did not disagree with my prescriptions but, being an entrepreneur, he also had doubts that workers would meet their work requirements in an undisciplined environment. He had been vice president of the national black newspapers association and knew Al McFarland, editor of *Insight News* in the Twin Cities. I spoke with Jones for almost half an hour. He said he would think about what coverage might be given to my campaign.

The newspaper in Belle Chasse, south of New Orleans, was also on my list for the day. Calling its office from downtown New Orleans, I was told that this was a bad day to visit. Try early next week. It appeared, then, that my appointments were done for the week. It had been a three-day week cut short by Mardi Gras. Speaking of which, I had not yet visited the French Quarter or done any late-night partying. This would be a good time to experience some of New Orleans' fabled night life. Could I leave Louisiana having ignored that part of its culture? Luckily, I found a parking space on St. Philip street and walked down Royal looking at window displays.

A fine arts shop had a box of large prints. Two caught my attention: portraits of Stonewall Jackson and of Robert E. Lee. The Lee portrait, in particular, would make a good souvenir. While in Milford in January, I had come across a letter from my father's sister, now deceased, disclosing that we were related to Robert E. Lee. Lee, she wrote, had been my father's maternal grandmother's first cousin. If only for this reason, I wanted to buy the Lee print. On the other hand, the night was reserved for partying. The print could wait. I did, however, buy my wife a cute feathered Mardi Gras mask with a bird-like beak at another shop.

A block over, on Bourbon Street near Bienville, there was a place called Red Rhino bar. Not many people were in the bar at this time of the day. An attractive young woman was talking with two men at a small table in the middle of the room. At one point, she did a solo dance, erotically running her fingers through her long hair. Beers cost $6.00 here but during happy-hour customers received three bottles for that price. I'm not a heavy beer drinker. I offered to give one of my bottles to the dancer when she came my way. She accepted and we struck up a conversation.

This woman told me that she was from Wisconsin and she had been in Louisiana for several months. She was living with her boy friend, also from Wisconsin. She was not happy about his apparent lack of interest in finding a job. She herself worked as a stripper at a club down the street. This may have been a result of low self-esteem brought on by a feeling that her father ignored her. We also talked about religion. She belonged to the religion of Wicca. It was hard for me to hear much of what she was saying because of the noise. We danced a rock 'n roll number together. I was proud of my ability to keep up with her lithe motions. Several minutes afterwards, she excused herself and walked out the door. After finishing my beer, I also exited the Red Rhino.

A block down Bourbon street, another woman came up to me on the street and asked if I would like to have a drink. Originally from New York, she had recently lost her job as a bartender in one of the French Quarter's drinking establishments. We went into the Famous Door bar where I bought drinks for her and myself. I think she was looking for a relationship more than drinks because she groaned when I said I was married and then groaned even more loudly when I said I had been married for only four years. I did not tell her why I was in Louisiana.

After drinking for awhile, this lady said she would call it a night. She would take a cab home. I was ready myself to drive back to Baton Rouge. I offered to drop her off on my way out of town. She was not up to walking the eight blocks to where my car was parked so I agreed to meet her at the Mango Daiquiri bar across the street. The woman was nowhere to be seen when I returned with the car. Having had enough post-Mardi Gras excitement for one evening, I returned to Baton Rouge. The alcohol content in my blood, diluted over time, did not seem to affect my driving.

CHAPTER TWENTY-SEVEN

Post–Mardi Gras Doldrums

The weekend which followed was a low point in my campaign from the standpoint of using time productively. As always, this was "down time" with respect to calling radio stations or visiting newspaper offices. It was not close enough to the date of the primary election to have a campaign event which local television crews might be interested in covering. That would be a possibility for the following weekend, prior to the election. The best use of my time, I thought, would be to scout locations for next weekend's events. Baton Rouge and New Orleans would be the places offering most voter exposure. I could pass out leaflets but, more importantly, decide where best to hold campaign events when the television crews covered them next week.

Saturday morning, February 28th, I returned to New Orleans. I first drove through Metairie to scout locations for an event in that area. There seemed not to be enough pedestrian traffic. Next I drove through downtown. Canal Street seemed the most promising place from a campaigner's point of view. The area above Magazine Street was lined with stores that attracted local cus-

tomers. The blocks toward the river were filled with tourists coming in and out of hotels. I could not find Woldenberg Park on my map; however, I did make note of the entrance to the

Riverwalk at the foot of Canal Street. A pelican statue marks the spot. A block up Canal Street was Harrah's Casino. Such places seemed to have plenty of people walking about who might have time to talk with me about politics.

A piece of unfinished business was to buy that print of Robert E. Lee from the fine-arts store. Unlike yesterday, there were no open parking spots in the French Quarter. I drove around for some time until I found an available space beyond Esplanade Avenue near the corner of Dauphine and Pauger. Then I walked ten blocks or so down Royal Street to the fine-arts store. The Lee print from yesterday was still unsold. While the sales person was wrapping the print in tissue paper before rolling it up and placing it inside a cardboard cylinder, I told her that I was a distant relative of Lee's. She treated me like a minor celebrity, shaking my hands warmly. I then told her that I was a candidate for President. Now she seemed to think I was nuts. Too many pieces of startling information at one time may be hard to accept.

Art work in hand, I walked back to my car. I knew the location since I had written the street names down on a scrap of paper but the car itself was nowhere to be seen. I walked up and down Pauger street for several blocks. The signs on the street said this was a "two-hour residential parking area". Did "residential parking" mean that only residents of the neighborhood could park there? Had the New Orleans police towed my car for violating that restriction? Or had I been a naive tourist who would leave a car packed with gear on the street in a high-crime city? Hopefully, car thieves would not want a 1995 Plymouth Acclaim. In any event, a sense of panic struck me. Eighty-five miles away from the night's confirmed motel reservation, I was standing on the streets of New Orleans with nothing more than a cardboard cylinder in my hand, keys to a vanished car, and a cell phone.

This cell phone was my link to the civilized world. I dialed Information for the numbers of the city's impound lot and the police department. Having written it down so often for motel-reservation clerks, I did know my license-plate number. No, the impound lot did not have a red Plymouth Acclaim with Minnesota plates displaying that number. Then I called the New Orleans police to report a "possibly stolen" car. What did "possibly stolen" mean? Was the car stolen or not? I did not know. The interrogator took some information about me and the car and said an officer would get back to me in a while.

Then I walked around the corner to Dauphine Street. There, half a block down, my bright red car sat unmolested at the side of the curb. I notified the police of this fortunate turn of events, turned the ignition key, and was on my way. It was around 4:30 p.m. I no longer felt like passing out leaflets. I had enough street-name information to write a press release for next week which would not embarrass me. My main mission had been accomplished as I drove back to Baton Rouge that evening.

Sunday, February 29th, was an unusual day in that this date appears on the calendar once every four years. I felt lucky to have an extra day for campaigning. As I had checked out locations for campaign events in New Orleans yesterday, so on this day I drove around Baton Rouge. The southern approach to the state capitol was a place that might be suitable for distributing political literature. The downtown area, several blocks away, was another. A third part of town, which I scouted first, was the campus of Louisiana State University - Baton Rouge.

I drove past the entrance to the Student Union near Highland Road. Several students were tossing frisbees on the lawn. On the other side of Highland, off campus, was a movie theater next to some food places. The sidewalk was crowded with young people. Was that because a film was letting out now? Would the same crowds be here next week? Along Nicholson Drive were people

heading for the LSU Tiger stadium to watch a baseball game. Would a game also be played next weekend? Would college sports fans be receptive to a presidential candidate passing out political literature? My uncertainty about these questions plus the lack of nearby parking spaces led me to seek a location elsewhere. Downtown Baton Rouge seemed largely deserted on Sundays except for church goers who would, of course, not want politicians to leaflet them after the service. That left the state capitol.

Small groups of people were walking up and down the marble steps that led to the front entrance of the capitol building. Most were Louisiana residents; some were from out of state. My campaign effort was directed at Louisiana voters. I went inside the building past the metal detectors. Cautiously, I asked a woman at an information booth what time of day most people visited this place. I had to be cautious. If I phrased my question the wrong way, she might think I was a terrorist. To identify myself as a presidential candidate might also set off alarms. The answer that I got from her and from a security guard was that on Sundays people often visited the state capitol after church. The building closed at 4 p.m. Any time between noon and closing time would be fine. The state capitol had one advantage over other Baton

Rouge locations: Visitors to this place would probably be interested in politics and, therefore, be less likely to be annoyed if a political candidate approached them. Yes, this was the place for next week's campaign event.

After ten days' lodging in Port Allen, I decided to spend Sunday night in Slidell to be closer to Monday's planned activities. That decision led to one of my best opportunities for media exposure. The cable-television selection at the Slidell Motel 6 included the New Orleans public-television station, WLAE-TV. One of that station's programs on Sunday evening was a political interview show called "Ringside: Politics with a Punch", hosted by Jeff Crouere. That night, February 29th, Crouere was interviewing a woman by phone about Mel Gibson's film "Passion of the Christ." Crouere also did personal commentary on political issues, personalities, and events. I liked the boxing theme as a metaphor for politics: It reminded me of my late friend in Minneapolis, Ray Whebbe, editor of the *Watchdog*, who was a wrestling and boxing promoter as well as a political journalist. I therefore made a note of this show.

Monday morning, March 1st, I drove west from Slidell on Interstate 12 toward Covington on the north side of Lake Pontchartrain. I had only two days left to visit the weekly newspapers before their deadlines for the last issue before the primary. In Covington, 
the editor of the *St. Tammany Farmer* had not yet come to work when I arrived. This was not an unwelcome event since it gave me time to catch up on a neglected chore. I began calling radio stations for interviews later in the week. These cell phone calls from the front seat of my car consumed nearly an hour. In the end, I had no firm commitments for interviews, just a request from a radio station in Opelousas to call when I came to town.

By that time, Danny Nowlin, editor of the Covington newspaper, was in the office. He interviewed me for fifteen minutes and took a photo. Then I was on my way to the second stop of the day. 

I was bound for the office of the *Plaquemines Gazette* in Belle Chasse on the southern edge of the New Orleans metropolitan area. The quickest route to that place was to take the Pontchartrain causeway across the lake. I had wanted to do that for some time. The twenty-five-mile trip went fast. Soon I was entering Metairie. The producer of the "Ringside" show, Jonathan McIntosh, had suggested that I send him a sample of my campaign literature. I was now able to deliver it in person at the studios of WLAE-TV on Causeway Boulevard. I then took I-10 through central New Orleans, turned onto U.S. 90, crossed the Mississippi River bridge, and took the exit for Belle Chasse. The newspaper office was about seven miles down this busy highway.

I arrived at lunch time. Gervais Joubert, the political reporter, was out on assignment. Did I care to wait? Fortunately, I was scheduled to be interviewed at 1:00 p.m. by Jayson Lee of the Thibodaux college radio station KNSU-FM. We had half an hour. I ordered a hamburger and soft drink at McDonald's and waited in the car. The cell-phone interview from the rear parking lot went well. I was able to make a smooth presentation of my economic proposals without sounding preachy or hurried. I then returned to the office of the *Plaquemines Gazette* two blocks away. Joubert had still not returned. I was looking through my papers when this reporter suddenly appeared. He explained that, while the paper was short on staff, he would write something about my campaign. I spent another ten minutes talking with him.

My final objective pushed the envelope. I drove more than one hundred miles down U.S. 90 and north on highway 1 to reach one

more newspaper office before the work day ended. This was the *Assumption Pioneer* in Napoleonville, which had a circulation of 2,600. At one point, I despaired of reaching this town by 5:00 p.m. and called the editor, Philip Gianelloni, to tell him so. He said they'd be working late that evening. I could decide if the trip was worthwhile. A kindly older man, Gianelloni took the time to talk with me while a female employee tried to figure out Quark, the computer software used to lay out the paper. No, I did not know Quark; I had some experience with Pagemaker. Economic issues were important to readers there. Gianelloni told me that politicians had plans for revitalizing the local economy by turning this area into a transportation hub. A new airport would be the key. I took leave of him and the woman at the computer and drove back to Port Allen by way of Plaquemine. Then, looking over the next day's schedule, I decided to drive an additional 110 miles to Alexandria.

Realistically, this was my last day to visit community newspapers before the primary. On the morning of Tuesday, March 2nd, I set forth from Alexandria bound for Jonesville on highways 28 and 84. The office of the *Jonesville Catahoula News Booster* had been closed when I last visited this town on February 13th. The editor, Will Clifton, talked with me in his office. There was still time to put something in the paper before tomorrow's deadline. I was not so lucky at the next place, Jena, 23 miles up the road. Sammy Franklin, editor of the *Jena Times Olla-Tullos Signal*, greeted me warmly and introduced me to his son. He remembered the message that I had left for him two weeks earlier. Unfortunately, the deadline for the last issue before the primary had passed. I left literature anyhow.

Two African American newspapers in Monroe, another 75 miles north, remained unvisited. The person who answered the phone at the *Monroe Dispatch* told me that they were not interested in a visit from me. At the other paper, the *Monroe Free Press*, I was told that I needed to speak with the publisher, Roosevelt Wright, and was given his home phone number. Wright's wife answered. Wright himself soon called back to report that he was tied up in a conference running into the afternoon. He might be free around 3 p.m. If so, he would call me and we could meet somewhere. I never did receive a call. By that time, however, I was traveling along country roads in the same northernmost parishes that I had visited on my first day of campaigning in Louisiana.

Farmerville was the first stop. Unfortunately, the paper's next issue came out on the Wednesday following the primary. Then I drove west to Bernice. I stopped at the city's Tourist Information Center to receive directions to Boyett Road where the office of the *Bernice Banner-News* was located. Boyett Road, named for the newspaper's publisher, was a small road off U.S. highway 63 two miles north of town leading back half a mile toward town. The paper was published in what looked like a farm house. Violet Lann, the advertising manager, kept me engaged in pleasant conversation for twenty minutes. She was a former school teacher from Arkansas who had closely followed Bill Clinton's career when he was governor.

The editor and publisher, Jesse Boyett, arrived twenty minutes later. Her husband, recently retired from Exxon/Mobil, was now helping her with the paper. Didn't I agree they put out a good product? Yes, I did. Jesse Boyett remembered having received my email. She also remembered some of Louisiana's recent political campaigns including the gubernatorial race a decade earlier where the choice was between a former Ku Klux Klan official (David Duke) and a man now serving a prison sentence (Edwin Edwards). These two women were well informed about politics. They gave me a copy of the *Banner-News* before I departed.

If I was lucky, I thought, I might catch one more newspaper before closing time, the *Springhill Press*. This newspaper I might have visited on the first day of my campaign had the receptionist been more encouraging. Springhill was sixty miles west and north of Bernice by way of Homer. I almost missed the newspaper office as I drove through town. Today was the paper's deadline. I handed a person at the counter my campaign leaflet along with a photo, trusting that something could be done before the primary. Next I called the office of the *Caddo Citizen* in Vivian in the northwest corner of the state. It was too late; their publishing deadline was yesterday. Then, sitting in the car across the street from the Springhill newspaper office, I made a number of cell phone calls.

Most of the calls were to radio stations. I lined up an interview with the Shreveport station KEEL-AM for the following morning. I left messages for Captain Glenn in Houma and Wandell Allegood in Opelousas. Other calls, however, were made to the advertising departments of newspapers where I planned to place paid ads. One-inch ads would be run Sunday, March 7th, through Tuesday, March 9th, in six different newspapers: New Orleans, Baton Rouge, Shreveport, Lafayette, Lake Charles, and Alexandria.

It was time to nail down Shreveport and Alexandria. In both cases, I encountered an unexpected obstacle. The rates previously quoted were invalid because someone had determined that, being a national political candidate, I needed to pay the national

advertising rate. For three days, a one-inch ad in *The Times* of Shreveport would cost me $272.00 rather than the $165.00 previously quoted. Sputtering into the phone, I told the sales representative to cancel the entire order. However, Shreveport was just too important to dismiss. Calling back later, I agreed to run the ad on Sunday only for $146.00. Likewise, the sales representative at the *Alexandria Daily Town Talk* quoted me a price at the national advertising rate that was higher than what was previously quoted. These people were stick-up artists. I drove through Shreveport and back to Alexandria to spend the night.

That evening, the results came in for the "Super Tuesday" primaries. John Kerry won convincingly in all contests. Little did I know then that this day's primaries would seal my own fate as a candidate in the Louisiana primary election that would be held the following week. A decision made next day by the man from North Carolina sucked the oxygen out of the race.

CHAPTER TWENTY-EIGHT

Wrapping up in Lafayette
and the Central Part of the State

I taped a radio interview with Mike Seavey of Shreveport station KEEL-AM at 9:00 a.m. on Wednesday, March 3rd, from my motel room in Alexandria. Several large-circulation newspapers south of the city remained to be visited that day. The most important was Lafayette's *Daily Advertiser*. I had a promise from its managing editor that reporter Lou Rom would do a story about my campaign.

Another paper not to be ignored was the *Bunkie Record* (and *Avoyelles Journal*) in Bunkie 25 miles down U.S. highway 71. I spoke with its editor, Garland Forman, after waiting for a short time in his office. He gave me the bad news first: Monday had been the deadline for the last issue before the primary. Even so, we had a good discussion about economic ideas. The subject of jobs was important to people in that area. It was a shame that I hadn't stopped by sooner. A Libertarian candidate, for instance, had visited Bunkie and received coverage in the paper. Forman advised me to go to Lafayette without further delay.

While driving south that day, I mulled over the election results from "Super Tuesday". North Carolina Senator John Edwards announced that he was dropping out of the race. This meant that John Kerry was the only serious contender left for the Democratic nomination. That being the case, the primary season was effectively over. It was over for the people hoping to be nominated though, of course, not for me. What to do now? I thought I should send a special message to Louisiana voters that they should consider voting for me in the primary even though John Kerry would be opposing President Bush in the general election. Yes, that was the formula: Vote for McGaughey in the primary and for Kerry in the general election. I would change the ads accordingly.

I also thought I needed stronger advertising support now that Kerry's nomination was assured. While driving, I composed a second one-inch ad which would run on the same days as the other. It began with a catchy phrase. The ad read: "We can't innovate, educate, or incarcerate our way out of this 'jobless recovery.' Try employer-specific tariffs. Vote for Bill McGaughey in the Louisiana Democratic primary and for John Kerry in the general election." The first ad was changed to: "Vote for Bill McGaughey in March 9th Democratic primary. He's for tariffs on imports from low-wage countries. Send a message on trade. In November, vote for John Kerry."

In both ads I was signaling my support of the Democratic nominee while asking people to vote for me in the primary. Why? Because of the trade problem. I was for tariffs, not the wishy-washy solutions proposed by other candidates. Send them a message.

While we were at it, why not advertise also in Monroe, Louisiana's eighth largest city? That would give coverage to Louisiana's nine largest cities. (Kenner would be covered by an ad in the New Orleans paper; Bossier City, by one in the Shreveport paper.) Monroe was a special case because of the State Farm job loss. Instead of using the boilerplate ad, I composed the following: "Life after State Farm? Save our jobs. Stop job loss to low-wage countries with employer-specific tariffs. Send a message on trade. Vote for Bill McGaughey in March 9th Dem. presidential primary and for John Kerry in the general election."

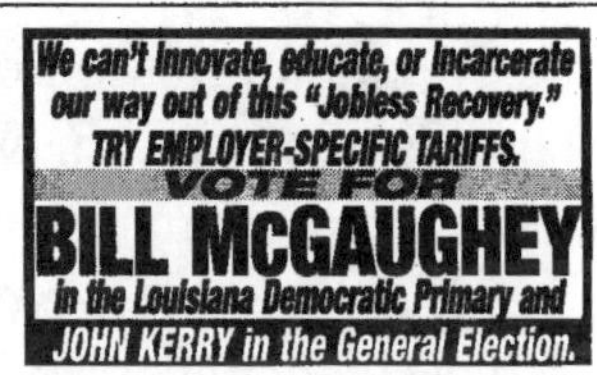

New Orleans

New Orleans

Baton Rouge

Baton Rouge

Lafayette

Lafayette

Alexandria

Alexandria

Shreveport

I called the sales representative at the *News-Star* in Monroe. Yes, I could place this ad in the paper but it would not fit in one column inch. My proposed ad would require three column inches of space. The price per insertion was $272.00. In other words, the Monroe newspaper, which had a weekday circulation of fewer than 40,000 readers, would charge me almost as much for a single insertion as the Baton Rouge paper did for three insertions including Sunday; and *The Advocate* had a weekday circulation of more than 100,000. True, the proposed copy for the *News-Star* ad had six more words than the longer of my two ads, but there was no way it could require three times as much space.

This time, I put my foot down: Reduce the ad to one column inch or it's no deal. The sales representative said he would double-check. In the late afternoon, I reached his assistant who confirmed that three column inches would be needed for the ad. Therefore, I did not advertise in Monroe.

I reached Lafayette in the early afternoon. Lou Rom was available to interview me for an article in the *Daily Advertiser*. I was in a feisty mood in defending my trade proposals. Rom was equally fired up. Here was a news reporter, much like Kevin Diaz, who was candid and to-the-point. What was the source of the information in my flier about overtime having risen by one third? I said the news clipping containing this information was in a folder in my car.

After we had talked about issues, Rom said I had to give him more personal information. Add a little color to the story. I thought Rom might be interested in my picking up the hitchhiker outside Lafayette and driving to the Mardi Gras parade in Lake Charles. That story did not make the cut. What did was the disclosure that I had once taken a literature course from Robert Penn Warren at Yale. The Louisiana connection was, of course, to Huey Long.

As always, the focus of Rom's story was: What was I doing in running for President? What was my motivation? The personal color took the form of reporting, among other things, that my car had 138,000 miles on it, that I wore "thrifty clothes (with) a short, fat circa '70s tie that stops a foot short of his belt buckle", and carried "a forest green tote bag stuffed with papers." This candidate was not exactly a spring chicken. Rom wanted a picture of me standing at my car next to the magnetic campaign sign. He and a photographer accompanied me to the parking spot a block away.

That mission accomplished, I was off to Opelousas and then to Ville Platte. In Opelousas, I visited radio station KSLO-AM, following up on the contact made two days earlier. A broadcaster named John Wright took me into the recording studio where he asked me to say something about the campaign. I talked non-stop for five minutes. Wright thought that this was what he wanted. Then, as an afterthought, he commented that not many politicians visited the station - except once when the Governor, a U.S. Senator, and a Congressman all showed up unannounced at the same time. He said I might enjoy a recording that a colorful sheriff had made in the same studio during a reelection campaign in 1964. This sheriff was a homespun character who, in his broadcast, referred to the use of government employees as campaign "volunteers". It was good for a laugh.

My last stop of the day was in Ville Platte. I spoke at the counter with an employee of the *Ville Platte Gazette* in its offices on Court Street, so-named because the Evangeline Parish court house was on the corner. The editor, Carissa Hebert, who handled this type of interview, was not in. An employee wrote her name and number on a green slip of paper, urging me to come back tomorrow. I left literature and a photo. Then I drove back to Lafayette to spend the night at the Motel 6. Along the way, I called the *Fort Polk Guardian* at the military base outside Leesville. The editor said that, being a military publication, her paper was not allowed to report on political campaigns. There had, of course, been much publicity during President Bush's visit.

I also called Ed Anderson at the New Orleans paper. It was then that he told me that Keith O'Brien, another *Times-Picayune* reporter, had been trying to contact me for some time. I called the New Orleans office immediately and spoke with O'Brien. He was working on deadline but would have time to talk after 6 p.m. When we did talk, O'Brien asked basic questions about my campaign. He would see if some of this material might be included in a wrap-up story about the Louisiana presidential primary before the election. The night's news was focusing on John Edwards' withdrawal from the race.

Next morning, Thursday, March 4th, I prepared for my final visit to a newspaper office. The *Daily World* in Opelousas was one of the few dailies in the state not yet covered. Fortunately, this city was only 24 miles north of Lafayette on I-49. I also called the *Leesville Leader* but could not make arrangements for a visit. For someone who had been to Opelousas the day before, I was extraordinarily inept in locating the newspaper office. It was along a service road paralleling I-49 on the south side of town. No reporters were available when I arrived early in the morning. Some were expected in an hour. So, as I had done in Covington Monday morning, I sat in the car phoning radio stations. The time went by quickly.

This round of telephoning brought bad news from Brittany Shay of Baton Rouge station WFMF-FM. They probably would not use me. If they did, it would be Monday or Tuesday morning of next week. On the other hand, when I called another Baton Rouge station, I spoke with Jim Engster, producer and host of a morning interview show. He asked me to call back at 10:15 a.m. When I did, Engster said he would put me on the air at 9:50 a.m. on Tuesday, March 9th, which was the day of the primary election. I wrote down both times in my notebook. The failure to label them properly would cost me dearly.

I also managed to reach Marsha Shuler by phone in her state-capitol office for the first time since February 6th. No, *The Advocate* still had not run anything about my campaign. Perhaps the material I had given her would be used in a wrap-up story about the primary which would appear next Tuesday. I stressed how hard I had campaigned in the state; I had traveled more than 7,000 miles and visited 60 plus cities since the campaign began a month earlier.

Returning to the office of the *Daily World*, I was assigned a reporter named Stephanie Kirk. She interviewed me in a conference room near the front door. We covered both my economic issues and the campaign's rationale. She had a picture taken of me. I was gone within twenty minutes. This was my last newspaper visit of the campaign.

The day's main event, I thought, would be the taping of Jeff Crouere's interview on WLAE-TV's "Ringside: Politics with a Punch." Yes, I was a political candidate with an issues-packed punch to deliver; or was I, by then, simply punch drunk? In any event, I took the engagement seriously. Television was the best way to connect with voters and I had ten full minutes on a New Orleans station with a well-known political personality.

Jonathan McIntosh, the producer, had requested that I be in the Metairie studio at 4:15 p.m. on Thursday. The show would air on Friday at 8:30 p.m. and then again on Sunday evening. The WLAE-TV studio was on the campus of New Orleans University - Jefferson. Although its park-ing lot was full, a security guard allowed me to park by the building in a reserved spot, seeing that I was a guest on the television show. After waiting in the lobby for several minutes, I was led to a back room where Jennifer, a make-up artist, prepared me for the interview.

Jeff Crouere was interviewing the first guest of the evening, a columnist who wrote for the *Times-Picayune*. I watched the studio monitors in another room. In my green canvas bag were copies of the three books that I had published on economic subjects. I hoped to use them as props during the interview. In the meanwhile, there seemed to be a delay in taping the segment with me. The first guest picked up his belongings near me. On the monitor, I could see Crouere relaxing in his seat in the studio, leafing through sheets of paper. A message on the screen told how viewers could order videotaped copies of the show by contacting WLAE-TV.

Then, suddenly, I saw another announcement to the effect that today's show would air on March 12th. WHAT? The primary election was on March 9th. What was the point of doing this show if it aired after the primary? When I ran into McIntosh in the hall, he confirmed that there had been a scheduling mix-up. The March 12th date was correct. However, Jeff Crouere was also the host of a radio talk show on New Orleans station WTIX-AM. He might arrange to put me on his radio show before the primary.

The interview itself was OK although I have a lot to learn about television. Crouere seemed pleased that I had contacted the show's producer because I had seen "Ringside" on cable television in my motel room in Slidell. He was a skilled interviewer. On the other hand, I may have tried too hard to force what I had to say into the discussion framed by Crouere's questioning. He let me go into my monologues for only so long before pulling me back to another subject. I never did find a suitable time to display my books.

We went through my arguments on trade and on the need for shorter working hours. I tried to explain why my presidential candidacy was worthwhile for Louisiana voters. Now that Kerry was effectively nominated, that motive for voting in a primary became less important while "sending a message on trade" made increasing sense. However, since the "Ringside" show would air after the primary, that appeal was itself less relevant. Crouere did confirm, however, that he would invite me to participate in his radio call-in show next week.

It was evening. I drove back to Port Allen to spend the night once again at the Motel 6. Angel was again at the front desk. First, however, I indulged myself in another dinner at Shoney's.

While pulling into the restaurant parking lot, I took a cell phone call from Lou Rom. He was putting the finishing touches on his story about my campaign. Did I know how many delegates Louisiana had at the Democratic convention? Embarrassingly, I had hardly thought about this question. Rom said he could find out. He asked about Robert Penn Warren. I suggested, once again, the story about me and the desperate hitchhiker. Rom said his article would be appearing in the next few days. If we were lucky, it would run in Sunday's paper. He proposed that I call him if I came to Lafayette again. Perhaps we could have coffee.

CHAPTER TWENTY-NINE

Fax Machines and Plantations in Baton Rouge

When I woke up in the morning of Friday, March 5th, television was on my mind. With the possible exception of the *Times-Picayune*, it was too late to seek newspaper coverage. I would have two separate ads running for three consecutive days in five big-city newspapers and a single ad appearing on Sunday in Shreveport. Maybe I could catch voters' attention by delivering a clear message on trade.

The open opportunities at this point lay with television. Hopefully, the stations' news departments would conclude, with the primary date drawing near, that viewers wanted more political coverage. Appearances on television so close to the election would give me a huge boost. On the other hand, political pundits had decided that the contest for the Democratic presidential nomination was over now that John Edwards had withdrawn from the race.

My first order of business Friday morning was to prepare press releases that I could fax to television stations in Baton Rouge and New Orleans announcing that, as a presidential candidate, I would be out on the street shaking handing with voters that weekend. How to identify me? First, I told the news reporters where and when I would be making campaign appearances. Second, I would be wearing a colorful hat. This was not the large purple sombrero worn during Mardi Gras but a white cowboy hat purchased recently at a gas station in Port Allen. Nowadays such hats seem unpresidential but I was not a conventional candidate. I thought this hat might have regional appeal - more so the closer one came to the Texas border. It might work, for instance, in a place like Shreveport.

Several times I tried to contact Melinda Deslatte of the Associated Press Baton Rouge bureau. She was away on assignment in New Orleans. I left cell phone messages for her which were never returned. This did not bode well for my "local event" in Baton Rouge. Also, there had been no response from the economics department at Louisiana State University. I had left a telephone message for the chairman of the department and not heard from him. Friday morning, I was still hoping for last-minute miracles.

I thought that my press releases should be typed rather than be handwritten. The Kinko's shop in downtown Baton Rouge rented computers with printers. I wrote out what I wanted to say and drove there. It cost about $10 to produce and print the press releases going to newspapers and television stations in four different cities. The fax machine was out of service at the Kinko's in downtown Baton Rouge. I knew that the one at the Motel 6 in Port Allen was also malfunctioning. Was there another Kinko's nearby which had a fax machine? Yes, the clerk suggested the one on Airline Highway. I drove to that store and was directed to its self-service fax machine. The faxes sent to Baton Rouge phone numbers could be sent at a reasonable price but those to out-of-town numbers would cost me $2.00 per page. I had twenty-two pages to send.

After sending the Baton Rouge faxes, I stormed out of the Kinko's unsure of my next move. By chance, I noticed that another Motel 6 was located on Airline Highway on the other side of a car dealership. Perhaps if I told the desk clerk that I was staying at its sister facility in Port Allen and that the fax machine there was broken, I could get my faxes done here at a reasonable rate. The ploy worked. A pleasant young woman behind the counter named Heidi agreed to send my faxes. We did not discuss price. She had first to take care of other business. That lasted about for ten minutes while I browsed through tourist brochures in the office.

This motel was having to evict a nonpaying tenant. Heidi's job was to call the police for assistance in removing the person. The Baton Rouge police dispatchers had made it clear that they did not appreciate taking such calls. As a landlord, I was familiar with that attitude. A sign on the wall said that Motel 6 allowed "well-behaved pets" in the rooms. How could they tell which pets were "well-behaved", I wondered. Actually, Heidi said, it was "one, small well-behaved pet." Someone had once tried to sneak a horse into the room. That wasn't allowed, of course. This type of conversation went on while Heidi was faxing my twenty-two pages. In the end, she charged me only $4.00 for the lot.

The stop here changed my plans in another way. Several of the tourist brochures had caught my eye. One was about touring an alligator-infested bayou in a motor boat. Several advertised tours of antebellum homes or  plantations in the area. The tourist instinct overcame me. I would be leaving Louisiana in the middle of next week and still had not done much sightseeing. There was a brochure for a place called "BREC's Magnolia Mound Plantation" not far from downtown Baton Rouge. Tours were available on weekdays during certain hours for $8.00 per adult. It was 2 p.m. and the day's work was done. I decided to spend the remaining hours of the day enjoying myself as a tourist at the Magnolia Mound Plantation which was located on Nicholson Drive.

A family from France pulled into the parking lot ahead of me. The woman in charge of the office found a French-speaking tour guide for them. She assigned to me a young woman named Cheryl who was dressed in period costume. I would be the only person on her tour. We first visited the main house, built in the

last decade of the 18th century. This house, Baton Rouge's oldest, was built of cypress wood. It was an example of Louisiana's creole culture. Cheryl told me about some of the early owners. One was a close friend of Lafayette's. In the early 20th century, a mayor of Baton Rouge had lived there. Later, a developer wanted to tear the building down to build a large apartment but historic preservationists had saved it.

We went through rooms in this mansion as Cheryl explained the furnishings. One could see differences between the boys' and girls' rooms. Bibles on tables in all the rooms showed the importance of Christianity to these people. Admittedly, some of their religious zeal reflected the fact that, under Spain, only Christians enjoyed the rights of citizenship. Cheryl also took me outside to see the kitchen garden. The slave quarters were across the lawn. She herself was dying to put on her regular clothes because the costume was hard to keep in place.

Besides information given as part of the tour, I was interested in what Cheryl had to say about herself and her people. She was a Cajun girl from Houma, studying psychology at LSU. After graduation, she hoped to attend seminary and then become a social worker who worked with troubled women - battered women, single mothers, etc. Her father and uncles were big sports fans who rooted for LSU. Cheryl told me that Huey Long was quite popular among LSU students and faculty because he had wangled the funds to build a sports stadium. When the legislature would not go for such a frivolous project, Long told them that he was building dormitories. He arranged the dormitories in a circle and put a stadium inside.

Also, did I know that right before the Civil War William Tecumseh Sherman had been the president of LSU? He had warned people in Louisiana not to secede from the union. It would have been better if they had listened to him. Cheryl explained the strategy of the northern forces during the Civil War: (1) gain control of the Mississippi river and cut off Texas, (2) blockade the South from the ocean, (3) let Sherman's armies devastate Georgia, thus isolating the southern forces further. I learned a lot from Cheryl.

I did not know then that, while I was having these interesting conversations in Baton Rouge, John Kerry was making his first and only campaign appearance in New Orleans. He held a noontime rally Friday along the Mississippi waterfront near Woldenberg Park and, of course, received much television and newspaper coverage. Kerry later had lunch with Louisiana's U.S. Senator, Mary Landrieu, rumored to be on his list of possible running mates.

Not only was I toiling in obscurity; I was also beginning to relax my campaign effort and have a little fun before I left the state. As far as the media was concerned, Kerry was the only candidate left to be covered in the presidential race.

The primary was effectively over. It was a waste of time and money even to hold an election. I was committed to carrying on the fight to the end. Tomorrow would be my big play for television coverage in New Orleans and then, in Baton Rouge, on the following day. But I was already feeling distracted and, like a distance runner short of breath, slackening my pace.

CHAPTER THIRTY

Available for Television

When I bought a copy of the *Times-Picayune* Saturday morning, March 6th, I was startled to read an article by Keith O'Brien about a presidential candidate named Bill Wyatt who was challenging President Bush in the Republican primary. This article took up an entire page of the newspaper - page A-14. Why couldn't it have been *me*?

Wyatt was a 43-year-old tee-shirt manufacturer from California who had entered several primaries. He had received only 153 votes in New Hampshire but, in Oklahoma, had captured nearly 10 percent of the vote as President Bush's sole challenger. O'Brien's article described some of Wyatt's campaign activities during the week spent in Louisiana. He had talked with customers at a 24-hour diner on Tulane Avenue in New Orleans. He had attended a candidates' forum at a sorority house. He hadn't yet been to Shreveport or Baton Rouge but was making plans. Why couldn't I have done this? How did the publicity bonanza come Wyatt's way?

I learned the truth only after returning to Minneapolis. There among my accumulated email messages was one from Keith O'Brien, dated February 3rd. After identifying himself, O'Brien wrote: "I am interested in doing a story about you, and the other lesser known candidates, who will be campaigning for president in Louisiana next month. What I was hoping to do is follow you around when you come here, if you are planning to come here, and essentially be a fly on the wall of your day, or days, on the road in Louisiana. And then write a story about it. So when you get a chance, drop me an email, call me at the number below, or let me know how I can reach you on the road."

Had I delayed my departure from Minnesota for just one day, I might have received this message. Had I bothered to access my email messages on the road from Earthlink's web message center, I might still have reached O'Brien in time for him to write a story. I assumed, however, that Ed Anderson was my link to the *Times-Picayune*. I had failed to cover all the bases.

This day, Saturday, March 6th, was devoted to New Orleans. In my faxed press release, I had promised to spend six hours walking along Canal Street between Magazine Street and the entrance to Riverwalk while wearing my white cowboy hat. I had long since decided not to lug the sign and metal stand around with me. I would, however, be carrying my green canvas bag stuffed with campaign leaflets, a bottle of water, and a few snacks. I would be wearing a tan sports coat to which was pinned a plastic badge identifying me as a presidential candidate. Saturday parking was no problem. Instead of seeking out my usual spot on Perdido Street, I parked a block off Canal on North Villere.

The pedestrian traffic on Canal Street was brisk. I approached a group of Christian street musicians who preparing for a performance. They asked if they could pray with me. In a small circle, we held hands and said a prayer. I gave my campaign pitch for a minute or so. They gave me a leaflet titled "This could be your last five minutes alive."

I spoke with people on the sidewalk, mostly blacks, and handed them campaign literature. Most people were friendly. Some were quite interested in talking with a presidential candi-

date. Below Magazine Street, I ran into mostly tourists. That meant that a majority of persons there were not eligible to vote in Louisiana. In theory, I was wasting their time. Therefore, I had to begin each campaign pitch with a question: Are you a Louisiana voter? Many were not. It might have been better to campaign in another location. Yet, this was where I had committed myself to be when the television crews tried to find me. I was doing this for television coverage.

Six hours on New Orleans' main street was tiring business. My energy level waxed and waned during the afternoon. I wandered about the Riverwalk area and saw the place where John Kerry had held his campaign rally on the previous day. I saw a Kerry flier announcing that event inside USA Today's locked newspaper stand. That's a candidate who has the inside track, I mused.

I talked with a young Chinese man who was attending LSU in Baton Rouge. He and his family posed for a picture. I spoke with a man from Memphis, Tennessee, who promised to give my campaign literature to some of his Louisiana friends. On Riverwalk, I walked down the boardwalk toward a cruise ship moored at the dock in the Mississippi river and read the many signs which told of Louisiana's history and culture. A magnificent fountain celebrated Spain's contribution to the history of this area. And, of course, 2004 was the 200th anniversary of the Louisiana Purchase made by our farsighted third President. Still no television crews had showed up to cover my campaign.

Around 4:30 p.m., I finally found Woldenberg Park. It was the stretch of Riverwalk in the opposite direction from the cruise boat. Yes, this was a good place for campaigning. Benches lined the walk

way which were filled with people tired of walking who were hopefully not too tired to talk with me about politics. But I was exhausted by that time. After working the crowd for twenty minutes, I bought a $3.00 bottle of beer and a $14.00 ticket to view a film about the Lewis and Clark Expedition in the Audubon I-Max theater starting at 5:00 p.m. The theater was cool and the beer relaxed me thoroughly.

So here I was in New Orleans watching an adventure story about an early 19th Century exploration of a river in the Upper Midwest - my part of the country - having temporarily suspended my presidential campaign. I was now counting the days before my own great adventure would come to an end. The movie was finished. Right after this, I walked up Canal Street, had dinner at Popeye's fast-food restaurant, saw a new type of Amhoist crane (my former employer), made a few cell-phone calls in the car to people in Minnesota, glanced down Basin Street, and then drove back to Baton Rouge. So long, New Orleans.

Sunday morning, March 7th, started the three-day run of newspaper campaign ads. The day's project was to purchase copies of these newspapers from as many of the cities as I could find. Copies of the *Times-Picayune* and *The Advocate* Sunday papers were available from news racks outside the Port Allen Motel 6 or across the road at Love's gas station. Since I drove to Shreveport that day, I was also able to pick up copies of the *Daily Advertiser* in Lafayette, the *Daily Town Talk* in Alexandria, and, of course, *The Times* in Shreveport. Yes, the newspapers delivered what was promised, each with its own creativity.

In the privacy of my motel room, I reflected upon the campaign. While yesterday's event was disappointing, I was still optimistic. I was telling people that I expected to attract 5% to 10% of the primary vote. I wrote in my notebook that the basis for expecting a good result was: (1) the 60 newspaper offices that I had visited, (2) the ads run in the state's largest-circulation newspapers, (3) the radio interviews already done with several more scheduled, (4) the personal handshaking and leafletting, and (5) the fact that some Louisiana voters would resent that Kerry had locked up the nomination so soon and might want to vote for someone else just to show that their vote counted.

Today's campaign effort was relatively modest. I had committed myself to campaigning on the front steps of the Louisiana state capitol between 1:30 p.m. and 4:30 p.m. Compared with yesterday, the crowds were sparse. One or two people passed by every ten minutes, worse than the previous week. My hopes were lifted when a mobile unit belonging to Baton Rouge station WAFB-TV (channel 9) parked in the state capitol lot not far from my car. The reporters ignored me. They were there because the Governor was convening a special session of the legislature that evening to consider tax reform. I later learned that Governor Blanco was hosting a reception at her mansion for John Kerry's wife, Teresa.

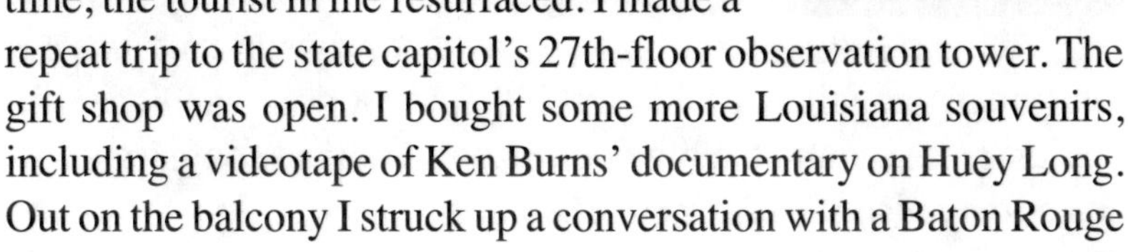

In an afternoon lull before closing time, the tourist in me resurfaced. I made a repeat trip to the state capitol's 27th-floor observation tower. The gift shop was open. I bought some more Louisiana souvenirs, including a videotape of Ken Burns' documentary on Huey Long. Out on the balcony I struck up a conversation with a Baton Rouge

couple who had taken my campaign literature on the front steps. They reminisced with me about Louisiana politics. Huey Long's brother, Earl K. Long, was mentally unstable. More than once, he was committed to a mental hospital but, being the Governor, he was able to check himself out. (Another version of this story has Long firing the hospital superintendent.) Residents of Louisiana, including this couple, were proud of the state's athletic accomplishments. LSU teams had won national championships both in football and baseball.

No Baton Rouge reporters covered my campaigning at the Louisiana state capitol. I had a long drive ahead of me. The night's motel reservation was in Bossier City where I had stayed during my first few days in Louisiana. There were 276 miles to drive before I would sleep. Interstate driving would take me most of the way there. I headed west to Lafayette on I-10 and then north on I-49 past Alexandria all the way to Shreveport, picking up Sunday newspapers along the way. I pulled into Shreveport well after dark, gassed up, and checked into the Bossier City Motel 6.

Here in the northern cities of Louisiana would be my last opportunity to attract television coverage. Despite recent disappointments, I felt that Shreveport and Monroe might come through for me where New Orleans and Baton Rouge had failed. I told myself that the serious candidates do not just hang around the big population centers of southern Louisiana; they also spend time in the north.

CHAPTER THIRTY-ONE

In Shreveport and Monroe on the Day before the Election

For better or worse, Monday, March 8th, may have been the most important day in my campaign. It was the day before the primary. On that day, I was seeking television news coverage in two large cities, Shreveport and Monroe. Additionally, there were promises from two radio talk-show hosts, Christopher Tidmore and Jeff Crouere, to put me on the air in New Orleans although specific arrangements had not yet been made. Portia Evans of station KFXZ-FM in Lafayette had said that she would call me for an interview in my motel room at 8:45 a.m. By the end of the day, I had done television events in both cities as well as the radio interview with Crouere. Everything else fell through.

I waited in my room at the Motel 6 for the call from Evans. It never came. I was not able to reach her for an explanation. The next item of business was the television appearance. My press release to Shreveport media had said that I would be standing on the corner of Texas and Marshall streets in front of the Caddo court house between 9:30 a.m. and 11:30 a.m. This place was not far from the motel but I had to hurry. A number of people walked past me. The traffic on Texas Street produced a certain level of noise.

Standing here on the corner, I placed cell phone calls to Jeff Crouere and Christopher Tidmore. Crouere said he would interview me for twenty minutes that afternoon starting at 12:45 p.m. Tidmore asked me to call him tomorrow - or so I thought - at 4:45 p.m. Our interview on New Orleans station WVOG-AM, the second with him, would be for fifteen minutes. Tidmore said listeners would be interested in local elections in places such as Kenner. I might refer to that fact but then add that a presidential primary was also taking place.

Wearing my white cowboy hat, I handed out leaflets to persons passing by. Then lightning struck. A man with a large television camera on his shoulder approached me to say that he would like to do an interview. He asked me to state my issues and say something about myself. In an uninspired way, I went on for five minutes or so as the camera rolled. Then the man taped statements from others. A slender black man confirmed that jobs were a big issue for him. Others declined to be interviewed. After he thought he had enough footage, the reporter walked down the block to take background shots of the court house. He said he was from the NBC affiliate in Shreveport, KTAL-TV, Channel 6.

The event had fulfilled its purpose. Even so, I continued to stand on the corner passing out literature until the two-hour period had elapsed. Then I had two-and-a-half hours to drive to Monroe, almost one hundred miles away, to see if the same type of event would work there. First I needed to do the interview with Jeff Crouere on WTIX-AM. I pulled off the highway and waited for his call. My cell phone rang at the expected time and we had the interview, covering some of the same topics as in the television interview. I was satisfied. However, this interview and other delays had put me behind schedule for the appearance in Monroe.

The press release had said that I would spend two hours campaigning in front of the Monroe Civic Center, starting at 2:30 p.m. I raced east on Interstate 20. The sights were familiar to me from having driven along the same highway weeks earlier. I arrived in Monroe with minutes to spare. With one eye on the map and the other on  the highway, I determined which exit to take in Monroe. I found the way to the Civic Center and pulled alongside the curb. The place was deserted.

Immediately my cell phone rang. "Paul" of KTVE-TV was on the line. How could this be? Paul (Turner) asked me to look up; he and a news reporter were standing near a van parked a hundred feet in front of me. I pulled my car up to the van. While Paul was setting his camera on the tripod, the reporter, whose name was Stephen Webster, introduced himself. He said they did not have much time for the interview. Both he and Paul were relatively new employees of the station. Their efficiency-minded employer had given them a number of assignments to complete that day. That's OK, I said, "I'm also new at this job of presidential campaigning."

When Paul was ready to shoot, Stephen asked me a number of questions. The Civic Center was our backdrop. Still under the spell of the high-speed drive to Monroe, I replied in a slick monologue as if on automatic pilot. After this performance Stephen said that I knew my issues and made the arguments sound interesting and clear. So it was a successful interview - maybe the best of the campaign. Paul and Stephen packed up their gear and were on their way to the next assignment. I stood there on the sidewalk wondering what to do next.

The area in front of the Monroe Civic Center was deserted. It was approaching 3:00 p.m. I had promised to stay there until 4:30 p.m. If another television crew showed up, I would look foolish campaigning when no one else was around. Where were the people? On the spur of the moment, I decided to drive through downtown Monroe in search of an alternative site. Once it was located, I would call the remaining television stations to inform them of my change in plans. I therefore drove up and down streets in the downtown area. None had significant pedestrian traffic. The city seemed a bit run-down.

From my visit to Monroe several weeks earlier, I remembered seeing a crowd of students when I did the public-radio interview on the LSU-Monroe campus. I drove back to the campus. This time, the students must have been in class. Nowhere did there seem to be a suitable alternative to the Civic Center. Therefore, I drove back there, arriving twenty minutes before 4:30 p.m. What was the use? The day was spent.

Had I known, I might soon have been speaking to a large radio audience in New Orleans. The fact is that Christopher Tidmore wanted to interview me at 4:45 p.m. on that day, not the next. In the bustle of arriving at a noisy street corner in Shreveport, I probably confused the time that Tidmore gave me for the interview. Come to think of it, there was no point to interviewing me late in the afternoon on primary day when many people would already have voted. But I was not thinking. I had written down in my notebook that the interview with Tidmore was tomorrow. So, at the time when I should have been calling him, I was driving back to Shreveport on Interstate 20.

The return trip presented another sightseeing opportunity. Several weeks earlier, I had picked up a copy of a magazine called *Louisiana Life*. On its front cover was a photograph of Bonnie and Clyde. Bonnie Parker was pointing a rifle at Clyde Barrow in jest. Why were they featured? It seemed that the place where Bonnie and Clyde were killed by law-enforcement officers in 1934 was located in northern Louisiana, south of the town of Mount Lebanon, not far from I-20.

That chance location of the couple's demise in a hail of gun fire has given the local economy a boost. There is a "Bonnie and Clyde Museum" in Gibsland. Arcadia hosts the "Bonnie and Clyde Trade Days" which attracted an estimated 65,000 visitors when it began in 1990 and continues to draw crowds of people each month. The event is held in the "Bonnie & Clyde Trade Days and RV Park". I was interested in the "Bonnie and Clyde monument", located 5.5 miles south of Mount Lebanon on Louisiana highway 154. This is where the two were shot. In the film "Bonnie and Clyde", I remember how Warren Beatty and Faye Dunnaway were peppered with bullets as they sat in their Ford along a country road. Now I would be visiting the actual spot.

From watching the film, I had the impression that Bonnie and Clyde were killed on a dusty road in open farm land. Highway 154, now paved, runs through a forested area. As one approaches the place of the killing, one sees a sign: "Historical Marker 1 Mile". At the location itself, there is a stone slab, perhaps four feet tall, on which is written: "(On) this site, March 23, 1934, Clyde Barrow and Bonnie Parker were killed by law-enforcement officials"; and, at the bottom: "Erected by Bienville Parish Police Jury".

The marker has been chipped away by souvenir seekers. Someone has spray-painted: "They were my hero's" in the middle of the marker. Below, the graffiti reads: "Bonnie and Clyde were killed by cold-blooded killers" (meaning the po-

lice). The back side is spray-painted: "God bless Bonnie and Clyde." The small gravel area containing the marker is littered with empty bottles and discarded tires. Obviously, this was a historical site which continues to be lived in. Bonnie and Clyde are folk legends who yet touch people's hearts. My only regret was that I did not have an unexposed roll of film with me to record the scene. I did when I returned two days later.

It remained for me to drive thirty-five miles on I-20 from the "Bonnie and Clyde" exit back to my motel room in Bossier City. There were no more activities for that day. I planned to rise at 5:00 a.m. on Tuesday to make one last attempt to stage a successful publicity event in Baton Rouge. I might pass out campaign literature there at noon in the downtown area hoping to influence persons who had not yet voted in the primary.

CHAPTER THIRTY-TWO

Primary Day

Tuesday, March 9th, was primary day in Louisiana and in three other states. My name would appear on the Louisiana ballot. My day began at 5:00 a.m. with Tom Bodett's facetious message about winning $10 million. Seeking the Presidency was, perhaps, equally preposterous. Yet, here I was. Much of what I had done during the past eight months led up to this day. By night fall, I would know if the effort had been worthwhile. In a way, I was relieved that this day had come. Except for one or two scheduled activities, the outcome was now out of my hands. I could sit back as a spectator and learn what the voters thought about me and my campaign.

All this time, I was telling myself that I could be reasonably proud of what I had done if it gave it my best shot. I had pursued a disciplined life during much of the campaign. Toward the end, however, my motivation began to wane. I no longer held myself in a high state of mental tension but was interested in enjoying myself with restaurant meals and sightseeing. This moment was an example.

As I lay in bed after Bodett's wake-up call, I thought about whether I really wanted to drive to Baton Rouge. It would mean a 275-mile trip from Shreveport. And for what? The trip would be based on the assumption that the same radio and television stations that had ignored my campaign appearance on Sunday would now be interested in my passing out literature during Tuesday's noon hour. No, the smart thing was to forget about further campaign activities beyond what had already been done. I lay in bed agonizing over such matters while intermittently gaining snatches of sleep.

I had arranged with Andrew Griffin to have dinner together at a sports bar in Alexandria and watch the election results come in on CNN or another news channel. I left the motel around 7 a.m. with a reservation at the Alexandria Motel 6. That destination was 125 miles from Shreveport, south on I-49. It would take me two hours to get there.

I purchased copies of the morning papers. In *The Times*, a front-page story quoted the Louisiana Secretary of State, the state's top election official, to the effect that this year's primary election was a complete waste of money. Perhaps it should be abolished in future years. The money would be better spent on education or preserving the Louisiana coast line. If it weren't for appearances' sake, he himself wouldn't vote. I listened to news commentary on the car radio in which people were saying the same thing. This year's presidential primary was a huge waste of time. Why go to the polls? For me, however, the primary election was my everything

I drove south on I-49 at a leisurely pace. In the back of my mind, I had the idea that I should check with Jim Engster, the Baton Rouge radio host, who had agreed to have me on his show on station WRKF-AM at 10:15 a.m. However, I was worried that I might incur roaming charges or become disconnected if I placed a call while driving between Shreveport and Alexandria. Realistically, that is not such a problem on major highways.

As I approached Alexandria, I stopped at a Tourist Information Center north of town to get an extra highway map and a free cup of coffee. Again, I was enjoying myself. I did not hurry but savored the coffee. Entering Alexandria, I drove straight to the Motel 6. Here I could place my phone call in a relaxed setting. Some workmen were making noise with a machine to clean the parking lot. I drove to a quieter side of the building and placed my call. It was a few minutes after 10:00 a.m. When Engster came to the phone, he informed me that I was supposed to have called him at 9:50 a.m. The show was off the air. There was nothing that he could do for me now. He wished me good luck.

Indeed, this had been my fault. When we had made the appointment, Engster asked me to call him back at 10:15 a.m. (because he was hosting a show until 10) to see if he would have me on his show. In my notebook, I had written: "Jim Engster 10:15". Then I had called Engster at 10:15 a.m. He had told me that I should call him at 9:50 a.m. on Tuesday, March 9th, at a certain telephone number. I wrote in my notebook: "March 9 Tuesday call 9:50 a.m." and then an 800-number. Looking at this note afterwards, I could not remember the reference. I had intended to call the 800-number to find out what it meant but had not done so. I thought that, with Engster's name written next to 10:15 a.m., I was supposed to call him then. Now I was paying dearly for the misunderstanding.

The Baton Rouge newspaper was sold at the Super One food store next to the motel. I bought Tuesday's paper. Marsha Shuler's article on the primary election began on page one and continued to page 4A. The headline was: "Democrats, GOP pick leaders today"; and the subtitle, "Primaries drawing scant attention." The article noted that both President Bush and John Kerry "have presidential nominations all but locked up" though party officials still encouraged people to vote. Secretary of State Fox McKeithen was predicting a 10 percent voter turnout. That was it. The rest of

the article was about elections to the parties' executive committees, especially on the Republican side.

Less than a week earlier, Shuler had told me that, while nothing yet had appeared in the paper about my campaign, she expected something in Tuesday's paper. This was Tuesday's paper and nothing was there. So I was skunked in Baton Rouge. My only hope at this point was that Keith O'Brien would write something about me for the *Times-Picayune*.

One more campaign activity remained: the interview with Christopher Tidmore on WVOG-AM at 4:45 p.m. In the intervening time, I might have passed out leaflets in Alexandria. I might have sought last-minute radio interviews. But I was drained of energy and ambition. I wanted to enjoy myself in the time I had left to spend in Louisiana. Also, I clung to a vague idea that gentlemen do not campaign on election day; they work hard right through the preceding day but then, as Mardi Gras ends abruptly at midnight on Tuesday, so campaigning stops on election day. Now, of course, if Engster would have me on his radio show that morning, the rule must be outdated. But it was time to enjoy myself having worked so hard during the past five weeks. I would go to the zoo. Alexandria reportedly had a fine one.

So it was that I spent much of the afternoon of election day at the Alexandria zoo. I like animals. In the zoo at Alexandria, there were nice-looking peacocks, alligators, apes, fish, and many other kinds of animals. Mothers with small children, boyfriends and girlfriends, grandmothers with their grandchildren, and many other types of people were walking along the paths of this zoo.

As a solitary person, I was somewhat unusual but I did enjoy myself. The only thing that kept me from becoming totally relaxed was the idea that I would have to do an interview with a New Orleans radio station at 4:45 p.m. My mind had to remain focused on what I would say.

Back in the motel room, I placed my call to Christopher Tidmore at 4:45 p.m. A switchboard operator took the call. I identified myself as a candidate in today's Democratic presidential primary. Soon I was put on the air - as a caller rather than a guest. "Hi, Bill," Tidmore said, after I had identified myself. "You were supposed to be on yesterday at this time." Then the discussion concerned my candidacy for President; today it was about gay marriage.

Improvising, Tidmore said he would give me a few minutes to state my views on gay marriage if I wished. Now I had to improvise. I said that I favored civil unions or another legal arrangement to give gays and lesbians the same rights to medical insurance and property inheritance which straight people had, but I did not favor gay marriage. Marriage was a religious structure and the courts had no right to make such decisions. Did I favor a constitutional amendment to ban gay marriage, Tidmore asked? No, I thought this was a sledgehammer approach to a problem which could be resolved by other means. Thus, my presidential campaign ended with a pronouncement on a question to which I had not previously given much thought.

Everything I attempted that day had turned to ashes. Would the election also turn out the same way? Would my unlucky streak continue or would fate bring balance to the day's events? The answer would be known in several hours. I placed a call to Marsha Shuler from my motel room. She was not at her desk.

Andrew Griffin and I had agreed to meet at 8:30 p.m. at Logan's Roadhouse restaurant a mile or two south of the motel on MacArthur Drive. He was not to do a story but share with me the experience of learning the election results after five hard weeks of campaigning. It could be a complete bust or a smashing victory, or something in between. Like a sporting contest, we would not know the result of the event until it happened. That meant watching the election returns come in on live television. At some point in the evening, CNN would flash the names of candidates in the Louisiana presidential primary and indicate percentages of

the vote which each candidate had received. When my name appeared, I would know whether I had won or lost.

Griffin greeted me in the parking lot outside Logan's Roadhouse restaurant. We sat in a booth near a large television screen and ordered dinners. He asked the waiter if we could turn to CNN. There was no objection. Griffin had opinions on many different subjects. Now a columnist on culture and entertainment, he had a keen interest in politics. He admired the late Paul Wellstone. Griffin had lived in many different cities, mostly in the south, both as a student and journalist. He had grown up in Arkansas. Now his parents lived in St. Louis. When I told him about spending the night in what I thought was Mena, he mentioned suspicions of a CIA connection. It was a mysterious place.

Griffin thought that the Louisiana press should have given my campaign more coverage. Maybe he would call Marsha Shuler to ask what had happened. He expressed disappointment that Moon Griffon, the highly popular talk-show host in Monroe, had failed to return my phone calls or put me on his program. Griffon was, in his view, overrated. This last name, "Griffon", was probably the same as his, but with a French affectation. He was more show biz than substance.

We discussed the state of Louisiana and the city of Alexandria. In many ways, Louisiana needs to catch up to the rest of the country, he said. There was its legacy of political corruption. Louisiana would lose out if it did not do more to retain its talented young people. The same was true of Alexandria. This was a good place to live but it lacked economic opportunity. State government and the gas utility were Alexandria's largest employers. Griffin asked the waiter about his career plans. A student at LSU-Alexandria, this young man thought he would leave Alexandria after graduation.

I proposed that Louisiana had a real asset in its regional culture - the Cajun food and music, Mardi Gras, jazz, even the legacy of Bonnie and Clyde. Griffin agreed this was important. He had enjoyed doing stories on some of Louisiana's local treasures - like the old Carmel church that he had discovered off the beaten path near Mansfield. We discussed the pattern in which an older and larger decaying city in Louisiana was paired with a smaller and more vibrant one, often across a river. Shreveport had its Bossier City; Monroe, its West Monroe; and Alexandria, its Pineville. Meanwhile, we kept an eye glued to the television screen.

Unlike its previous election-night coverage, CNN's program did not report returns from the day's primary states. Instead, it showed John Kerry giving a speech in Illinois where a primary would be held next week. Kerry was saying that he expected to cinch the Democratic nomination in that state. Bush had already done it this evening. Briefly, the CNN coverage focused on Florida which also reported primary-election results this evening. It also mentioned Texas. But, there was nothing about Louisiana. The conversation implied that Kerry was sweeping every contest.

This was not the type of evening that I had expected. Last week's "Super Tuesday" contest, which had brought John Edwards' withdrawal as an active candidate, had changed everything. We had a ringside seat to nothing. The national media had decided that the race for the Democratic nomination was over. It was now focusing on Kerry exclusively. If I wanted to learn the results of my own campaign, it would not be from a television news report.

Andrew Griffin had an idea. On his cell phone, he called the office of the *Daily Town Talk* and spoke with one of his colleagues. After a moment, this colleague reported that she thought I was receiving around 4 percent of the vote. My heart fell. I had expected to do better than that. In fact, as I learned the following day, I did worse. My final statewide percentage of the Democratic primary vote was around 2 percent. Actually, it was even less: 1.955%. But I did not finish last.

And so, with a general idea of how well I had done in the primary, Andrew Griffin and I finished our meal and bade farewell, promising to stay in contact. I returned to the Motel 6 and prepared for a long trip back to Minnesota.

CHAPTER THIRTY-THREE

Going Home to Minnesota

The morning of Wednesday, March 10th, began the first day without pressure that I had experienced in many weeks. I had only to drive home to Minnesota. Before leaving Louisiana, I bought newspapers from several different cities to check the election results. None gave statewide totals, reporting instead at the parish level. My vote count in Rapides Parish (Alexandria) was disappointing in view of the time spent here and coverage received in the *Daily Town Talk*. I received 1.35% of the votes in that parish compared with 2% statewide. I checked out of the Motel 6 and was on my way home.

There remained one sightseeing objective before leaving the state. Having run out of film to shoot the Bonnie and Clyde monument, I wanted to return to that site with film in my camera. I

drove north on I-49 as far as Natchitoches and then took Louisiana highway 1 to Armistead near Coushatta where I took U.S. highway 371 through Ringgold to the highway 516 turnoff. That led straight to the place where the monument was located. Passing through rustic landscape, I felt the peacefulness of nature.

The monument to human violence was still there with the same graffiti. Andrew Griffin called my cellphone number just as I was pulling up to the site. I took some photos and continued on my way. A few miles up the road, I joined I-20 heading west and, at Minden, exited to U.S. highway 371. There was a truck stop where I bought gas and local newspapers including Shreveport's. Then came a quick journey to Springhill and the Arkansas border. My last stop in Louisiana was at a Wal-Mart to replenish my film supply and buy snacks.

My plan was to take a different route through Arkansas than the one (U.S. highway 71) taken in early February. Hope, Arkansas, was a familiar name. Why not drive through the home town of the last Democrat to be elected President? U.S. highway 371 from Springhill did not go to Hope. The most direct route, I thought, was to take several small roads (Arkansas 53 and 313) to the town of Lewisville, where I could join Arkansas highway 29 leading to Hope. The problem was that, as I approached Lewisville, a line of cars and trucks was backed up on highway 29 waiting to cross a bridge. A man holding a stop sign was standing at the entrance to the bridge.

I waited for twenty minutes before realizing this was not a normal construction delay. I left my car and walked up to the traffic controller to ask how much longer we would have to wait. He could not say but suggested I take an alternative route. Glancing at the map of Arkansas, I thought I might take a small road behind me which seemed to head north. I drove several miles down the barely paved road until I reached a small town. There were no highway signs at all. Realizing I was lost, I decided to cut my losses by returning on the same road to the bridge at Lewisville. The line of traffic was just starting to move when I arrived.

While I was driving back to Lewisville, my cell phone rang. The call was from Seth Fox at the Bossier City newspaper. Fox congratulated me on the election results. He thought I had polled about 1,000 more votes than either Kucinich or LaRouche. Was I planning any more political campaigns? I told him that I had no such plans but might do something to promote my trade proposals. Perhaps I would lobby people in Washington. The call made me think.

Previously, I was feeling disappointed with the election results. I had predicted I would receive 5% to 10% of the vote and had fallen well short of that goal. But Fox was telling me that the glass was half full. Why was I insisting it was half empty? I needed to do further thinking about how to interpret the election. Was my claim to fame that I had beaten Kucinich and LaRouche? I had no axe to grind with either of them. They were candidates much like me - little guys in the race, persons serious about issues. My advantage over them was that I had spent five weeks campaigning in the state.

Hope, Arkansas, did not make much of an impression on me. There no signs at the city limits saying that this was the home town of President Clinton. I did see a community college. Of more practical significance, Interstate 30 passed by Hope, two miles out of town. I would enjoy fast driving on this highway for more than a hundred miles and then, at Little Rock, pick up roads which would head due north. This way, I would be driving back to Minnesota in a generally northerly direction through the middle of Arkansas, Missouri, and Iowa, instead of

along the western fringe. It would offer new scenery, new places where I could say I had been.

The drive around Little Rock was a bit stressful because of road construction and rush-hour traffic. I then took Interstate 40 to Conway and then joined U.S. highway 65 which ran all the way to Des Moines. This road started to wind through more rugged terrain thirty miles farther north. I was again passing through territory associated with the Ozark mountains. There were long, steep climbs followed by comparable descents. I was rolling along through this beautiful country when the sun set. One after another, towns were passed until I reached Harrison, Arkansas, the area's largest city. At a gas station there, the attendant told me that, heading north out of town, I could expect another twenty miles of difficult driving but then the highway would become straight and fast.

I crossed over into Missouri and soon afterwards drove by Branson. This was the famous Branson, Missouri, which country western fans often visit. It had a bucolic appeal, so accurately captured in tourist brochures. But it was late at night and I was driving home. Should I stay at a motel in the area? No, I would continue my practice of driving through the night and catnapping when I became tired and a suitable opportunity for rest presented itself. That opportunity came near the town of Buffalo, another eighty miles up the road. I pulled off U.S. highway 65, drove several hundred yards to a gravel farm road, turned right, parked the car and put the seat back. There I would not be disturbed.

These cat naps are never totally restful. After an uncertain period of time, I woke up and continued my journey north through farm country. Although it was a two-lane highway, the driving was not difficult. The early-morning traffic was light. I passed through Sedalia and then Marshall after passing under Interstate 70 (the east-west highway between St. Louis and Kansas City). After that, U.S. highway 65 continued north through Chillicothe and Trenton into an area adjoining Iowa. There fatigue overcame me again. I catnapped in a rest area just south of the state line. Missouri was behind me.

As I woke up, it was mid morning. I entered southern Iowa and thought of stopping at a small-town cafe for a cup of coffee. I spotted such a cafe in Lineville, near the border, but decided to drive on. The opportunity did not repeat itself. I had to settle for gas-station coffee. In the town of Lucas, there was a museum honoring John L. Lewis, arguably the most important U.S. labor leader during the 1930s. The association of big labor unions with this small town seemed incongruous, but Lucas was his birth place.

I began to think that in towns such as this, as well as in Iowa's larger cities, the outcome of the race for the 2004 Democratic presidential nomination had effectively been de-cided. John Kerry had won here and he never lost his lead. A bare two months ago, one might have seen 

Kerry, or Gephardt, or Howard Dean visiting small towns such as these in the winter time. Farther north a short distance was Des Moines, then the center of the political universe. Attention had now shifted elsewhere, but this was where Kerry won the nomination. I was a bit player returning from a campaign which was too little and too late.

At Des Moines, I thought I might continue on U.S. highway 65 to Mason City but took a turn that brought me to I-35, a few miles west. I could see the golden dome of the Iowa state capitol in the distance. Now I was on familiar ground. I had made this trip numerous times - all in connection with a political undertak-ing which was now coming to an end.

As I continued on I-35, the needle on my speedometer began to swing wildly. Then it would stay on zero even with the car traveling at a high rate of speed. I noticed that, in this case, the odometer did not function either. That meant that not all the miles traveled on the Louisiana trip would be counted. I had begun the trip with 132,608 miles showing on the odometer and ended back in Minneapolis with 141,331 miles showing. Ignoring the effect of the malfunctioning odometer, I had traveled 8,724 miles. Roughly 1,100 miles each way were required for travel between Minneapolis and the northern Louisiana border. The rest pertained to travel inside the state.

I arrived back in Minneapolis around 2 p.m. on Thursday, March 11th. My cat greeted me as someone returning from the dead. There were trays of mail held by the post office, many recorded telephone messages, and over 500 email messages waiting to be read. The most important of these was the February 3rd message from Keith O'Brien offering to follow me around on the campaign trail and write a story. Now it was all water over the dam.

I did manage to find a copy of Wednesday's *Star Tribune*. There on page three was a box score of the four presidential primaries held on March 9th - in Louisiana, Florida, Mississippi, and Texas. My name was listed among the Louisiana contenders. In round numbers, I had two percent of the vote, compared with one percent each for LaRouche and Kucinich. For a newspaper which had declined to print the results of my 2002 Senate race, this was outstanding coverage. Several friends saw it.

My wife returned from China in the evening of Sunday, March 14th. My stepdaughter and I greeted her at the Minneapolis-St. Paul International Airport. I wore strands of Mardi Gras beads around my neck and surprised my wife at the airport by wearing her feathered mask. Now the family was back together. I had to do income taxes and many other things.

Kerry went on to continuing success in the Democratic primaries. The race was now clearly between

him and President Bush. Kucinich, LaRouche, and Sharpton slogged on. One night, I watched Dennis Kucinich on the David Letterman Show. He was giving the "top ten reasons" how he could get elected President. One was that, if 300 other people died, the succession might fall to a certain congressman from Ohio. The top way, though, was to find good sex scandals involving the other candidates. Kucinich, the issues man, was learning to adjust to the politics of entertainment. I empathized with him and wished him well.

The Democratic National Committee held a "unity dinner" to honor John Kerry on March 24th. Kucinich was pointedly not invited. Party officials were miffed that he refused to drop out after his chances of winning the nomination became hopeless. Evidently, these were the same DNC creeps who had knocked me off the South Carolina ballot. Their mission seemed to be to shoot the stragglers. I wrote a letter of protest to Kerry, copying Kucinich and Terence McAuliffe. A Kerry volunteer answered the letter thanking me for my support.

I had another bright idea. Considering that President Bush had raised over $200 million for his reelection campaign and much of this would be spent on anti-Kerry television commercials, I thought that persons supporting Kerry might take to the streets and sing patriotic songs. The theme would be: "Sing past the Bush attack ads." I would myself be willing to sing and do organizing work for such an event. Ed Eubanks and I drove to St. Paul to present this idea to Democratic-Farmer-Labor (DFL) state party officials in charge of volunteer activities. We wanted to rent a table at the DFL state convention, where Ed would be a delegate, for the purpose of recruiting volunteers. We were told that no tables were available.

So, as a former presidential candidate, I have quickly sunk back into the deep personal obscurity in which my campaign began on June 20, 2003. Before it becomes a fading memory, I have tried to relive the experience in writing this book.

For whatever it's worth, I do support John Kerry's election in 2004. He is a seasoned political leader with knowledge on a wide range of issues and a moderate temperament. What the Bush campaign claims is a tendency to "flip flop" on issues is, to my mind, a personal strength. Kerry makes up his mind on a case-by-case basis. While his stump speech may not be as inspiring as Howard Dean's, we are looking for an intelligent, balanced, and sober decision maker as President. John Kerry fits the bill.

I do not fault Kerry for not being as forthright on certain issues as I might have wished or for being slavishly faithful to the Democrats' special interests, if that's what it takes to win elections. This year, it's important to remove George W. Bush from office - not that I have anything against the President personally but that it was a terrible thing to invade someone else's country. It's also quite negligent to preside over the destruction of our country's industrial base and let the federal budget run amok.

Let Kerry take over the White House then. My role in the Louisiana primary was, I hoped, to lay a foundation for pervasive political change.

CHAPTER THIRTY-FOUR

Results of the Primary Election

It usually takes several days or perhaps weeks for the final election results to be determined. A month after the March 9th primary, the Louisiana secretary of state published the following vote totals and percentages for candidates in the Democratic presidential primary:

7,091	4%	Clark, Wesley K.
7,948	5%	Dean, Howard
26,074	16%	Edwards, John
112,639	70%	Kerry, John F.
2,411	1%	Kucinich, Dennis J.
2,329	1%	LaRouche, Jr., Lyndon H.
3,161	2%	McGaughey, "Bill"

On the Republican side, the results were:

69,205	96%	Bush, George W.
2,805	4%	Wyatt, "Bill"

The published percentages exaggerate my margin of victory over the candidates who finished behind me. Carried out to three decimal points, I had 1.955% of the total votes, Dennis Kucinich had 1.491% of the votes, and Lyndon LaRouche had 1.441% of the votes. John Kerry's percentage of the vote was 69.679%.

Kerry obviously did quite well. So did the three candidates on the ballot who had dropped out of the presidential race before March 9th. Louisiana voters continued to support them although they had declared they were no longer candidates for the presidential nomination. I had naively assumed that would not be the case. The result shows the power of the branding process associated with televised debates.

Here is where I miscalculated in predicting that I would receive 5% to 10% of the primary vote. Had Louisiana voters not given the three withdrawn candidates any votes but instead voted for the remaining candidates other than Kerry (assuming they wanted to protest the lack of a contest) in the same proportion what they actually received, I would have received more than 12% of the primary vote instead of 2%. But that is pure fantasy.

It's interesting that the Republican challenger, Bill Wyatt, received fewer votes than I did while gaining twice as large a percentage of the votes cast in his party's race. Republican voters were even less motivated than Democrats to come to the polls on this occasion. Bush had an even stronger lock on his nomination.

That's the "what" of the story. In the rest of this chapter, we will discuss the "why". Why did John Kerry win by such a convincing margin? He was obviously a popular candidate but also someone generally acknowledged to be the Democratic nominee by the time of the Louisiana primary. That might have helped him with party regulars and have hurt everyone else. If Kerry had the nomination sewn up, it also affected voter turnout. What was the point of voting if the ultimate end, the Democratic nomination, was already determined?

With respect to Kucinich, LaRouche, and me, one cannot assume that John Edwards' withdrawal from the race a week earlier favored one of us more than another. Fewer people voted, but the proportion of votes should not have been affected. Before the campaign, no one knew who I was. People did know LaRouche and Kucinich. I had more media coverage than they in the preceding five weeks because I was the only candidate actively campaigning in Louisiana. But was I helped or hurt more than the other two by the fact that the media considered the race over after Edwards withdrew?

Where it might have made a difference was in publicity given us during the last week. It seems clear that Marsha Shuler's election-day article in the Baton Rouge paper omitted any mention of the primary contestants because Shuler thought there was no contest. Had there been a contest, she might have included some of that long-kept information about my campaign in her article.

For the New Orleans paper, I know that was the case. Keith O'Brien was also sitting on information about my campaign. In response to a subsequent inquiry, he emailed me: "I apologize for not being able to write about you and your campaign here in Louisiana. It just didn't work out this time. After Edwards conceded the election days before our primary, the campaign just wasn't much news here anymore." I can't complain about his decision. Chairman McAuliffe knew what he was doing when he made sure that I would not be a candidate in a live contest.

What interests me here is not what happened externally but how my own efforts might have affected the election result. For meaningful analysis, we must look to the votes and percentages by parish. I did better in some parishes than in others. How do the results correlate with known campaign activities in each parish? If, for instance, the dominant newspaper in a parish published a glowing account of my campaign right before the election, one would expect that I would receive an unusually high percentage of the votes cast in that parish. If I lacked publicity in the parish or received negative publicity, then one should expect me to do poorly. Since I have seen few of the newspaper articles that were published about my campaign, I do not know in most cases whether the publicity was positive or negative or even if there was any.

From the standpoint of the number of votes cast, it's clear that parishes with more persons voting in the Democratic primary affect the total votes cast more than parishes with few voters. The vote that I received would be a product of the total votes and my percentage of them. If I had a large percentage of a small number of total votes cast in the parish, my number of votes would be small. Therefore, even if my publicity effort in that parish had been effective, it would not affect my statewide total or percentage of votes very much.

What happened in this particular election was that some of my lowest percentages were in parishes that cast the largest numbers of votes; and some of my highest vote percentages were in parishes with the fewest votes cast. Orleans Parish, where New Orleans is located, is the prime example. There were 30,788 votes cast here in the Democratic primary, which was twice as many as the next largest parish, Jefferson. Unfortunately for me, I received my lowest percentage of votes here among Louisiana's 64 parishes - 0.656% compared with 1.955% statewide. East Baton Rouge Parish, site of Baton Rouge, gave me my fourth lowest vote percentage - 1.351%. Rapides Parish, where Alexandria is located, also gave me 1.351% of the total votes.

The election results showed, then, that I did poorly in the larger cities. Why was this? Was the urban voter less receptive to my trade message? Had I unknowingly received bad publicity? In both New Orleans and Baton Rouge, I had been a "no show" on a radio talk show within 24 hours of the election. That could have had an impact. On the other hand, I had participated in Jeff Crouere's radio program in New Orleans during the same period. Christopher Tidmore had written a generally positive column about my campaign which appeared in the New Orleans publication, *Louisiana Weekly*, three weeks before the election. But, of course, I had given my uninformed thoughts on gay marriage on his radio show on primary day.

Another reason for my relatively poor performance in New Orleans might be that the other candidates put forth a greater or more effective effort here than I did. They might have had more active campaign organizations. They might have attracted more or better publicity. I do know that John Kerry's campaign appearance in New Orleans on the Friday before the primary was extensively covered by the media. In Orleans Parish, Kerry received 83.757% of the Democratic primary vote compared with 69.679% statewide.

In Baton Rouge, I am assuming that I received no publicity due to Marsha Shuler's decision to hold back information about my campaign. Also, Brittany Shay's Baton Rouge station WFMF-FM decided not to interview me after once expressing an interest. And there was my "no show" on Jim Engster's program. In Alexandria, I was interviewed by Dave Graichen and Bob Madison on station KSYL and by William Taylor in the *Daily Town Talk* early in the campaign. Did I come across poorly in those interviews? Did the publicity come too soon to leave an impression in voters' minds?

Something that appeared in the *Daily Town Talk* the day before the election might have had an impact. A story by Julia Robb reported: "When asked about (Bill) McGaughey, Rapides Parish Democratic Executive Committee Chairman Brian Cespiva said, 'Bill who?'" The article also disclosed that I was a landlord and I was interested in a shorter workweek and "ideas like the comparison between rhythm and form as philosophical concepts." Also, my typical method of campaigning was to carry a sign.

Some of this personal information may have turned off voters. However, I believe that such publicity, even if negative, does not hurt less-known candidates like me so much. Most people, having never heard of me, would not be inclined to give me their vote. Bad publicity would not change that. Good publicity, on the other hand, gives people a positive reason to vote for relatively unknown candidates. Any publicity, good or bad, creates name recognition. It creates buzz.

With 3.044% of the vote, I did better in Louisiana's fourth largest city, Lafayette. That superior result must certainly be attributed to Lou Rom's article about my campaign in the *Daily Advertiser* on Monday, March 8th, although there may also have been lingering name recognition from the television coverage received during Mardi Gras. In Lake Charles, Louisiana's fifth largest city, I received 1.85% of the votes - below the statewide average but better than in Baton Rouge or New Orleans.

In the state's third largest city, Shreveport, my vote percentage was slightly higher than the statewide average: 2.121%. It was 1.98% - about average - in Monroe, the state's eighth largest city. Surprisingly, however, I received more votes in Monroe than in Shreveport because more people there voted in the Democratic primary. The relatively strong result in the two northern cities may have reflected the television news coverage that I received on the day before the primary. When I report votes in "cities", I mean, of course, in the parishes where the cities are located.

One conclusion that can be drawn from my weak showing in Louisiana's larger cities was that the one-inch retail ads in six big-city newspapers before the election did my campaign little good. I had spent $2,000 on them, hoping to tip the scales in my favor. I had doubled the campaign's advertising budget in the last week in a sudden surge of confidence. How mistaken this was! Persons with greater marketing expertise than I will have to provide the explanation. Was it because I supported tariffs? Was it because I also plugged John Kerry in the ads? Was it because the ads had a poor visual appearance or, being one-inch ads, seemed cheap? Again, I have no answer.

On a more positive note, I did well in a number of parishes with small populations and voter turnouts, especially in the western and in the northeastern parts of the state. Concordia Parish, where Ferriday is located, tops the list at 3.974% of the vote. I did not visit the newspaper office there but do know that an article written by Rod Elrod of the *Franklin Sun* in Winnsboro also ran in Ferriday.

Sabine Parish gave me the second highest percentage of votes. Its principal newspaper is the *Sabine Index* in Many. This is where political reporter, Pam Russell, promised to run a story about my campaign on the front page of the newspaper and where I had interesting discussions with others in the office. Union Parish, third on the list, is the parish where Farmerville is located. I visited this town's newspaper after the deadline had passed. (What happened here?) The fourth, Winn Parish, is where Bob Holeman, editor of the *Winn Parish Enterprise*, took me to lunch at the Rotary Club.

Natchitoches Parish, including the city of Natchitoches, gave me the fifth highest percentage and also the fifth largest number of votes in absolute terms. I spent two nights and a day in Natchitoches attending the Governor's Conference on Rural Economic Development. That was may not have been why my campaign was successful here. Most conference attendees were from other communities. I did visit the local newspaper, the *Natchitoches Times*, and, just as important, had a 12-minute interview on radio station KNOC in Natchitoches on the morning of February 20th. It's likely that these two pieces of publicity did more to produce the 179 votes and 3.716% of the vote total that I received in Natchitoches.

Interestingly, my campaign received the largest number of votes in Jefferson Parish, which is part of the New Orleans metropolitan area. The parish seat is Gretna, across the river from downtown New Orleans, but the parish also includes Metairie and Kenner to the west. Jefferson Parish gave me 254 votes representing 1.838% of the total votes, which was slightly below my statewide average. Since New Orleans media also cover this parish, I have no idea why my campaign did so much better here than in Orleans Parish.

The parish giving me the second largest number of votes, and also an above-average percentage, was Tangipahoa Parish, north of Lake Pontchartrain. Here I had an interview at the office of the *Ponchatoula Times*, a good one. This is where Bryan McMahon and I reminisced about Detroit. I also dropped off literature at Hammond and had a short interview at Amite. Orleans Parish, my worst in terms of percentage, gave me the third largest number of votes, thanks to the large number of votes cast in total. Then came Ouachita Parish (Monroe), Natchitoches Parish (Natchitoches), Lafayette Parish (Lafayette), Caddo Parish (Shreveport), and East Baton Rouge Parish (Baton Rouge) in that order.

It would have been nice to have had a full page of coverage in the state's largest newspaper, as Bill Wyatt had, but my style was more to drive around the state seeking coverage in small- and middle-sized newspapers. For an unknown candidate like me, this works well. The media people in these cities and towns are not so apt to have "presidential" candidates calling on them. They're more willing to spend time in conversation. Their readers may also appreciate the effort made by candidates in visiting their community. In such places one feels that the voters, editors, reporters, and candidates are partners in that great enterprise which we call democracy.

Part

IV

CHAPTER THIRTY-FIVE

Business versus Government: Historical Perspectives

Epic events in world history focus on conflicts between representatives of different civilizations. A power struggle takes place between institutions embodying different functions within society. In western Europe a thousand years ago, the struggle was between government and religion. Royal governments demanded the right to invest (appoint) local clergy. The church fought back by excommunicating monarchs who opposed its will. Such monarchs would be denied Christian sacraments and therefore entrance to Heaven. A poignant moment occurred in 1076 A.D. when the Holy Roman Emperor, Henry IV, stood barefoot in the snow for three days before Pope Gregory VII granted him absolution from excommunication. In those days, business was not yet a fully organized sector within society. Religion and government were the two power centers.

Business emerged as an activity focused on the market place. As merchants bought and sold merchandise, wealth accumulated throughout the realm. Parliaments were organized to help the monarch collect taxes. Its  members testified to the tax-producing capacity of areas which they represented. This branch of government grew in power. The Puritan revolution of the mid 17th century and the American and French revolutions of the late 18th century deposed the king in favor of parliamentary government. It was the culminating act of a new civilization.

Where the king had derived his authority from God, the authority of parliament rested upon popular elections. This is democratic government. Its method of selecting a ruler reflects mechanisms of the marketplace. The outcome - election to a position in government - is the result of a contest between competing candidates supported by voters who exercise their individual judgment. In a like manner, free markets allow individuals to determine prices and quantities of commercial products by their separate decisions to buy or sell. Money and votes are the media through which decisions are made.

In the United States, the politics of the new democratic republic took the form of a struggle between rich merchants, traders, and bankers on the east coast and farmers and workers who were settling the western territories. President Andrew Jackson's decision not to recharter the national bank brought this politics into sharp focus. During the period of "Jacksonian democracy", labor unions arose as working people organized around the struggle for a shorter working day. In the 1880s, labor's campaign for the 8-hour day gave rise to the international holiday known as May Day. Labor unions were organized at the level of the business firm to bargain with employers. Also, a labor-friendly political movement appeared in the form of international socialism (or communism).

Socialist politics represented an extreme tipping of the political scales against business. Government used its monopoly of force to expropriate private property and put it into collective hands. Government took over the ownership and management of business often without compensating the previous owners. Worse yet, the communists used physical violence against property owners as when Stalin liquidated the kulaks of Russia and the Ukraine. In the power struggle between private businesses and government, socialism shifted the balance of power completely in favor of government.

As we know, the socialist regime known as the Soviet Union became an ideological rival to nations which had capitalistic economies and a democratic form of government. In the latter nations, some balance was maintained between business and government. The Soviet bloc engaged in a costly arms race with the western democracies which eventually led to the downfall of the Soviet Union. President Reagan shrewdly pushed that nation into bankruptcy by its need to respond to his "Star Wars" initiative. Communist society was also showing internal strains, both economic and moral. The totalitarian government which resulted from destruction of the rival commercial and religious power centers practiced brutal acts against its own people. Today this form of government is largely discredited.

With the fall of the Soviet Union and other communist governments in the late 1980s, the United States became the world's only military superpower. Our nation came to dominate the world politically, culturally, and economically. In the power struggle between business and government, the pendulum now swung the other way. The communist menace was defeated. Organized labor went into political decline.

I attribute this decline, in part, to the fact that labor abandoned the struggle to reduce work hours. This had been its mission in a time when the unions were built. Those battles won, union members saw the overtime provision as an opportunity to earn more money than a deterrent to scheduling long hours of work. Also, labor hopped aboard the Civil Rights movement, the women's movement, and the immigrant-rights movement, casting a blind eye on the weakening of the solidarity principle upon which its strength had been based. A defining moment occurred when President Reagan, himself a former union president, fired the striking air-traffic controllers and broke their union.

At the same time, business began to squeeze government for favors. Changes in election law allowed business to form political-action committees, undoing a previous rule that corporations could not contribute to political candidates. Business lobbyists, as well as those from other interest groups, swarmed Washington and the fifty state capitols seeking an advantage for their clients. Public office was linked with this type of influence-peddling job in a revolving door. Business influence increased with the increasing amount of money donated to political candidates and the thick presence of lobbyists. Elected officials were forced to solicit campaign contributions to keep up with the escalating cost of elections. They were begging for someone to buy them. And buyers were not hard to find.

It used to be that the news media would communicate information about government activities free of charge as part of their news coverage. As journalists have inserted themselves as gatekeepers into the news process, political candidates have been forced to communicate with their constituents through paid advertising. The high cost of television commercials explains why political campaigns have become so expensive and why, consequently, moneyed interests have gained such influence over government. The television broadcasters are using a public resource free of charge. The private companies which control the broadcasting industry have, in effect, exercised "squatters' rights" to monopolize certain broadcast frequencies. They are now making political candidates pay to communicate with the voters in election campaigns.

Yet, elected officials are afraid to challenge this arrangement for fear of offending the powerful broadcast industry. Newspaper reporters increasingly cover political campaigns from the standpoint of how much money is raised or what television commercials have been run, suggesting that only the best-financed candidates can win elections and therefore interest their readers. So, this corrupt relationship between journalism and moneyed interests feeds on itself. Business, which has the most money to spend on advertising, necessarily gains the upper hand in political affairs.

Organized labor, the main political counterweight to business, has acquired an entrenched interest in certain business firms.

Over the years, union members have gained in wages and benefits to the point that labor costs in unionized firms are out of line with costs elsewhere. Meanwhile, business has steadily invested in labor-saving technologies, allowing its operations to be handled by a smaller complement of workers. Proportionately fewer workers are employed in the more highly paid union shops. As a result, the labor movement is no longer seen as a idealistic effort to upgrade the condition of working people generally. Instead, the public increasingly regards unions as a selfish enterprise designed to allow a shrinking group of overpaid workers to retain their privilege. The political influence of labor has declined accordingly.

Business managers are eager to cut costs and remain competitive. Because top managers would risk losing their jobs if they resisted union demands and a costly strike ensued, they look for alternative ways to achieve the same end more smoothly. One way is to make investments in capital equipment by which a smaller number of employees can handle the production. Another is to work employees for longer hours. A third way is to close down operations where unions have become entrenched and outsource production to facilities with lower costs. They could be nonunion shops in a part of the country where labor is weaker or plants in low-wage countries abroad.

The ideology of "free trade" took hold during the Reagan administration. A free-trade pact was first concluded with Canada. Then, under the first President Bush, it was extended to Mexico. President Clinton arm-twisted the U.S. Congress to approve the North American Free-Trade Agreement (NAFTA). Where the U.S.-Canada pact had given Canadian businesses access to lower-cost production in the United States, NAFTA gave U.S. and Canadian business access to cheap Mexican labor. The free-trade principle has since been extended to commercial relations with other countries.

Essentially, national governments have agreed to reduce tariffs and non-tariff trade barriers to the lowest possible level in their trade with each other. The term "trade" may be a misnomer. The idea is to let multinational businesses shift production to low-wage countries and export the production with minimal restrictions back to the high-wage countries where it will be sold. It's a device to bypass high-priced union labor.

The doctrine of free trade, enjoying strong bipartisan support, has organized labor on the run. American consumers appreciate the low-cost imported goods that they can buy at Wal-Mart. "Buy American" has less appeal if it means supporting those angry people who strike for higher pay while making more money than the average consumer. On the other hand, as production outsourcing is applied to more functions in the economy, people are starting to realize that their jobs, too, could be eliminated. It has been a shock to realize that well-educated but less well-paid Indians, who speak good English, are taking many of clerical, technical, and professional jobs once handled by Americans. No job is safe from outsourcing.

Meanwhile, Wall Street fund managers and stock analysts are relentlessly demanding higher profit margins from business firms. Hungry CEO's need to be paid. Financial managers need their fees. It's the people down the corporate ladder who pay for this, either in reduced pay and benefits, increased work pressures, or loss of employment. Wages are flat. A smaller percentage of private firms offer paid vacations, health insurance, or pensions. Work hours are increasing. Job security is nonexistent. The health-care system has reached a state of crisis. "Affordable housing" for working Americans has become an important political issue not because there are not enough homes but because people cannot afford them on their current salaries. The general taxpayer will have to subsidize what businesses are unwilling to pay in wages.

What we have, then, is a kind of business totalitarianism, milder perhaps than the political totalitarianism of the 1930s but still a menace to the community. Any extreme swing of the pendulum creates a dangerous situation. Only a reasonable balance of power between business, government, and other institutions within the society will provide safe conditions. That is why government must become stronger in relation to business. Organized labor must also become stronger by becoming less selfish. Such things are possible if a political consensus can be formed which is based in a vision of a better society. With such a consensus, government can bring its superior power to bear upon the problems created by business overreaching; for government has the power of the gun.

The preferred strategy would be to use this power sparingly. Build flexibility into government regulation. Use taxation policy and financial penalties to encourage certain behavior without requiring it. The overtime-penalty provision of the Fair Labor Standards Act provides a model of such regulation. Hours worked beyond the standard number of weekly hours are not forbidden but financially discouraged. Likewise, tariffs on imported goods place a financial burden on production outside the country but do not legally forbid it.

Business has the power to make decisions about where to locate its facilities and the jobs that go with them. This power has been used to wrest financial concessions from government. Government has the power, however, to penalize or restrict access to markets within its jurisdiction. National governments should use that power to control business firms which in a free-trade regime ignore social and environmental needs to increase profits. To increase the share of national wealth for working people would pump new money into the consumer market. In that kind of power struggle, the long-term interests of business are served. No one needs stand barefoot in the snow.

I suggest that the politically conservative maxim, "that government governs best which governs least", should be targeted to the monetary and fiscal policies of government. Government needs to cut subsidies to the bone. It needs to purchase fewer goods and services. It needs to stay out of wars. Government should forgo direct spending and return to basic regulation. Its regulations should be disinterested and uniform. Politicians in a position to do special favors for contractors, taxpayers, or anyone else should work themselves out of a job. Let our laws, once set, go on automatic pilot. Shrink the discretionary powers invested in public officials so that private interest groups will find it less rewarding to contribute to political campaigns. Forget the policies of Lord Keynes.

In the years ahead, the federal government's huge debts and its immense trust-fund deficits will force governmental operations to contract. Also, the earth's finite natural resources cannot sustain present modes of economic activity. No longer able to "grow" our way out of economic problems, we will need to develop a strategy for dealing with that new situation.

What positive scenario which can be imagined in those circumstances? If past history is any indication, our future society will be one where economic activity, after self-destructive convulsions, shrinks down to a stable arrangement. Those kinds of activity which require fewer material resources will set the pace of creative change. A society of more general leisure represents my best guess of how humanity can prosper in the years ahead. Given sufficient (but not abundant) material resources, individuals would have freedom to shape their own lives. This vision of personal opportunity should extend to everyone.

In theory, the people control the government. Shareholders control the management of corporations. In practice, those arrangements don't work because the ownership interest is hopelessly divided. Yes, the people could dictate their wishes to government if they were of one mind. Yes, shareholders banding together could tell corporate management how to run the company. But, in fact, the hirelings rule the roost. The shareholders of any large corporation, being so numerous and diverse, must defer to the paid managers in making decisions for the company. The managers will, of course, reward themselves to the extent that they can. Likewise, those lower-ranking employees who have organized themselves into a union take advantage of their incumbency in functional positions to squeeze what they can from the corporation. This has little to do with decisions of the free market. It's tenancy in a position of trust. Today labor and management resemble each other more closely than either would admit.

Henry Ford once said that every private fortune was really a public trust. Socialism may have erred in letting government assume direct control of productive enterprise, but, where the managers and operators of this enterprise fail to serve the public, government has a right to step in to correct the situation. Certainly government has the power. The solution lies, first, in gaining government power and making it amenable to those ends; and, then, in establishing a workable arrangement to benefit all the world's people and the earth itself.

So where does this leave us as Democrats and Republicans? The Republicans are where they have been for a century - aligned with business interests. While the failures of socialist government have discredited the idea of across-the-board wealth redistribution, a new redistributive system, targeting specific beneficiaries, has emerged through the legal system. The Democrats and trial lawyers work together on this. Lawyers extract huge fees for their work. "The sky's the limit" in jury awards. The Democratic Party wins votes by sending a general message that the same groups of people are victimized by discrimination.

In addition, then, to what business can be made to pay for injuries related to its products, new types of injuries based on "discrimination" have been devised to allow a more plentiful harvest of grievances for lawyers to mine. We cease to be governed by uniform laws but instead use the courts to pry wealth from the productive sectors of society. This system resembles justice less than, in Elizabethan times, the licensing of "privateers" to plunder treasure ships on the high seas.

My sympathies lie with the Republicans on this one. Why reshape society to create or exacerbate grievances? Somehow, democratic society must regain control over those who call themselves "servants of the court" and proponents of "justice". In moderate numbers they may not be such a threat; but the population of lawyers is increasing at a faster rate than the general population, and lawyers produce little of tangible worth.

I believe that business can be, and usually is, an honorable vocation. There is nothing inherently wrong with making profits. The person who creates a commercial product which is sought by the public, who successfully markets the product, or who manages a large enterprise involved in a productive, wealth-creating activity is someone who deserves to be admired.

Why, then, do I, Ralph Nader, and others pursue a politics of attacking "big business"? It is because of today's business ideology - the idea of extracting special favors from government, the idea of begrudging working people a livelihood, the idea of putting personal gain ahead of the needs of the community. If "class warfare" is to become a relic of history, business zealots who battle against working people or the poor need also to lay down their arms. Business and labor are customers of each other. In a free market, you do not want to destroy your customers.

Successful businessmen can be popular heroes. In the 1920s, a poll showed that Henry Ford was the first choice for President of the United States by nearly one voter in three. In our own time, Ross Perot attracted much political support. A man of great wealth such as Warren Buffett is also popular because he appears to have community interests at heart. But these business people were or are popular because they offered something to the people.

Sadly, the same cannot be said of others in the business community today who pursue an inhumane ideal. The same cannot be said of the Bush administration which goes to war to enrich preferred contractors. The "slave labor" required to pursue that war in the form of army reservists made to serve repeated terms and of persons "volunteering" for service because their economic prospects at home are so bleak is a stain on our national honor. For this reason alone, the President deserves not to be reelected.

CHAPTER THIRTY-SIX

Creative Uses of Statistics

In October 1992, the St. Paul *Pioneer Press* ran a story about the presidential campaign of Ross Perot, purporting to do a reality check on his campaign issues. Perot had referred to a "giant sucking sound" as U.S. jobs went south of the border. "FACT: A study by the Institute for International Economics found that the United States would gain 130,000 jobs by 1995 if the North American Free-Trade Agreement were approved," read the bullet-point item in this newspaper report. By implication, Perot was talking through his hat.

I happened to have purchased a copy of the book which contained that statistic. Published by the Washington-based Institute for International Economics, it was *North American Free Trade: Issues and Recommendations* by economics Gary C. Hufbauer and Jeffrey J. Schott. The net gain of 130,000 jobs by 1995, I found in reviewing the authors' argument, was based purely on an assumption. There was no empirical basis for the claim of a net gain in jobs. Yet, this study was widely touted in the press as providing evidence for a gain in jobs under free trade.

I outlined Hufbauer's and Schott's calculation on a sheet of paper. (See the Appendix.) I then called the editor of the *Pioneer Press* to inform him of my work. No, it was not a "fact" that 130,000 jobs would be created, merely an assumption. I offered to walk a Pioneer Press reporter through my analysis of the two economists' argument. The editor said he would look at these materials. Some time later, he wrote me to suggest that my rebuttal would better take the form of an opinion article. I wrote it up in that form. Eventually, I received a postcard from another editor stating that my opinion piece was "a bit dense & technical"; but, he added, "try us with something else." In the meanwhile, the 1992 presidential election was held. Many people in St. Paul believed that Ross Perot was misinformed on trade issues.

This was my introduction to how the news media play the game of statistical studies. The statistic did not have to be true. All that was required was that it be authoritative - issued by a prestigious organization or individual. Certainly the Institute for International Economics was that: Its letterhead listed such persons as Peter G. Peterson, Michael Blumenthal, Alan Greenspan, Donna Shalala, Lawrence H. Summers, Andrew Young, and David Rockefeller. And, even if the media were presented with evidence that the statistic was suspect, they were not interested.

As an accountant, I had the patience to review detailed calculations or chains of statistical reasoning. Most others did not. The fact that a statistic appeared in the newspaper meant that it was probably true; and newspapers did not seem to care about truth if a published piece of "information" supported the conventional wisdom.

On March 22, 2004, *U.S. News & World Report* published a column by its editor-in-chief which said that "according to a McKinsey Global Institute study, for every dollar a U.S. company spends on outsourcing, our economy gains $1.14." I wrote that magazine challenging the editors to produce details of the study. What did the statistic mean? If the results of outsourcing were that good, we might as well shut down our economy, outsource everything, and pocket the 14% margin. Or was something else meant? There was no response to my letter. The rest of the column did not seem all that factual. Its author was calling opposition to outsourcing "delusional". Democrats, he said, were "demagoguing" the issue. Arguments opposing free trade were "economic nonsense" and "the old protectionist dodge."

To be honest, I do not know how one demonstrates that NAFTA will create 130,000 jobs in three years or even how, after the fact, one can show that this many jobs were created as a result of the agreement. I have absolutely no idea how the U.S. economy can gain $1.14 for each dollar of something sent abroad for production. This makes little sense to me.

As a former accountant, however, I have seen how statistics are made. Assumptions, changes in definitions or methodology, or totaling mechanisms often drive the results. To understand what is happening, one needs to know where the numbers come from and see how all the elements work together. In news reports one typically sees only the numerical result. The media plug these factoids into arguments. A prestigious organization lends them its seal of approval. That's all that is required to make a fact-based argument nowadays.

I prefer to let intuition and experience play a part in forming such judgments. An actual person who has been laid off is a good source of information about unemployment. As one lives each day in this world, one has experiences of various kinds and, after awhile, begins to see a pattern. This type of evidence should count for something. Statistical studies also have a place if they are transparent. In political discussions, references to authority mean little. We know that interest groups support think tanks and universities financially. Professional reputations depend on affiliation with them. Research funds will not be available to scholars likely to reach unwanted conclusions; or else, their work will not be publicized.

I listened to a press conference of John Donahue, president of the U.S. Chamber of Commerce, which was broadcast on C-SPAN. His world view contradicts mine. According to Donahue, job outsourcing is a necessity in today's business world because employers can't find enough qualified workers in the United States to handle the available work. What's more, the shortage of workers will only get worse. To plug the gap, employers must look to places like India to find the needed skills. Alternatively, they may have to require even longer hours of work from their employees.

Why is that so? Are Americans stupid? Donahue would not go that far, but he did say that our school system is no good. There's not enough emphasis on math and science. On the other hand, American universities are the best in the world as evidenced by the fact that so many foreigners want to attend them. American industry had a "lock" on certain kinds of knowledge which would assure our economic supremacy well into the future.

Later, Donahue said that only 25% of U.S. jobs today required a college education. He said that labor productivity was advancing at a breakneck pace. This, rather than outsourcing, caused most of the job loss that Americans have experienced recently.

Donahue stressed that his arguments were supported by facts rather than emotion. Each statement was delivered with impressive certitude. But the presentation as a whole did not add up. To wit: Why is a bad educational system the source of our employment problems if uneducated people can qualify for most of today's jobs? How can our knowledge-based industries stay ahead of foreign competition if so many foreigners are attending American universities or working for U.S. firms on skill-related visas? If productivity advances are eliminating so many jobs, why is a labor shortage meanwhile developing? Finally, if this "shortage" could be filled, what were all these highly qualified persons from India or elsewhere supposed to be producing? To what end was their labor required?

That, indeed, is the question. The man from the U.S. Chamber of Commerce was stressing the need for more workers with more sophisticated job skills - but to what end? Design computers? How much of the work force is engaged in that pursuit? The reality is that, when I drove around Louisiana, I saw casinos, not computer factories. I saw expensive-looking universities in places of economic decline. Nearly every day, telemarketers call me to urge me to refinance my mortgage or to sign me up for a free vacation trip that will require me and my wife to spend time listening to a sales pitch. Perhaps some of these people were calling from India because Americans lack telemarketing skills? The junk mail pours in with financial solicitations. Is this labor increasing my prosperity? Isn't the point of economic input to produce a wanted output? Where is the output, Mr. Donahue? Where is this better life for the American people?

The U.S. Government attempts to measure economic output by a numerical construct called Gross Domestic Product (GDP). This is the presumed volume of goods and services produced in the domestic economy. If per-capita GDP rises, it is assumed that we are becoming more prosperous. Output is a hodgepodge of products defined in terms of dollars which have been adjusted for quality and for price. If new features have been added to a product, that increases its quality and therefore its quantity (in terms of GDP) even if the number of physical units are the same. Also, if the per-unit price of a product drops, the same dollar amount spent on the product translates into more units and therefore higher GDP. So, measuring GDP with its infinite variety of goods and services is a tricky business.

I would focus on the changing mix of goods and services in the U.S. economy. It is not that consumer preferences have changed that much or that new and better kinds of products are being developed for the same function. With the statistical rise in GDP, we Americans are not consuming so much more food, clothing, and shelter. Rather, its content has shifted from goods and services needed for living to those which one would regard more as a necessary evil.

In an earlier time, for instance, we might not have had to worry about the security of our homes when we went to work each day. As urban crime has risen, we are now having to pay the additional cost of installing burglar alarms in our homes or repairing damage done by vandals. Such expenses, borne reluctantly, do not increase our prosperity in a real sense although, as a component of GDP, they may seem to do so. The government does not compile statistics which distinguish truly beneficial from "remedial" types of spending.

It becomes a significant policy question if GDP growth is concentrated in the remedial areas. If there were some way that the problems could be avoided which necessitated this extra spending, then common sense would say we should go that route even if GDP rose more slowly. It would be better never to have been sick than to experience both the illness and treatment.

In fact, health-care expenditures have been rising far more rapidly than expenditures for other consumer products. It is not that we are becoming a healthier nation but that more medicine is being pushed at us. More consumer debt is also being pushed at us. More education, driven by career-related fears rather than the joy of learning, is being pushed at us. Television commercials urge us to pester doctors to prescribe certain drugs to relieve our pain and make us feel better.

We, of course, have to deal with the escalating costs of crime, the criminal-justice system, and the corrections system. We have to support a large military force although no other nations are threatening to attack us. On certain "holidays", we must buy gifts for family members to show we love them. We have to support a growing class of lawyers needing to be fed. We must sustain a huge increase in gambling expenditures. We need more and more advertising inserted in our entertainment, much of it directed at children. We need to drink branded soft drinks. We need professional help to solve our personal problems. We need to spend money on what used to be had for free and then borrow the money with interest on credit cards which are aggressively hawked through the mail. When is enough?

I think that our economic policymakers tolerate these financially blossoming but humanly problematic types of activity because they provide jobs. Indistinguishable from expenditures on products which do contribute to human happiness and well being within dollar-denominated GDP, such activities generate increased taxes for the government. They postpone the day when its fiscal irresponsibility will come home to roost. They allow today's business empires to become impressively larger and a certain class to stay on top. So, whatever happens to people, the financial bubble must continue to grow.

My view is that, slimmed down, the economy might be refocused on products needed in daily life and that the bulk of what constitutes GDP could be eliminated without being missed. In a better world, individuals would choose how to spend their time and money, not have decisions forced on them. Leisure would be a priority in this world. The fuller and more productive employment that would come from providing more leisure, combined with greater personal autonomy, would address the despair which many people feel in their lives. A sounder basis of personal life should make it possible to escape many of our social ills.

Let not statistics mislead us into believing that dollars spent for the current purposes equate with better, happier, or more prosperous lives. Money is a fiction. Time is the substance of our lives. Free time, materially equipped, is a free society's greatest achievement.

CHAPTER THIRTY-SEVEN

My Vision of a Better World

Yes, we are living in a global economy. Immigrants from all countries make their home in the United States. The situation of people living outside our country critically affects the well being of the American people. We depend on trade with other countries for many important raw materials. We depend on foreigners for new products, new ideas, and creative influences. We depend on them for cooperation in protecting the natural environment, global security, and basic human rights. We are citizens of the world as well as U.S. citizens. Some outsourcing of U.S. jobs will and should continue.

That said, the U.S. Government has a duty to protect the interests of its own people. In our pursuit of a better world, we ought not allow the U.S. economy to collapse or be weighted down with hopeless debt to serve the interest of a few.

Political conservatives often suggest that government is bad. Huge government bureaucracies are wasteful and corrupt. Free the private sector from the shackles of government and watch the economy bloom. I think, however, that eliminating government from involvement in the economy is like eliminating the police officer on the street. In the absence of centralized power, individuals tend to abuse each other. We do need a structure of power to enforce community cooperation and bring peace and justice to our land. I do agree, though, that government does tend to become corrupt if its leaders lack a vision of a better society. Given that vision, they will be proud of their community-building role. Lacking it, they will use their positions in government to enrich themselves and betray the public trust.

While not everyone will agree, I think that we're seeing the end of a commercial and business culture that has existed for hundreds of years. Every living organism goes through a life cycle that includes both growth and decline. The signs of economic decline are quite evident. This emphasis on reviving the entrepreneurial spirit is a symptom of its malaise. Growing economies don't need to revive spirit because entrepreneurial types know how to respond to the opportunities around them. Although the drug dealers on the streets in my neighborhood are spirited entrepreneurs, I would prefer that they peddle their wares elsewhere.

No culture lasts forever and ours is no exception. When a priesthood of money managers and business graduates takes charge of business, that is a sign of its decay. The Henry Fords and Thomas Edisons who created our basic industries will not return. "Been there, done that." Contemporary life is not going to improve through a continuing stream of new products. We should set our eyes on opportunities of another sort as we begin to build civilizations of the future. The business sector will not disappear but it will significantly change. Government will play a role in that process.

I would expand the government's role in economic life. Governmental authority should embrace a new concept. One of the government's functions should be to regulate the supply of basic commodities including labor. This means that government should limit supply. Government should not take over production and distribution of goods and services (as socialism would propose) but limit their supply. The reason is that limited supply stabilizes or increases prices. Prices provide income for people who furnish the products. Adequate incomes stabilize employment.

Stable, well-paid employment is the foundation of better lives for working people. National and global economies can be sustained on that basis despite scarce resources.

In my discussions with people in Louisiana, I was struck by the importance of commodities to the local economy. Louisiana farmers and fishermen were facing competition from Central American and Asian producers. As more supply of crawfish, rice, sugar, or other commodities was put on the market, prices fell. All those producers who thought they would become rich by selling more product found that falling prices defeated that purpose. Yes, there was a gain in income when a surge of new product hit the market, but eventually prices and income dropped and everyone in the industry was hurt.

What's more, overproduction of farm commodities and over-harvesting of fish depleted the natural environment. Countless acres of rain forest in Brazil were being deforested so that more crops could be grown and more product be put on the market. U.S. farmers wanted to sell more corn in Mexico, but, when that happened, small Mexican corn growers could not support themselves due to falling corn prices. They flocked to the cities in search of work. Some came across the border into the United States.

What can government do about this situation? It could pay farmers to take their fields out of production. It could supplement farm income by providing crop subsidies. Better still, it could buy up and preserve farmland, rain forests, timber land, and wild grass lands so that no crops were grown in these places, at least not until demand warrants the added production and the price levels can be maintained. Price is the key to agricultural prosperity. Even with smaller volumes of production, farmers can remain prosperous if price levels are adequate. It also helps to have small industries in rural areas so that farm people can have seasonal jobs to supplement their incomes.

The perspective, however, should be global. Limits on supply must be maintained throughout the world or else each nation's farm producers will be threatened by foreign competition. The idea of each nation encouraging its farmers to maximize their "comparative advantage" as foreign markets are pried open by free trade is self-defeating from the standpoint of the world economy. The advantage of low prices for agricultural commodities costs a nation more than the benefits gained. The important thing is to keep people in the world productively employed at a level of income which will adequately support them. Even if keeping a large number of producers on small farms is not the most efficient way to produce farm commodities, it may be the best way to manage an economy.

The economist E.F. Schumacher, who was a friend of my mother, popularized the idea of appropriate technology. This said that productive efficiency was not the only consideration in deciding which technologies to employ. In countries with teeming populations, it was important to keep people employed even if production techniques were less efficient. Therefore, obsolete technologies of production were appropriate in rural India or Latin America where labor was abundant and capital was scarce. One had to look at the whole picture.

The most important type of commodity is human labor. Most people do not own farm land or enough business equipment to support themselves. Their livelihoods depend on selling their personal time, knowledge, disciplined effort, and commitment to perform a task which is embodied in that commodity called labor. They have contracted with an employer to sell their labor in exchange for money. This is the moral basis of economic life in our society. We encourage people to advance themselves economically and socially through labor.

How can government limit labor supply? An obvious way is to limit the time when people are required to work for wages. That was the idea behind the Fair Labor Standards Act of 1938. During the Great Depression, federal policymakers believed that an effective response to the limited demand for labor might be to limit labor supply. They established a standard workweek and imposed financial penalties on work hours exceeding the standard. Employers had to pay their employees one-and-one-half times the regular hourly rate of pay for each hour worked beyond the standard number per week. As employers cut back on weekly hours to avoid this expense, they hired additional workers to maintain labor supply at a level appropriate to demand.

The quantity of labor is expressed in terms of man-hours of work. This quantity is the product of the hours worked per person and the number of people employed. It makes no difference whether fewer people work more hours or more people work fewer hours: the quantity of work is expressed in their product. Therefore, if an economy is having difficulty in providing full employment, an appropriate response is to cut the average hours of work.

In terms of the Fair Labor Standards Act, one can either reduce the standard workweek - change it from 40 to some smaller number of hours - or increase the penalty rate so that more employers find it financially advantageous not to work people overtime. Still another approach to cutting work time is to make more people eligible to receive overtime pay. Eliminate exemptions to FLSA coverage. Also, the government should not reward people for working these extra hours but discourage employers from allowing such hours to be worked. Since overtime pay currently rewards employees for working overtime hours, I favor government's taxing away all or part of the extra pay. Then more people can be employed.

What about people who need the money? Wouldn't a shorter workweek mean less pay? In the short run, that may be so. Employers will argue that they cannot afford to pay the same amount of money for less work each week. In the long run, however, shorter work hours do not mean that wages will drop. If labor supply is reduced in the face of constant or rising demand, the price of labor increases. Supply is reduced as the amount of work time per person decreases. Shorter work hours also tend to increase demand as more people are employed at an adequate wage. That is why, in the long run, wages do not decline as working hours are cut. By the law of supply and demand, the price of labor rises. Wage levels are higher.

Come on, critics will say, there's no such thing as a free lunch. Someone needs physically to work to produce whatever output the market requires. How the economy will get all its work done if people work for shorter periods of time? There are two answers.

First, the increase in labor productivity (which may already have taken place) through the introduction of labor-saving equipment, better production methods, and other efficiencies make it possible to maintain required levels of output when labor supply is reduced. Capital investment makes up for the reduction in human labor.

Second - and this is controversial - much of the work being done in today's economy really does not have to be done. If we had more people employed at an adequate wage, I believe we would have less crime and, therefore, less need for prisons. Shorter work hours would mean less stress and less medication. And so it would be in other areas of remedial activity as well.

Generally speaking, the more pressure which is put on the economy to get work done, the more of this work will go toward producing goods and services which people need and want. Less will go toward satisfying "necessary evils". The public will insist on having its real needs met before these "services" are provided. Enough jobs will be related to useful functions that make-work projects will be unnecessary.

I must admit, however, that the time-based model of labor is not perfect. Not all labor is the same. A man-hour of Einstein's deliberations is worth more than an hour of attending a parking lot. Another element, then, is knowledge. In paying a wage or salary, the employer is buying access to an employee's knowledge of handling certain functions. This knowledge is applied instantaneously, not in proportion to time. Sometimes knowledgeable workers are "on call" to provide a service whenever it is needed; they are not really "working" during that time. Knowledge is the result of previous education or work. It is a stored commodity, specific to a person's brain.

A similar dynamic applies in all industrialized societies. Most national economies are experiencing both the benefit and curse of improved labor productivity. Unemployment is high almost everywhere. Underemployment is also a problem. Of course, we need to cut the developing countries some slack in doing what they must to start the process of industrialization. Some labor exploitation may have to take place for the sake of capital accumulation. At a certain point, though, the health of the world economy requires that all nations get behind a program to develop their industries in ways that benefit the mass of people. Real wages need to increase. Hours of work need to be reduced. Wealth needs to be shared by a broad segment of the population. And the natural environment should not be ruined while this is happening.

Although there is resistance in this country to the idea of economic planning, the present individualistic approach will not meet the needs of the future, given resource constraints and the threat of political instability. The nations of the world can, I believe, cooperate in seeking to build a better world society. If the U.S. government throws its weight behind such an approach, that would go a long way toward making it a reality. As the power to execute economic policies currently rests with national governments, I am writing primarily from the standpoint of that which the U.S. Government is able to control.

This brings us to employer-specific tariffs. Were it not for free-trade agreements and the WTO which tie our hands in this respect, the federal government could set tariffs any way it wished. The U.S. Constitution gives Congress unquestioned power to regulate both foreign and interstate commerce.

Assuming that power remains in force, I have proposed a new type of tariff to be imposed by the federal government. The government might set tariffs specific to the employer. It would develop individual tariff rates for business firms which produced goods or services in a foreign country and exported them to the United States. These rates might be adjusted each year to encourage a certain kind of corporate behavior. The tariff rates would be lowered when the behavior improves; or remain at a high level if the behavior remains substandard.

When I presented this concept in Louisiana, employer-specific tariffs were proposed as a way to save U.S. jobs. I said that the federal government might discourage outsourcing of U.S. jobs by imposing tariffs on imported products whose rate recaptured the cost savings from this practice. The companies already knew how much money they saved in labor costs by closing a facility in the United States and opening one in a low-wage country. The government would calculate the percentage of total product cost represented by this saving and develop a tariff which neutralizes the cost advantage. That way, business firms could still outsource their production if they wished but there would be no financial incentive to do so.

Some saw this proposal as a nationalistic device that would invite retaliation by other national governments. I suggested that the U.S. Government could minimize that risk by directing the tariff at employers rather than products imported from particular countries. Other countries might be encouraged to do the same thing. Really the purpose would be to create a tool by which national governments could effectively pressure multinational businesses to upgrade what they offer to labor as well as protect the natural environment. Right now, business has outgrown political regulation. It's a race to the bottom.

As I envision my system of tariffs, wages could be dirt-cheap when industry first came to a Third World country but employers would eventually be expected to raise them. If wages were not raised on schedule, then the importing country, acting on behalf of the world community, might impose a tariff to make the company pay the cost anyhow. The same would be true of working hours. Weekly hours might start high, but, as the business became established, they would have to come down for the company to avoid paying the tariff. It's better to apply regulation at the point of entry to the consuming nation than at the product's point of production because the multinationals can so easily move production to evade government-imposed costs.

It is in the interest of both the developing nations and developed nations that living standards rise in all countries. From our standpoint, if wages stayed low in China, the Chinese people would not have money to buy products made in the United States. Higher wages there mean a larger market for our products. Reduced working hours in China would mean that employment opportunities would be spread more broadly through the Chinese population, again increasing the size of its consumer market. Eventually, we could have real two-way trade.

Under the present "free trade" system, the name of the game is for a business firm to save money by cutting out high-priced U.S. labor. The same product may be sold at about the same price to U.S. consumers, but production costs will be lower. The cost savings become profit. Then top management will claim its reward for good performance. This gives them the money to retire comfortably to a luxurious place while the U.S. economy falters. The U.S. Government needs to protect U.S. workers (who are also consumers) from this practice, perhaps not to the extent of protecting abnormally large wages at particular firms but, at least, of bridging the wage differential between economies at different stages of development.

Alan Greenspan has pointed out that if employers were pressured to raise wages in China, they would simply move to another low-wage country. Many companies have short-term contracts to lease facilities in foreign industrial parks. Successful union drives would mean that employers would cease operations there and find another place to maintain low-wage production.

Playing the job-location game, they cannot lose. On the other hand, these employers cannot avoid abiding by the rules of the nations to which they export their products unless they engage in smuggling operations. I see no way other than tariffs to control the situation.

I do not claim that my scheme of tariffs is politically feasible. The business community may be too strong at the present time to allow something like this to happen. I do claim, however, that it is technically feasible. To those who argue that such a scheme would entail a large bureaucracy or much paperwork, I respond that computer technology, bar coding, etc. makes it possible to do today what could not have been done in the past. Companies already collect cost and operational data. They are already audited by outside professionals for compliance with quality-control and environmental standards. Some companies even employ labor-standards auditors. The technology and organization is in place for employer-specific tariffs.

My vision of a better world in the future would be for the earth's population to be spread out in small villages and towns, and in farms, as well as in large cities. Every able and willing adult might be working in a useful enterprise of some kind, receiving an adequate wage and having enough leisure to pursue family and personal interests. The governments of all nations as well as international bodies would cooperatively regulate international trade to promote a better world society. Would this be a lethargic, colorless place filled with persons of middling incomes and meaningless leisure, living in a drab government-controlled environment? Would we miss all the wars?

No, the positive aspect of this future society would be, not what I or anyone else might prescribe, but what people are able to create for themselves within the space afforded by adequate income and leisure. Though the earth's supply of oil and gas may no longer support modes of transportation to which we have become accustomed, we will have more advanced communication technology which will let us "go" quickly anywhere in the world.

We will have more culture, knowledge, and entertainment. Hopefully, we will have more personal freedom. There is a politics out there waiting to advance that better society which it is possible for us to have, even with the mistakes already made. I had the privilege of trying to act upon that vision while campaigning for President in Louisiana in 2004.

The United States stands at the proverbial "crossroads" between two prospective futures. Will American continue in the superpower mode, aggressively advancing "our interests" through military and economic muscle; or will we seize the opportunity to build a better society at home? Backing down from the Iraq misadventure, we can perhaps redirect our attention to use political power as a tool to create what we would want for ourselves and our children in our own land. As I see it, America's unique future - its "exceptionalism" if you will - consists of several elements.

First, we are a society based on the principle of human freedom. This starts with freedom of thought and personal expression, which must be defended against lies imposed by powerful interest groups. We need to create small-scale free-speech forums that can compete against the big media.

Freedom also extends to the economic sphere. Free markets need to be encouraged. To the greatest extent possible, individuals should have freedom to contract with employers to sell their labor or to go elsewhere if the offering is inadequate. This means that a reasonable balance should exist in the supply and demand for labor. It means that impediments to labor mobility should be removed, such as vacations or pensions tied to length of service or the provision of health-care services. Another aspect of economic freedom is free time - time away from work and other pressing obligations, time to fulfill one's personal desires.

A second element of the better society in America is its democratic form of government. This "democracy" should, of course, be put back in the hands of the people. The influence of money in the political process is intolerable for a nation which professes democratic ideals. However, the restoration of democracy in America starts with the communication process. It's scandalous how privately owned broadcast interests have taken control of political discussion and debate while making the candidates pay for it. The lack of transparency in the communications media is also a threat to democracy. The solution to this problem may not be only government regulation but also a grassroots effort to create alternative media and build political parties that serve as centers of communication with respect to certain issues.

Finally, the United States of America is unique among the earth's nations in the extent to which our society consists of different races and nationalities living together in a single community. We are unique in having the headquarters of the United Nations located in our nation's largest city. This is our institution as much as anyone's; we should be proud of the United Nations and of the peaceful aspirations it represents. In the years ahead the United States will be at the center of an emerging global society. Our people will individually have close ties with people in other nations. The Internet will make global consciousness a practical reality. This is to be welcomed. Given skill and restraint in our own foreign policy, America would be surrounded not by enemies but by friends.

Having said this, I must also speak to the needs of America's core population. I am referring primarily to white people or, more precisely, to those who have no identity other than as part of America's "majority" population. Is your culture only to eat at McDonald's, attend college, and root for the area's professional sports team? This is selling yourself short. You will need to do something about the self-hating message that emanates from your own cultural and political elite class. The Civil Rights model of politics, which envisions someone else's bright future and your own decline, is no longer a healthy one - certainly not for you. That economic model which sees you only as a consumer of products profiting someone else scarcely contributes to your personal self-esteem. Cast off these demoralizing influences and reclaim your heritage.

If America is to be spiritually strong in the future, we Americans need to take the initiative now to make it so. We will need to be resourceful and courageous. Who are our people? What is their bright future? Only after we have confidence in ourselves as a people of some worth with an honorable place in this world will we be able to deal with others in a spirit of true friendship and good will. We will then be immune to the appeals of a false patriotism, urging us on to kick someone else's butt. It is we, not media pundits or self-serving politicians, who define what it is to be an American. So let that process of political and cultural self-definition begin.

Appendix

(A)   Calculations supporting Gary Hufbauer's and Jeffrey Schott's Claim that Passage of NAFTA would Create 130,000 Net Jobs in the United States by 1995   (page 346)

(B)   McGaughey campaign leaflet: biographical information (page 349)

(C)   McGaughey campaign leaflet: The Democratic Presidential Candidates' Job Proposals   (page 351)

(D)   January 2004 correspondence about McGaughey's appearance on the ballot for the Democratic presidential primary in South Carolina:
        (1) Joe Erwin to William McGaughey   (page 354)
        (2) Terence McAuliffe to Joe Erwin   (page 355)
        (3) Wm. McGaughey to Terence McAuliffe   (page 357)

(E)   Louisiana's Thirty Largest Cities   (page 360)

(F)   Date and place of each night's lodging in McGaughey Louisiana primary campaign   (page 361)

(G)   Schedule of visits to newspaper offices   (page 362)

(H)   McGaughey's vote total and percentage of votes by parish in 2004 Louisiana Democratic presidential primary   (page 364)

(I)   Map of Louisiana: largest cities   (page 366)

(J)   Map of Louisiana: interstate highways   (page 367)

(K) A Standard Campaign Pitch   (page 368)

Appendix A

Calculations supporting Gary Hufbauer's and Jeffrey Schott's Claim that Passage of NAFTA would Create 130,000 Net Jobs in the United States by 1995

(A) In "North American Free Trade: Issues and Recommendations", Hufbauer and Schott write on pages 55 and 56: "U.S. jobs are assumed to be created at the rate of 14,500 jobs per billion dollars of net improvement in the U.S. trade balance. Thus, about 130,000 additional U.S. jobs are created under a NAFTA scenario." ($9.0 billion times 14,500 jobs per billion dollars) The ratio of 14,500 jobs per one billion dollars comes from 1986 statistics on dollars and workers involved in exported manufactured products as published in the *Statistical Abstract of the United States, 1990*. Where does the $9.0 billion figure come from?

(B) Hufbauer and Schott write on page 53: "Mexican imports of goods and nonfactor services in 1995 are assumed to equal the sum of Mexican exports in 1995, plus remittances from abroad (about $3.9 billion), plus the excess of capital inflows over debt-service requirements." In this sentence, we can see that the authors define the dollar amount of Mexican imports as being greater than the dollar amount of Mexican exports - namely, imports equal exports plus remittances plus excess capital inflows. So long as remittances and excess capital inflows are a positive number, Mexico will run a trade deficit with respect to the United States, by this definition. Conversely, the United States will run a trade surplus with respect to Mexico.

(C) Now the authors calculate the difference between Mexican imports from the U.S. if NAFTA passed and if it did not pass; and also the difference between Mexican exports to the U.S. if NAFTA passed and if it did not. This difference represents the imports or exports attributable to NAFTA. Notice that Mexican imports will always be greater than exports because of assumptions made in (B).

(1) For imports, this is the difference between $78.1 billion (if NAFTA passed) and $55.8 billion (if NAFTA did not pass), or $22.3 billion.

(2) For exports, this is the difference between $62.2 billion (if NAFTA passed) and $51.9 billion (if NAFTA did not pass), or $10.3 billion.

(D) The difference between Mexican imports and exports attributable to NAFTA is $12.0 billion ($22.3 billion - $10.3 billion). However, the authors state on page 55: "Mexico is assumed to purchase 75 percent of its imports ... from the United States and to sell 75% of its exports ... to the United States." Therefore, to determine the U.S.-Mexican bilateral trade, we need to multiply both the imports and exports by .75. The same applies to their difference. $12.0 billion times .75 equals $9.0 billion. This is where the $9.0 billion figure in (A) comes from. The United States has a bilateral trade surplus in an amount equal to Mexico's bilateral trade deficit. But Mexico's deficit is assumed.

(E) To show the source of the numbers in (C), the authors assume that Mexican exports will increase by 11.2% annually if NAFTA passes but only by 7.9% annually if NAFTA does not pass. The starting point is $32.9 billion of Mexican exports in 1989. Therefore, if NAFTA passes, Mexican exports will be $62.2 billion in 1995; and, if NAFTA does not pass, they will be $51.9 billion in 1995.

(1) For imports: If NAFTA passes, we have the $62.2 billion in Mexican exports plus $3.9 billion in remittances from abroad plus $12 billion for net capital inflow, or $78.1 billion. If NAFTA does not pass, we have only $51.9 billion in Mexican exports plus the $3.9 billion in remittances from abroad and no net capital inflows, equaling $55.8 billion.

(2) For exports: If NAFTA passes, we have only the $62.2 billion in annual exports shown above. If NAFTA does not pass, we have only the $51.9 billion shown above.

(F) Looking sharply at the numbers in (E), we can see that the $12 billion difference identified in (D) is simply the $12 billion in net capital inflow which Hufbauer and Schott assume would come to Mexico if NAFTA passed but would not if NAFTA did not pass. The math is: $62.2 billion plus $3.9 billion plus $12 billion minus ($51.9

billion plus $3.9 billion) minus (62.2 billion minus $5l.9 billion). Remove the brackets and watch the pairs of numbers zero out until only the $12.0 billion is left. This figure comes from Hufbauer's and Schott's statement on page 55 that "a good part of the increment, some $12.0 billion, is financed by capital inflows attracted by the NAFTA."

There's nothing empirical about this study. Its conclusion is driven entirely by Hufbauer's and Schott's assumption of a net capital inflow to Mexico if NAFTA passed. Yet, the *St. Paul Pioneer Press*, the *Wall Street Journal*, and other respected publications passed this study off to the public as factual evidence that NAFTA's passage would create jobs.

Appendix B

Biographical information about the candidate

HEY - there's a tenth candidate for President seeking the Democratic nomination! He'll be at (but not in) the MSNBC-DNC debate in Des Moines, Iowa, on Monday, November 24th.

Bill McGaughey, a Minneapolis landlord and author, is also a candidate for President in 2004. If you want a real outsider (in this case, a man standing with a sign outside the Polk County Convention Center in Des Moines), check out this candidate:

* McGaughey is one of the nation's leading experts on the economics of work time, having authored a book to support the last major drive for federal shorter-workweek legislation (*A Shorter Workweek in the 1980s*) and coauthored another with Sen. Eugene McCarthy (*Nonfinancial Economics: The Case for Shorter Hours of Work*), which provided an economic and moral justification for reducing work time.

* He has a strong sense of history and of historical trends. He is author of *Five Epochs of Civilization: World History as Emerging in Five Civilizations* published in 2000. A Chinese-language version was published this year. (See the book's multilingual web site, http://www.worldhistorysite.com. If you type "predict the future" in the Google or Yahoo search engine, this website comes up #1 on the list.)

* He was an early critic of NAFTA and free trade. His 1992 book *A U.S.-Mexico-Canada Free Trade Agreement: Do We Just Say No?*, outlined a positive alternative to free trade. It was used by leading opponents of NAFTA (and even by the Clinton Administration) to bring their people up to speed on these issues.

* As a small landlord in a less affluent neighborhood of Minneapolis, he is intimately acquainted with big-city problems, including racial and neighborhood politics, housing, and crime. He has prospered in the city despite the efforts of elected officials and neighborhood groups to run him out of business in 1995.

* A scrappy political fighter, he helped engineer the defeat of top Minneapolis city officials in the 2001 city election. The following year, he ran for U.S. Senate in the Independence Party primary against the party-endorsed candidate. Embracing issues that were anathema to the political establishment, he finished second (of three) in the primary with 8,482 votes, or 31% of the total. There is a new book out about this campaign.

* A CPA, he is financially literate. His accounting career included employment in manufacturing and public transportation. He has made money as a stock-market investor.

* Not totally an outsider, he attended the same college as President Bush and was in the same graduating class as Senator Joe Lieberman.

Bill McGaughey is a man with a vision of a better society. While the other candidates tinker around the edge of problems, he puts forth basic solutions. Having written the (world history) book, he is comfortable with doing politics in an age of entertainment (which is a basis of the fourth civilization).

Website: http://www.billforpresident.org   Telephone: (612) 374-5916
Email: 2wmcg@earthlink.net   Address: P.O. Box 50256, Minneapolis, MN 55405

Appendix C

The Democratic Presidential Candidates' Job Proposals

As the federal debt and personal debt rise to record levels, a sense of anxiety hangs over the U.S. economy. Our "jobless recovery" in the context of robust stimulus from tax cuts and an obliging monetary policy is deeply troubling. If not taxpaying workers with adequate incomes, who will pay back this debt, much of which is owed to foreigners?

Jobs are the most important issue in this campaign, acknowledged as such by most of the Democratic presidential candidates. What is the cause of the job erosion? What can the federal government do about it? These are the questions that ought to be asked.

One element of the problem is that, even with increased production, employers are asking their employees to work longer hours instead of hiring new people. In 2003, U.S. workers put in 32.7% more overtime than in 2000. Even then, overtime was at historically high levels.

Another element is the increase in labor productivity due to investment in equipment. You don't need as many people to do the work. Productivity increases hit a 20-year high in the 3rd quarter of 2003.

Still another element is the outsourcing of U.S. jobs to low-wage countries. The Chinese do much of our manufacturing. Well-educated workers in India and the Philippines can do our office work. The U.S. trade deficit is expected to approach $500 billion this year. Much is due to intracorporate trade between the United States and low-wage countries.

Fine, what do the leading Democratic candidates for President propose to do about job loss? The following is taken from the candidates' web sites:

John Kerry: Kerry promises to "restore the (3 million) jobs lost under Bush in the first 500 days of his administration. Kerry has proposed creating jobs through a new manufacturing jobs credit, by investing in new energy industries, restoring technology, and stopping layoffs in education."

He proposes "new tax breaks to manufacturers who produce goods and create jobs in the United States" and will "provide relief for companies that provide quality health care and retirement. John Kerry will strongly enforce trade laws to assure that American industries are on a level playing field with our trading partners." He will also "invest in research and development, give tax incentives to help industries upgrade, and work to assure a highly qualified work force", which means invest in education.

With respect to trade, Kerry promises a "120-day review of all trade agreements" to make sure that foreign governments are living up to them. All trade agreements should include "core labor standards and environmental protection." Countries such as China should not manipulate their currencies. Displaced workers should be retrained. Also, Kerry would lower the corporate tax rate for firms staying in the U.S.

Howard Dean: Dean wants a 2-year $100 billion "Fund to Restore America" to create one million new jobs especially in disadvantaged communities. He would create a Small Business Capital Corporation within the Small Business Administration. He, too, wants to put "core labor standards" in trade agreements. His "four fundamentals" are: (1) Repeal the Bush tax cuts. (2) Shoot for a balanced budget. (3) Create a fairer and simpler tax system. (4) Adequately fund Social Security and Medicare.

John Edwards: "John Edwards has a plan to create jobs with a 10 percent tax credit for companies that keep jobs in America, a venture capital fund to bring jobs to those hardest hit in the Bush economy, new tax credits for working Americans to buy their first home, save for retirement, or save for child's education." Edwards also wants trade agreements to contain "strong labor and environmental protections." He would crack down on "lax Chinese trade law enforcement."

Wesley Clark: Clark would "devote $100 billion over two years to jump start job creation without increasing the deficit." $80 billion of this would be for homeland security and aid to state governments. More money would be put into improved public infrastructure. Clark also supports a "Job Creation Tax Credit" that gives "up to a $5,000 tax credit for each additional full-time employee that any business hires." He also wants to crack down on Chinese currency manipulation.

Comments: The idea of paying manufacturers to stay in this country is laughable. We don't have the money to do that. The same is true of all these "job-creation" funds. Any federal fund will be funded either through taxes or borrowing which will crowd out other job creation in the private sector. Linking labor standards to trade is fine, except it is no violation of any labor standard for Third World workers to be paid so much less.

Bill McGaughey's Approach: (A) Address the productivity and overtime problems by amending the Fair Labor Standards Act to reduce work time. Priorities: (1) Raise the overtime penalty to double time and tax away the extra 1/2 time premium for the employee. (2) Tighten overtime exemption for administrative and professional employees. (3) Reduce standard workweek to 32 hours over 4-year period. (B) Address job outsourcing by abolishing free trade. Rescind NAFTA and WTO. Create new system of tariffs targeted to individual employers. As emergency measure, impose tariff on imported products whose rate equalizes the cost advantage in low-wage countries. Long range, work with other nations to use adjustable tariffs as a tool to encourage firms worldwide to raise pay, cut work hours, and operate in environmentally sound ways.

McGaughey for President Campaign   www.BillforPresident.org
Candidate cell phone   (612) 280-xxxx

Appendix D

January 2004 correspondence about McGaughey's appearance on the ballot for the Democratic presidential primary in South Carolina

(1)

January 6. 2004

William McGaughey
P.O. Box 50256
Minneapolis, MN 55405

Dear Mr. McGaughey:

This is to confirm receipt of your application to participate as a candidate in South Carolina's February 3rd Democratic Presidential Preference Primary. Under the South Carolina Delegate Selection Rules, (Section VI.A.1) no one may gain access to the Primary ballot unless he or she is entitled to obtain delegates to the 2004 Democratic National Convention.

The Chair of the Democratic National Committee has advised me that in accordance with Section 11.K.(1)(b) of the Delegate selection rules for the 2004 Democratic National Convention, you do not qualify to obtain delegates. Accordingly, I am returning the check that you included with your filing form.

Thank you for your interest in the South Carolina Democratic Presidential Primary.

Yours truly,

Joe Erwin, Chair
South Carolina Democratic Party

(2)

January 5, 2003

Joe Erwin, State Chair
South Carolina Democratic Party
P.O. Box 5965
Columbia, SC 29250

Dear Chair Erwin:

Rule 11.K of the Delegate Selection Rules for the 2004 Democratic National Convention (the "Delegate Selection Rules") adopted by the Democratic National Committee on January 19, 2002 provides that, for purposes of the Delegate Selection rules, a qualified candidate for the nomination of the Democratic Party for President shall -

(1)(a) be registered to vote, and shall have been registered to vote in the last election for the office of President and Vice President; and

(1)(b) have demonstrated a commitment to the goals and objectives of the Democratic Party as determined by the National Chair and will participate in the Convention in good faith.

Under Article VI of the Call for the 2004 Democratic National Convention (the "Call"), adopted by the Democratic National Committee on August 10, 2002, the term "presidential candidate" means:

... any person who, as determined by the National Chairperson of the Democratic National Committee, has accrued delegates in the nominating process and plans to seek the nomination, has established substantial support for his or her nomination as the Democratic candidate for the Office of the President of the United States, is a bona fide Democrat whose record of public service, accomplishments, public writings and/or public statements affirmatively demonstrates that he or she is faithful to the interests, welfare and success of the Democratic Party of the United States, and will participate in the Convention in good faith.

This is to notify you that:

1.   William McGaughey of Hennipin (sic) County, Minnesota ran as a candidate for Mayor of Minneapolis in 2001 as a member of the "Affordable Housing Preservation Party," against the incumbent Democratic Mayor. In 2002, Mr. McGaughey sought the nomination of the Independence Party as a candidate for United States Senate from Minnesota, and ran in that party's primary election. Mr. McGaughey has publicly stated that he "remains a member of the Independence Party of Minnesota"; and "has reservations about joining the current Democratic Party."

2.   Under the authority granted to me by Rule 11.K.(1)(b) of the Delegate Selection Rules and Article VI of the Call, I have determined that William McGaughey is not a bona fide Democrat and does not possess a record affirmatively demonstrating that he is faithful to, or has at heart, the interests, welfare and success of the Democratic Party of the United States. This determination is based on Mr. McGaughey's candidacies as members of other parties; his continuing professed membership in another party; and his express refusal to affiliate with the Democratic Party of the United States.

Accordingly, Mr. McGaughey is not to be considered a qualified candidate for nomination of the Democratic Party for President under the Delegate Selection rules and is not to be considered a "presidential candidate" within the meaning of Article VI of the Call. Therefore, state and territorial parties, in the implementation of their delegate selection plans, should disregard any votes that might be cast for Mr. McGaughey, should not allocate delegate positions to Mr. McGaughey and should not recognize the selection of delegates pledged to him at any stage of the delegate selection process.

Further, Mr. McGaughey will not be entitled to have his name placed in nomination for the office of President at the 2004 Democratic National Convention. No certification of a delegate pledged to Mr. McGaughey will be accepted by the secretary of the Democratic National Committee and no such delegate shall be placed on the Temporary Roll of the Convention. The National Chair will, if necessary, and upon the proper filing of a challenge, recommend to the

Credentials Committee of the 2004 Democratic National Convention that the Committee resolve that any such delegate not be seated at the Convention.

If you have any questions about the implementation of this notice, please do not hesitate to contact me or Phil McNamara, the DNC's Director of Party Affairs and Delegate Selection, at (202) 479-5131.

Sincerely,

Terence R. McAuliffe
National Chair

(3)

January 9, 2004

Terence R. McAuliffe, Chair
Democratic National Committee
430 South Capitol Street S.E.
Washington, DC 20003

Dear Mr. McAuliffe:

On my way to South Carolina to participate in the Democratic presidential primary, I learned from a reporter that the party had taken my name off the ballot. I drove to Columbia to learn the reason for that decision. Staff at the Democratic Party headquarters showed me a copy of a letter which you wrote to the state chair, Joe Erwin. I found several factual inaccuracies in that letter which I communicated to Phil McNamara. He indicated that he would be passing this information on to you. I would be hearing from him next week. I suggested that I drive to Washington, D.C., to meet in person, but Mr. McNamara discouraged that suggestion. I will return to Minneapolis tomorrow.

Your reasons for declaring me ineligible to receive delegates have to do with a perceived insufficient commitment to "the goals and objectives of the Democratic Party" and an unwillingness to "participate in the convention in good faith." Yes, it is true that I sought the Independence Party's endorsement for U.S. Senate in 2002, and that, technically, I remain a member of the Independence Party of Minnesota. However, in a telephone conversation with a member of your staff on or about December 29, 2003, I indicated that I would be willing to affiliate with the Democratic Party this year. I did express some reluctance to attend the DFL caucus on March 2nd since I intended to be in Louisiana campaigning in that state's presidential primary until March 9th. However, if it is necessary to disrupt that campaign (assuming that I will be on the ballot) for the purpose of traveling back to Minnesota to attend the DFL caucus and thus, officially, become a Democrat, I would be willing to do so.

I tried to convey to Phil McNamara that my issues were consistent with the philosophy of the Democratic Party. If I participated in the national convention in Boston, it would certainly be in good faith. My main issue is jobs; secondarily, it is to criticize the divisive politics of gender and race. I have published several books on employment-related topics which I showed to Wyeth Ruthven and other staff of the South Carolina party. "A Shorter Workweek in the 1980s", published in 1981, (ISBN 0-9605630-0-8) contains a foreword by Rep. John Conyers. "Nonfinancial Economics: The Case for Shorter Hours of Work", published in 1989 (ISBN 0-275-92514-5) is coauthored by former U.S. Senator Eugene McCarthy. "A U.S.-Mexico-Canada Free Trade Agreement: Do We Just Say No?" (ISBN 0-9605630-2-4) was used to inform opposition to NAFTA in the early 1990s. I am also enclosing a copy of the cover letter which I used in my latest mailing dated January 1, 2004, as well as an email "Why this is a jobless recovery and what to do about it" sent to more than 1,000 political reporters and editors. I believe these communications are consistent with those of a candidate representing the Democratic Party.

You apparently felt that I was an opponent of Paul Wellstone because I had run for his seat in the Independence Party primary. In fact, I knew Paul Wellstone for more than twenty years. I was a financial contributor to his Senate campaigns through the early months of 2002 until I became a candidate myself. My disagreement with Wellstone was that he would not support shorter-workweek legislation because he did not think it enjoyed enough public support. I hoped to demonstrate support through my candidacy. My campaign for U.S. Senate with the Independence Party stressed federal legislation to reduce the workweek to 32 hours by 2010. I received 31% of the vote in a 3-way contest. By my standards, it was a success. I had proven my point. However, tragic fate intervened in that race. It is untrue that I contributed in any way to Norm Coleman's victory. Had Wellstone lived to be reelected, I feel sure he would have taken a new look at shorter-workweek legislation.

In summary, I would urge you to reconsider your decision and let me run in the South Carolina and Louisiana primaries. I would run as a candidate of "new ideas", contributing useful proposals in the employment area. Please do not apply a purity test to my candidacy. The Democratic Party stands to gain by encouraging many different types of candidates to participate.

Sincerely,

William McGaughey

Appendix E

Louisiana's Thirty Largest Cities

rank	Name	population
1	New Orleans	460,913
2	Baton Rouge	210,667
3	Shreveport	187,393
4	Lafayette	116,806
5	Lake Charles	72,163
6	Kenner	71,567
7	Bossier City	56,413
8	Monroe	52,114
9	Alexandria	45,959
10	New Iberia	33,317
11	Houma	32,541
12	Chalmette	31,860
13	Slidell	27,138
14	Sulphur	21,151
15	Ruston	20,241
16	Opelousas	19,315
17	Hammond	18,593
18	Natchitoches	16,834
19	Gretna	16,169
20	Thibodaux	15,163
21	Pineville	14,917
22	Crowley	13,850
23	Morgan City	13,756
24	Baker	13,648
25	West Monroe	13,641
26	Bastrop	13,607
27	Minden	13,413
28	Bogalusa	13,374
29	Abbeville	12,882
30	Zachary	11,924

Appendix F

Date and place of each night's lodging in McGaughey
Louisiana primary campaign

day of week	date	spent night in	room number
Monday	Feb. 2	Alma, Ark.	
Tuesday	Feb. 3	Bossier City	101
Wednesday	Feb. 4	Bossier City	101
Thursday	Feb. 5	Port Allen	212
Friday	Feb. 6	Port Allen	130
Saturday	Feb. 7	Port Allen	130
Sunday	Feb. 8	Alexandria	121
Monday	Feb. 9	Natchitoches	
Tuesday	Feb. 10	Natchitoches	
Wednesday	Feb. 11	Monroe	132
Thursday	Feb. 12	Monroe	132
Friday	Feb. 13	Alexandria	129
Saturday	Feb. 14	Alexandria	129
Sunday	Feb. 15	Alexandria	129
Monday	Feb. 16	Lake Charles	137
Tuesday	Feb. 17	Port Allen	136
Wednesday	Feb. 18	Lafayette	143
Thursday	Feb. 19	Slidell	207
Friday	Feb. 20	Port Allen	107
Saturday	Feb. 21	Lafayette	123
Sunday	Feb. 22	Port Allen	107
Monday	Feb. 23	Port Allen	107
Tuesday	Feb. 24	Port Allen	107
Wednesday	Feb. 25	Port Allen	107
Thursday	Feb. 26	Port Allen	107
Friday	Feb. 27	Port Allen	107
Saturday	Feb. 28	Port Allen	107
Sunday	Feb. 29	Slidell	166

Monday	March 1	Alexandria	110
Tuesday	March 2	Alexandria	110
Wednesday	March 3	Lafayette	113
Thursday	March 4	Port Allen	
Friday	March 5	Port Allen	
Saturday	March 6	Port Allen	
Sunday	March 7	Bossier City	101
Monday	March 8	Bossier City	101
Tuesday	March 9	Alexandria	153
Wednesday	March 10	Buffalo, MO	
Thursday	March 11	Minneapolis, MN	

Appendix G

Schedule of Visits to Newspaper Offices

day	date	city of newspaper visited that day
Tues.	Feb. 3	
Wed.	Feb. 4	Minden, Homer, Haynesville, Ruston
Thurs.	Feb. 5	Shreveport, Bossier City, Mansfield, Many, Deridder
Fri.	Feb. 6	Baton Rouge, New Orleans, Plaquemine
Sat.	Feb. 7	
Sun.	Feb. 8	
Mon.	Feb. 9	Alexandria, Natchitoches
Tues.	Feb. 10	
Wedn.	Feb. 11	Coushatta, Winnfield, (nobody at Jonesboro)
Thurs.	Feb. 12	Monroe, Arcadia, West Monroe, Bastrop, Oak Grove
Fri.	Feb. 13	Rayville, Winnsboro

day   date   city of newspaper visited that day

Sat.   Feb. 14
Sun.   Feb. 15
Mon.   Feb. 16   Lake Charles
Tues.   Feb. 17   Dequincy, Welsh, Jennings, Rayne, Crowley
Wed.   Feb. 18   Gonzales, Donaldsonville, Thibodaux
Thurs.   Feb. 19   Abbeville, New Iberia, St. Martinville, Franklin
Fri.   Feb. 20   Bogalusa, Franklinton, Amite
Sat.   Feb. 21
Sun.   Feb. 22
Mon.   Feb. 23   Slidell
Tues.   Feb. 24
Wed.   Feb. 25   Ponchatoula, Port Allen
Thurs.   Feb. 26   Larose, Morgan City, Jeanerette, Church Point
Fri.   Feb. 27   Laplace, Boutte, Metairie, Arabi, New Orleans
Sat.   Feb. 28
Sun.   Feb. 29
Mon.   March 1   Covington, Belle Chasse, Napoleonville
Tues.   March 2   Jonesville, Bernice, Springhill
Wed.   March 3   Lafayette, Ville Platte
Thurs.   March 4   Opelousas
Fri.   March 5
Sat.   March 6
Sun.   March 7
Mon.   March 8
Tues.   March 9

Appendix H

McGaughey's vote total and percentage of votes by parish in 2004 Louisiana Democratic presidential primary

Parish	big city in parish	total votes	McGaughey votes	percent
Acadia	Crowley	1,772	55	3.1%
Allen	Oakdale	646	21	3.3%
Ascension	Gonzales	6,059	112	1.8%
Assumption	Napoleonville	646	9	1.4%
Avoyelles	Bunkie	1,013	19	1.9%
Beauregard	Deridder	653	17	2.6%
Bienville	Arcadia	779	23	3.0%
Bossier	Bossier City	1,295	16	1.2%
Caddo	Shreveport	5,798	123	2.1%
Calcasieu	Lake Charles	5,190	96	1.8%
Caldwell	Columbia	789	18	2.3%
Cameron	Cameron	620	12	1.9%
Catahoula	Jonesville	1,110	39	3.5%
Claiborne	Homer	472	8	1.7%
Concordia	Ferriday	2,768	110	4.0%
Desoto	Mansfield	858	23	2.7%
East Baton Rouge	Baton Rouge	8,884	120	1.4%
East Carroll	Lake Providence	671	23	3.4%
East Feliciana	Clinton	927	25	2.7%
Evangeline	Ville Platte	989	21	2.1%
Franklin	Winnsboro	876	29	3.3%
Grant	Colfax	474	10	2.1%
Iberia	New Iberia	1,120	27	2.4%
Iberville	Plaquemine	671	14	2.1%
Jackson	Jonesboro	1,099	23	2.1%
Jefferson	Gretna	13,820	254	1.8%
Jefferson Davis	Jennings	998	24	2.4%
Lafayette	Lafayette	4,369	133	3.0%
Lafourche	Larose	2,208	41	1.9%
Lasalle	Jena	321	11	3.4%
Lincoln	Ruston	2,975	65	2.2%
Livingston	Denham Springs	1,344	43	3.2%

Parish	big city in parish	total votes	McGaughey votes	percent
Madison	Tallulah	404	13	3.2%
Morehouse	Bastrop	648	14	2.2%
Natchitoches	Natchitoches	4,817	179	3.7%
Orleans	New Orleans	30,788	202	0.7%
Ouachita	Monroe	9,244	183	2.0%
Plaquemines	Belle Chasse	1,065	16	1.5%
Pointe Coupee	New Roads	577	11	1.9%
Rapides	Alexandria	2,369	32	1.4%
Red River	Coushatta	375	11	2.9%
Richland	Rayville	901	27	3.0%
Sabine	Many	713	28	3.9%
St. Bernard	Arabi	3,122	93	3.0%
St. Charles	Boutte	877	7	0.8%
St. Helena	Greensburg	538	17	3.2%
St. James	Gramercy	1,566	31	2.0%
St. John the Baptist	Laplace	1,034	21	2.0%
St. Landry	Opelousas	3,344	76	2.3%
St. Martin	St. Martinville	1,219	29	2.4%
St. Mary	Morgan City	821	12	1.5%
Tangipahoa	Ponchatoula	8,655	212	2.4%
Tensas	St. Joseph	274	7	2.6%
Terrebonne	Houma	3,509	68	1.9%
Union	Farmerville	499	19	3.8%
Vermillion	Abbeville	1,018	36	3.5%
Vernon	Leesville	2,816	73	2.6%
Washington	Franklinton	882	21	2.4%
Webster	Minden	1,372	27	2.0%
West Baton Rouge	Port Allen	399	10	2.5%
West Carroll	Oak Grove	213	5	2.3%
West Feliciana	St. Francisville	329	5	1.5%
Winn	Winnfield	400	15	3.8%
total		161,653	3,161	2.0%

Appendix I   Map of Louisiana: largest cities

Alexandria, LA	Monroe, LA
Baton Rouge, LA	New Orleans, LA
Lafayette, LA	Shreveport, LA
Lake Charles, LA	Slidell, LA

Appendix J   Map of Louisiana: interstate highways

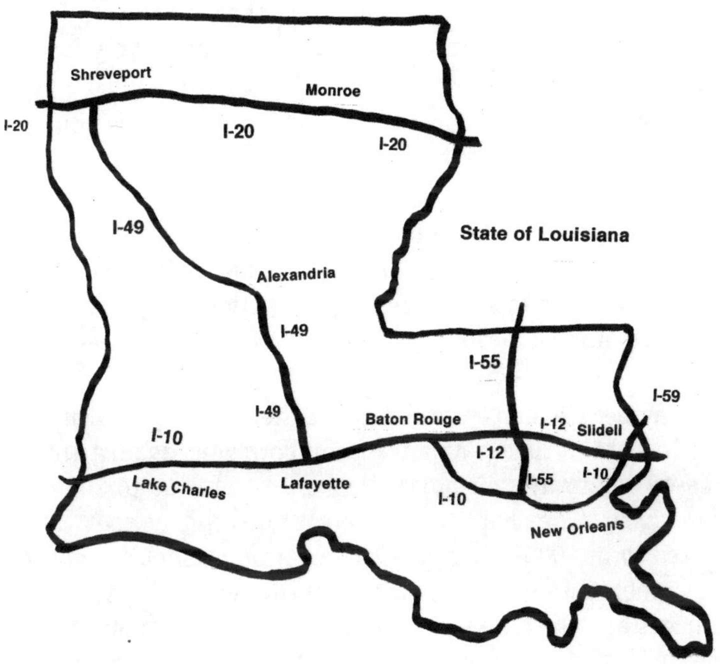

Appendix K   A Standard Campaign Pitch

Hi, I'm Bill McGaughey of Minneapolis. I'm one of seven candidates on the ballot in the March 9th Democratic presidential primary - the one you haven't heard of. You may not be able to pronounce my name when you read it on the ballot. It's spelled "McGaughey" but pronounced "McGoy". I'm running only in Louisiana.

You might ask: Why on earth are you running. Are you crazy? Do you expect to win the nomination? Perhaps not. But I do expect to win votes.

I'm running for President because I think this country is in crisis. We have a projected $520 billion budget deficit combined with a $500 billion trade deficit. The country is bogged down in a war in Iraq. And we have a "jobless recovery". Jobs are my main issue.

Many people aren't worried about the economy. Housing prices have been rising. Americans are borrowing against the increased equity in their homes to the tune of $400 to $600 billion a year. What happens if interest rates rise, as they are expected to in 2005? That puts a damper on the housing market. With variable interest rates, many homeowners can't pay their mortgages and the banks foreclose. Housing prices tumble as more homes are thrown on the market. What could save us would be a strong structure of jobs. But the job market is weak.

I'm a small-scale landlord in Minneapolis. Before that, I was an accountant. For almost 30 years, I've been studying labor economics and trade. I've been an advocate of shorter working hours. I've published six books - three on employment-related topics. So I think I have something to contribute to the discussion of jobs.

The other candidates for President say that jobs are their top issue but they have no realistic answers for this problem. Kerry says he'll create three million news jobs during the first 500 days of his administration. That's a goal, not a program. Kerry does propose to lower the tax for companies that stay in the United

States. But no amount of tax reduction can overcome the cost advantage in moving production to a low-wage country. Besides, with a $520 billion budget deficit, the government doesn't have the money to pay manufacturers to stay in this country.

I analyze the "jobless recovery" as having two causes:

(1) the outsourcing of U.S. jobs to low-wage countries, and

(2) continued improvements in labor productivity combined with chronic overtime.

With respect to outsourcing of jobs, it won't work to try to shame companies into stay in the United States when their competitors go offshore. The federal government needs to create a compulsory "level playing field".

I think tariffs are the only answer. However, the traditional type of tariff won't work. We need tariffs targeted to individual employers. As an emergency, the tariffs might take into consideration the cost advantage derived from producing in low-wage country. Its rate would be set to neutralize the cost advantage from going off shore. I published a book in 1992 and, later, two articles in Green Party publications that spelled out this concept in detail.

With respect to overtime, we need to stiffen the disincentive to working long hours by raising the overtime penalty rate from time-and-a-half to double-time and tax away the extra half-time premium so that the employee does not have a windfall. A health-insurance system decoupled from employment would also help to remove the disincentive to hiring more people.

I think the Democrats have become too pragmatic and not idealistic enough. We need to get back to pursuing ideas of a better society. That's what I'm trying to do. On a global scale, I would envision national governments employing a system of flexible tariffs to encourage multinational employers to raise wages, reduce work hours, and operate in environmentally responsible ways. Domestically, I want more economic "growth" to be taken in the form of leisure. The use of automated equipment should allow people to work fewer hours without lowering their standard of living.

If the Democrats are not idealistic, they either become corrupt or beholden to special interests. How else would they be motivated? In Minneapolis, the Democratic leadership of city government became corrupt and they were defeated at the polls.

I intend to win votes in my campaign. In voting for me, Louisiana voters can signal to the political establishment and to the media that they want Democratic candidates to offer specific, realistic solutions to the problem of job loss.

By March 9th, John Kerry will have sewn up the nomination. Louisiana voters will not be able to affect the outcome of the nomination but they can help put jobs on the national agenda by voting for me. That's because jobs are my only issue. I want to create a statistic by doing unexpectedly well in the primary election. Voting for me will not be a "throwaway vote".

Believe me, the political establishment will pay attention to the result in Louisiana even if I don't get nearly as many votes as Kerry does. It will be interpreted as a desire of Louisiana voters for the candidates to present better proposals for jobs. Shifting the debate away from Iraq and toward jobs will help the Democrats in the general election.

I am not just using this campaign as a platform to express my issues. I need to get votes. It's not important what I say but what Louisiana voters say. People will listen to that voice.

Politics is a game of expectations. Even a relatively modest result will have a big impact on the political process. If I got, say, 10 percent of the Democratic primary vote, that would be interpreted as a great victory - for me, certainly, but, more importantly, for my approach to creating jobs. Together, we can put the issue of jobs on the political map.

Some doubt that my scheme for a "better society" will work. They doubt that government has the capacity to be honest. I disagree. I also believe that the Democratic Party will be able to recapture its idealism so that it becomes rooted in the vision of a better world, benefiting not only its traditional "special interests" but everyone.

Index

A

"a bit dense & technical" 324
"a bone to pick" 103
"A Challenge to my Opponents" 97
A Shorter Workweek in the 1980s 349, 358
A U.S.-Mexico-Canada Free Trade Agreement 349, 358
AARP discount 149
Abbeville, LA 201, 360, 363, 365
Abbeville Meridional 201
Abita Brewing Company 216
Abita Springs, LA 216
abortion 174, 69
Abrams, Mary 193, 194, 241
academic hired guns 104
Acadia Parish 364
Acadian Tribune 241
accent 145
accountant 33, 324, 325
action 45
action rather than legislation 39, 44
ad hominem attacks 25, 53
Adams County, Ohio 164
adjustable tariffs 353
Administrative Services Dept. 75
Advanced Placement 167
advertising 185, 193, 260, 308, 316, 328
advertising costs per reader 187
advertising department 189, 196, 205, 241
affirmative action 26, 56
affordable housing 318
"Affordable Housing Preservation Party" 123, 356
Africa 169
African American 142, 164, 206
African Americans 26, 215, 43, 58, 74
African reviewer 61
African-American newspaper 160, 232, 256
After the New Economy 134
agent provocateur 68
agricultural commodities 334
Aiken Standard 120
Ailes, Roger 51
air-traffic controllers 315
Airline Highway (in Baton Rouge) 211, 270
Alabama 83
alcohol content in blood 248
Alexander, Jim 189
Alexandria, LA 11, 12, 16, 17, 18, 107, 152, 157, 158, 159, 161, 179, 184, 185, 187, 188, 232, 255, 257, 258, 259, 279, 280, 288, 290, 292, 293, 306, 307, 86, 360, 361, 362, 365, 366
Alexandria News Weekly 160, 232
Alexandria public library 185, 186
Alexandria zoo 14, 15, 17, 290
algebra 167
All the King's Men 156
Allegood, Wandell 257
Allen Parish 364
Allen, Teddy 139, 141, 142
alley in Alma 132
alligators 14, 190, 218
Alma, AR 132, 133, 361
alternative media 342
aluminum-boat factories 203
American dream 22
American Jews 26
American people 22, 99, 31, 331, 343
American revolution 313
American South 52
Amhoist crane 278
Amite, LA 10, 13, 207, 208, 212, 309, 363
Amite Tangi-Digest 208
Anderson, Ed 131, 143, 144, 145, 185, 195, 206, 223, 233, 263, 276
Anderson Independent-Mail 120
Angel, desk clerk at Motel 6 11, 143, 267
angry black man 77
animals 290

H

I

Copies of this book may be ordered directly from the publisher
for the list price of $16.95 per copy plus $3.95 for shipping and
handling. Residents of Minnesota should add 6.5% for sales
tax.

Please make checks or money orders payable to "Thistlerose
Publications". Prepayment is required.

Thistlerose Publications
1702 Glenwood Avenue
Minneapolis, MN 55405
U.S.A.

Other books written by the author include:

The Independence Party and the Future of Third-Party Politics:
Adventures & Opinions of an IP Senate Candidate
ISBN 0-9605630-5-9   471 pages   List price $18.95

Rhythm and Self-Consciousness: New Ideals for an Electronic
Civilization ISBN 0-9605630-4-0   262 pages   List price $14.95

Five Epochs of Civilization: World History as Emerging in Five
Civilizations   ISBN 0-9605630-3-2   590 pages   List price $18.95

These books may also be ordered through Thistlerose Publications at
the list price plus $3.95 for shipping and handling.

www.thistlerose.com   (877) 537-6247